Reading the Way to Heaven

Journal of Theological Interpretation Supplements

MURRAY RAE
University of Otago, New Zealand
Editor-in-Chief

---

1. Thomas Holsinger-Friesen, *Irenaeus and Genesis: A Study of Competition in Early Christian Hermeneutics*
2. Douglas S. Earl, *Reading Joshua as Christian Scripture*
3. Joshua N. Moon, *Jeremiah's New Covenant: An Augustinian Reading*
4. Csilla Saysell, *"According to the Law": Reading Ezra 9–10 as Christian Scripture*
5. Joshua Marshall Strahan, *The Limits of a Text: Luke 23:34a as a Case Study in Theological Interpretation*
6. Seth B. Tarrer, *Reading with the Faithful: Interpretation of True and False Prophecy in the Book of Jeremiah from Ancient Times to Modern*
7. Zoltán S. Schwáb, *Toward an Interpretation of the Book of Proverbs: Selfishness and Secularity Reconsidered*
8. Steven Joe Koskie Jr., *Reading the Way to Heaven: A Wesleyan Theological Hermeneutic of Scripture*
9. Hubert James Keener, *A Canonical Exegesis of the Eighth Psalm: YHWH's Maintenance of the Created Order through Divine Intervention*

Reading the Way to Heaven

A Wesleyan Theological Hermeneutic of Scripture

Steven Joe Koskie, Jr.

Winona Lake, Indiana
Eisenbrauns
2014

Copyright © 2014 Eisenbrauns
All rights reserved.

Printed in the United States of America

www.eisenbrauns.com

Library of Congress Cataloging-in-Publication Data

Koskie, Steven Joe.
　Reading the way to heaven : a Wesleyan theological hermeneutic of scripture / by Steven Joe Koskie, Jr.
　　　page　cm. — (Journal of theological interpretation supplements ; 8)
　Includes bibliographical references and index.
　ISBN 978-1-57506-706-3 (pbk. : alk. paper)
　 1. Bible—Hermeneutics.　 2. Bible—Criticism, interpretation, etc.
 3. Wesley, John, 1703–1791.　 4. Wesleyan Church—Doctrines.　 I. Title.
　BS476.K665　2013
　220.601—dc23
　　　　　　　　　　　　　　　　　　　　　　　　　　　　2013040736

The paper used in this publication meets the minimum requirements of the American National Standard for Information Sciences—Permanence of Paper for Printed Library Materials, ANSI Z39.48-1984.♾™

Table of Contents

Acknowledgements	vii
1. A Survey of Theological Hermeneutics	1
Introduction	1
Contemporary Theological Hermeneutics	2
Theological Hermeneutics: Summary of the Issues	11
Toward a Wesleyan Theological Hermeneutic: A Preview	17
2. The Wesleyan Conversation	19
In Search of a Wesleyan Theological Hermeneutic of Scripture	19
MacIntyre and Reading Wesley in the Wesleyan Tradition	31
3. A Postliberal Contribution	34
Hans Frei's Theological Hermeneutics	36
In Dialogue with Frei	47
4. Wesley's Theological Hermeneutics	53
John Wesley's Soteriological Vision	53
Hermeneutics and Holiness	61
5. Wesley's Hermeneutics in Action	71
Sermons	72
Explanatory Notes	82
The Literal Sense in Wesley's Hermeneutics	92
6. Appropriating Wesley I	97
Church as Spirit-Formed Context	98
Toward a Wesleyan Hermeneutical Context	104
7. Appropriating Wesley II	120
Umberto Eco's Reception Theory	121
Forming the Wesleyan Model Reader	130
8. A Wesleyan Theological Hermeneutic of Scripture	143
From Wesley to Wesleyan	143
Demonstration of a Wesleyan Theological Hermeneutic of Scripture	155
Conclusion	162
Bibliography	165
Index of Authors and Subjects	188
Index of Scripture	193

Acknowledgements

I am grateful to Murray Rae, Jim Eisenbraun, and everyone associated with the *Journal of Theological Interpretation* for including my work in the Supplement Series. Their forbearance is to their credit.

As this manuscript began life as a Ph.D. thesis for London School of Theology, special thanks goes also to my examiners, David Wilkinson of Durham University and Graham McFarlane of LST, for their interaction and helpful feedback at my viva.

My doctoral supervisor, Joel B. Green, is a rare combination of accomplished scholar and generous teacher. I could not have even begun this project, much less seen it through to completion, without his guidance.

Above all, my family has been my stalwart support throughout my educational odyssey. To my daughters, Simone and Sophia—who for the longest time did not know life without a Ph.D. student for a dad—and, as ever, to my wife, Melanie, I express my deepest gratitude.

1. A Survey of Theological Hermeneutics

Introduction

In recent decades theological hermeneutics, as a topic, has moved from the margins of academic discourse to the center. The pressures of philosophical and theological shifts in the latter twentieth century have propelled this movement, as the methodological sureties of modernism have been questioned and displaced. In the 1990s several theoretical monographs appeared, and by the turn of the century the conversation was well underway.[1] Within the last several years, that theoretical conversation has begun to bear fruit, as commentary series, dictionaries, and professional journals and study groups have begun to populate the landscape of theological hermeneutics.[2]

This study will develop and demonstrate a Wesleyan theological hermeneutic of Scripture. In so doing, I will attend to many of the issues and positions that define the present conversation. Yet, as the goal of my study indicates, I will not simply work within those parameters, but proceed within a particular tradition of enquiry that is identifiably *Wesleyan*, though even to say that is to invite another level of questions and problems. Navigating the terrain of those Wesleyan questions and problems will begin in chapter two. For now, I will take up theological hermeneutics more generally.

To that end, in what follows I will refine the sense in which I will be using the term "theological hermeneutics," then examine major contributors and issues to the subject as it presently stands. Scholars today have generally converged around a similar set of concerns regarding the theological interpretation of Scripture, though they of course bring differences of emphasis and opinion to these concerns. Surveying these differences will bring the issues into focus, and

---

1. E.g., Anthony C. Thiselton, *New Horizons in Hermeneutics* (Grand Rapids, MI: Zondervan, 1992); Francis Watson, *Text, Church, and World: Biblical Interpretation in Theological Perspective* (Grand Rapids, MI: Eerdmans, 1994); idem, *Text and Truth: Redefining Biblical Theology* (Grand Rapids, MI: Eerdmans, 1997); Stephen E. Fowl, *Engaging Scripture: A Model for Theological Interpretation* (Challenges in Contemporary Theology; Oxford: Blackwell, 1998); Kevin J. Vanhoozer, *Is There a Meaning in This Text? The Bible, the Reader, and the Morality of Literary Knowledge* (Grand Rapids, MI: Zondervan, 1998); Joel B. Green and Max Turner, eds., *Between Two Horizons: Spanning New Testament Studies and Systematic Theology* (Grand Rapids, MI: Eerdmans, 2000).

2. Regarding commentaries, there are the Brazos and Two Horizons series; among dictionaries, see esp. Kevin J. Vanhoozer, ed., *Dictionary for Theological Interpretation of the Bible* (Grand Rapids, MI: Baker Academic, 2005); the *Journal of Theological Interpretation* was launched in 2007; the Society of Biblical Literature has two study groups on theological hermeneutics: Theological Hermeneutics of Christian Scripture and Christian Theology and the Bible.

set the stage in a general way for the particular task I have set for myself in this study of developing and demonstrating a Wesleyan theological hermeneutic of Scripture.

Contemporary Theological Hermeneutics

Theological Hermeneutics: Orientating the Discussion
A survey of recent literature shows little consensus on the content of the term "theological hermeneutics." We can roughly identify two orientations however. Some scholars, such as Charles M. Wood and Werner Jeanrond, take the term "hermeneutics" in the sense of "understanding," only understanding as now occurring through the theological interpretation of texts. For Wood, "[Theological hermeneutics] aids the inquiry into the character of truly Christian witness by a continually renewed effort to determine what constitutes the Christian understanding of those texts upon which Christian witness depends; to identify and study the conditions and practices which enable that understanding; and to bring the endeavor of Christian understanding into proper relationship to its norm."[3] In a similar vein, Jeanrond thinks theological hermeneutics "aims at understanding this universe as God's universe." It is a "macro-hermeneutical" goal accomplished through the "micro-hermeneutical" exercise of interpreting texts from a theological perspective.[4] Jens Zimmermann argues that "hermeneutics is all about self-knowledge, and self-knowledge is impossible without knowledge of God." Opposed to the "progressive secularization" of philosophical hermeneutics, theological hermeneutics is the attempt to understand based on an unapologetically theological ontology made possible by the incarnation.[5]

All three definitions are concerned with understanding as such. In the cases of Wood and Zimmermann, this understanding is theological in a way that is indigenous to the particularity of the Christian faith; it does not make theological hermeneutics a subset of the discipline of philosophical hermeneutics, and therefore does not allow Christianity to be a localized version of some larger human phenomenon called "religion." Jeanrond, on the other hand, does subscribe to this latter view, understanding theological hermeneutics as a species of the genus philosophical hermeneutics. In putting understanding front and center in theological hermeneutics, all three occupy familiar territory created by the shift in hermeneutics that occurred in the twentieth century. Up to then, "hermeneutics" meant "interpretation" as the interpretation of texts, particularly

---

3. Charles M. Wood, *The Formation of Christian Understanding: Theological Hermeneutics* (2nd ed.; Valley Forge, PA: Trinity, 1993), 29.

4. Werner G. Jeanrond, *Theological Hermeneutics: Development and Significance* (New York: Crossroad, 1991), 8.

5. Jens Zimmermann, *Recovering Theological Hermeneutics: An Incarnational-Trinitarian Theory of Interpretation* (Grand Rapids, MI: Baker Academic, 2004), 7-9.

biblical texts.[6] Beginning with Martin Heidegger, however, and especially with his pupil, Hans-Georg Gadamer, hermeneutics became the universal and ontological problem of understanding itself.[7]

There is a second orientation to theological hermeneutics. Stephen E. Fowl offers that "theological interpretation [is] that practice whereby theological concerns and interests inform and are informed by a reading of scripture."[8] Similarly, Daniel J. Treier construes theological hermeneutics as "an account of how biblical interpretation should shape, and be shaped by, Christian theology."[9] Kevin J. Vanhoozer, eschewing precise definition, discusses theological interpretation via what he sees as its primary concerns: the responsibility to theologically interpret for "all the theological disciplines and the whole people of God," not professional exegetes only; theological interpretation's "governing interest in God, the word and works of God, and [its] governing intention to engage in what we might call 'theological criticism'"; and finally, theological interpretation is the designation for "a broad ecclesial concern that embraces a number of academic approaches."[10]

It is this orientation to theological hermeneutics as the interpretation of Scripture that will dictate the course of investigation here. For Wood and Jeanrond, at least, scriptural interpretation is still important to understanding, but it is secondary.[11] For this study, the priority is reversed. The insights of twentieth-century philosophy and theology into the hermeneutical nature of understanding are important, but here "hermeneutics" will reassume its older meaning of textual interpretation, specifically the interpretation of Christian Scripture. In this sense, "theological hermeneutics," "theological interpretation," and "theological exegesis" will all be used synonymously.[12]

---

6. Jeanrond, *Theological Hermeneutics*, 12.

7. For more on this shift, see Hans-Georg Gadamer, *Truth and Method* (2nd ed.; London: Continuum, 2004).

8. Stephen E. Fowl, "Introduction," in *The Theological Interpretation of Scripture: Classic and Contemporary Readings* (ed. Stephen E. Fowl; Blackwell Readings in Modern Theology; Cambridge: Blackwell, 1997), xiii.

9. Daniel J. Treier, "Theological Hermeneutics, Contemporary," in *Dictionary for Theological Interpretation*, 787.

10. Kevin J. Vanhoozer, "Introduction: What Is Theological Interpretation of the Bible?" in *Dictionary for Theological Interpretation*, 21-23.

11. Zimmermann's take on hermeneutics is so ontologically focused that the status of scriptural interpretation is unclear. If one assumes the incarnation to be a scripturally mediated reality, however, surely the interpretation of the Bible should fit within his concerns.

12. Given the distinction sometimes made between hermeneutics (the theory of interpretation) and exegesis (the practice of interpretation), this usage may seem confused, but there is precedent in the literature. See, e.g., R. R. Reno, "Biblical Theology and Theological Exegesis," in *Out of Egypt: Biblical Theology and Biblical Interpretation* (ed. Craig Bartholomew, et al.; Scripture and Hermeneutics Series 5;

Theological Hermeneutics and Biblical Theology
Along these lines it will be helpful to clarify the distinction between "theological hermeneutics" and "biblical theology." I will not be using biblical theology as a synonym for theological hermeneutics here, partially because of the traditional understanding of biblical theology as an intermediary discipline. In 1787, J. P. Gabler posited biblical theology as an intermediary step between historical study of the Bible and dogmatic theology.[13] According to Gabler, the purpose of biblical theology is to distill the timeless teachings of the Bible from its temporal depository in the text. Once distilled, these teachings could then be made useful to the dogmatic theologian. Gabler's proposal eventually begot the conception of biblical theology as it is found in Stendahl, who argues for a two-step approach moving from what the text "meant" to what it now "means."[14]

Today the term biblical theology is used in various ways, adding to the need to distance a study in theological hermeneutics from it. Heikki Räisänen, for instance, moves fluidly between "biblical theology" and "New Testament theology,"[15] arguing that New Testament theology "may be a legitimate part of self-consciously ecclesial theology," but that certain scholars may set it aside in favor of either "the 'history of early Christian thought' (or theology, if you like), evolving in the context of early Judaism," or "critical philosophical, ethical, and/or theological 'reflection on the New Testament," as well as on its influence on our history and its significance for contemporary life."[16]

James K. Mead presents biblical theology as a development from within biblical studies that answers the question, "What is the Bible all about?"[17] Biblical theology focuses on the whole of the Bible, not just particular passages, and is to be distinguished from historical, sociological, and literary studies of the Bible's background, though it should not ignore these endeavors. It tries to discern the Bible's message and themes, demonstrating what its pages say about God and God's relationship to creation and humanity. Mead distinguishes between biblical theology and theological interpretation, claiming the former is the work of biblical scholars desiring to describe the entire Bible's message and themes, while systematic theologians who focus on smaller passages and their

---

Grand Rapids, MI: Zondervan, 2004), 385-408, whose use of "theological exegesis" is akin to mine; also Daniel J. Treier, *Introducing Theological Interpretation of Scripture: Recovering a Christian Practice* (Grand Rapids, MI: Baker Academic, 2008), 14.

13. John Sandys-Wunsch and Laurence Eldredge, "J. P. Gabler and the Distinction between Biblical and Dogmatic Theology: Translation, Commentary, and Discussion of His Originality," *Scottish Journal of Theology* 33 (1980): 133-58.

14. See Krister Stendahl, "Biblical Theology, Contemporary," in *Interpreter's Dictionary of the Bible* (ed. G. A. Buttrick; vol. 1; New York: Abingdon, 1962), 418-32.

15. Heikki Räisänen, *Beyond New Testament Theology: A Story and a Programme* (2nd ed.; London: SCM, 2001), see esp. 1-8.

16. Räisänen, *Beyond New Testament Theology*, 8.

17. James K. Mead, *Biblical Theology: Issues, Methods, and Themes* (Louisville, KY: Westminster John Knox, 2007), 2.

relation to confessional traditions do the latter.[18] Mead feels the tension of the descriptive and normative aspects of biblical theology ("what it meant" versus "what it means"), and attempts to find a way forward.[19] However, for Mead biblical theology is still at base a descriptive enterprise performed by biblical scholars, even if it might concern itself with the contemporary relevance of its descriptions.

By itself, this is enough to show that biblical theology is not synonymous with theological hermeneutics as I am using that term here. Theological hermeneutics is not an intermediate, descriptive step between biblical studies and systematic or dogmatic theology that must somehow find a way to be relevant. I will not be offering here an approach where first the theology of a particular New Testament book is described, then its relevance for Wesleyan systematic theology is established. Instead, the approach here will consider the interpretation of Scripture as vital to the formation of Christian identity, specifically within the Wesleyan tradition. It will pursue, through interaction with John Wesley's hermeneutics, how Wesleyan beliefs and practices inform the reading of Scripture, and in turn how Scripture informs Wesleyan beliefs and practices. It will assume that reading Scripture is not a set of steps—say, from grammatico-historical exegesis, to theological description, to constructive theology—but rather an ongoing, living interaction that has no clear starting point, and whose end is not the execution of a methodology but God. In other words, historical, literary, and other types of "critical" approaches will not be disqualified, but they will be subsumed to the goal of theological interpretation as that is understood in the Wesleyan tradition, a tradition that is part of the larger tradition of the Christian faith, which claims the Bible as its Scripture.

Theological Hermeneutics: Contributions
Within this orientation to the theological interpretation of Scripture, many different approaches and emphases can be discerned. For Francis Watson, theological hermeneutics means offering "theological justification for particular hermeneutical decisions."[20] Watson's primary theological commitment is to Jesus Christ as God's self-revelatory Word mediated through the Bible.[21] He therefore argues that "all Christian theology must be 'biblical theology'—not in the sense that it should consist in nothing but biblical exegesis but in the sense that the particular truth attested in the biblical texts must constitute its centre and

---

18. Mead, *Biblical Theology*, 11.
19. See esp. Mead, *Biblical Theology*, ch. 3.
20. Watson, *Text, Church, and World*, 221.
21. John Webster echoes Watson, both in his Barthian commitment to the preeminence of the revelation of the Word, and to doctrine's position vis-à-vis hermeneutics (John Webster, *Holy Scripture: A Dogmatic Sketch* [Current Issues in Theology; Cambridge: Cambridge University Press, 2003]).

foundation."[22] Watson wants to protect the reality of Jesus "in the flesh," so to speak, and so he advocates reading the Gospels as a form of historiography. Watson turns to literary theory, in particular speech-act theory, in service to his theological commitment, making the Word God's speech-act. As a result, although a text's meaning cannot be known apart from its communal reception, God is the primary author of the text, and a given text's authorial intent is the literal sense of Scripture a community receives.

On the one hand, Watson states that the worshiping community is the primary context for biblical interpretation, and preaching is the preferred genre of exposition. On the other hand, Watson envisions from within the academy a truly interdisciplinary approach to biblical interpretation that draws together confessionally both biblical studies and systematic theology around the textually mediated Jesus Christ. Either way, he seeks a newly revived "biblical theology" that prioritizes God's scriptural self-communication in Jesus.

Kevin Vanhoozer's contributions demonstrate some similarities with Watson's. Vanhoozer stresses Christ's centrality in biblical interpretation, since it is through the canon of Scripture that Christ communicates with the church. More than most writing in theological hermeneutics, Vanhoozer wants a criterion that validates interpretation.[23] In other words, the authority of Scripture is foremost on his agenda. The need for verification, for an established criterion to distinguish interpretations, is a consequence of Vanhoozer's theological adherence to the Reformed tradition and his hermeneutical adherence to speech-act theory. As a trinitarian operation of self-disclosure, God's use of Scripture takes priority over the church's use. The communicative priority of God in history cannot be gainsaid in any way, and this is the driving force behind Vanhoozer's desire for verification. This is most obvious in his recent book *The Drama of Doctrine*, where he turns to performance theory to contend that God is the dramatic director of the Bible-as-script, which the church performs.[24] The interpretative approach Vanhoozer describes is a *canonical-linguistic* one: "Canonical-linguistic theology attends both to the drama in the text—what God is doing in the world through Christ—and to the drama that continues in the

---

22. Watson, *Text and Truth*, 2. Watson's use of "biblical theology" is framed within a discussion of the failures of the Biblical Theology Movement of the mid-twentieth century. Aside from the reasons I have already given for resisting the use of the term, Watson's resuscitation of it does little to alleviate possible confusion.

23. This is as true in his earlier contributions (Vanhoozer, *Is There a Meaning in This Text?*) as it is in his more recent ones (e.g., see his essays in A. K. M. Adam, et al, *Reading Scripture with the Church: Toward a Hermeneutic for Theological Interpretation* [Grand Rapids, MI: Baker Academic, 2006]).

24. Kevin J. Vanhoozer, *The Drama of Doctrine: A Canonical-Linguistic Approach to Christian Theology* (Louisville, KY: Westminster John Knox, 2005). Vanhoozer's work always evinces a deep interaction with theory of different stripes. His later proposal is more theological than his earlier. See, e.g., *Is There a Meaning in This Text?*, with its heavy reliance on literary theory and linguistic philosophy.

church as God uses Scripture to address, edify, and confront its readers."[25] With such a proposal, Vanhoozer hopes to hold together both the whole of Scripture as God's communicative vehicle within the church (the "canonical"), with the place of context-specific interpretation as a practice by human readers (the "linguistic").

Stephen Fowl takes a somewhat different tack. Stressing less than either Watson or Vanhoozer the priority of God's self-revelation, Fowl focuses attention on the life of the ecclesial community that interprets Scripture—its aims, dispositions, and interests in reading the Bible. This he deems a far more fruitful path for discussing interpretation than other paths that require a theory of meaning. In fact, distinguishing himself from both *determinate* interpretation (which sees meaning as a property of the text and stresses proper methodology abstracted from Christian doctrine and practices) and *anti-determinative* interpretation (which is parasitic on a determinative view and dismisses it as a mistake of western metaphysics, favoring interpretive instability), Fowl argues for *underdetermined* interpretation, foregoing theories of meaning for looking at what it is that drives readers to read and keep reading. And whereas Vanhoozer especially wants a validation of a certain meaning of a text, Fowl celebrates interpretive pluralism and whatever "set of doctrinal, moral, ecclesial and communal concerns" precipitates it.[26] These elements shape readers' identities, equipping them to adroitly interpret according to the normed life of the community of faith. Fowl is interested in the interplay between the ethical life of the community and how this relates to biblical interpretation.[27] Recovering premodern interpretive practices, especially looking to Thomas Aquinas, Fowl has developed a view of the literal sense that allows for different readings of a text in different situations.[28] As a result, it is practical wisdom, or *phronesis*, that he favors in adjudicating the validity of readings.

Matthew Levering's *Participatory Biblical Exegesis* is a Catholic recapitulation of biblical interpretation as *sacra doctrina*, a perspective and practice undermined in the era of modern historical criticism.[29] However, in building the scaffolding for his proposal, Levering goes beyond historical criticism to the conception of history that underlay it, a linear view of human

---

25. Vanhoozer, *The Drama of Doctrine*, 17.
26. Fowl, *Engaging Scripture*, 59. This continues to be an issue between Vanhoozer and Fowl. See Kevin Vanhoozer, "Four Theological Faces of Biblical Interpretation," in *Reading Scripture*, 136-37.
27. A theme earlier explored in Stephen E. Fowl and L. Gregory Jones, *Reading in Communion: Scripture and Ethics in Christian Life* (Eugene, OR: Wipf and Stock, 1998).
28. For Fowl's more recent use of Aquinas, see Stephen E. Fowl, "The Importance of Multivoiced Literal Sense of Scripture," in *Reading Scripture*, 37-50. He also argues for appropriation of premodern interpretation in Fowl, "Introduction," xvii-xviii.
29. Matthew Levering, *Participatory Biblical Exegesis: A Theology of Biblical Interpretation* (Notre Dame, IN: University of Notre Dame Press, 2008).

time traceable to fourteenth-century nominalism. In this view, human life is a basically secular, linear continuum, and the study of a human-produced text like the Bible requires tools and assumptions that bracket Christian doctrine, and ultimately the sacramental life that is the essence of the church. Levering proposes as corrective a *participatory* exegesis, which (re-)introduces patristic-medieval assumptions about metaphysics and the pneumatological-christologically based doctrines and practices of the church to historically serious biblical interpretation. "Participatory biblical exegesis," writes Levering, "locates the linear-historical details within a participatory-historical frame, a frame established by God's creative and redemptive work in history."[30] Human and divine agency are held together, bridged by the literal sense, which possesses the resources to in turn bridge past and present—a biblical text produced in the past with a church presently reading it.

Christopher R. Seitz has made one of the more substantive contributions to theological interpretation from the area of Old Testament studies. Inspired by Brevard Childs' theme of the Old Testament's "discrete witness," Seitz has sought to defend the unity of Scripture as a true two-testament witness, where the Old Testament is heard as an "abiding theological witness," rather than subordinated to a New Testament that is "the developmental culmination of and correction of the Old Testament."[31] Sensitive to the impact of historical criticism on this developmental approach, Seitz attempts to recover a typological or figural reading of Scripture that protects his interests in canonical unity and the Old Testament's discrete witness, and does so in the wake of historical criticism's failure "to do constructive theological work involving the identity of God in the most basic sense."[32] What Seitz wants by "typological," or "figural," is a reading of Scripture that identifies the God of Israel with the God and Father of Jesus Christ, and allows Scripture a prophetic voice in the church today. Disciplined by the rule of faith—that "credal deposit or précis of the apostolic faith"[33]—the unity of Father and Son, and the unity of the Old Testament and New Testament, are perceivable again within the church thanks to the providential work of the Holy Spirit.

Important contributions to theological hermeneutics have come not only from individual authors, but from collaborative efforts as well. Participants in *The Art of Reading Scripture* offer nine theses on biblical interpretation, including an affirmation of God's identity truthfully told through the biblical accounts; the role of the rule of faith in seeing the dramatic unity of biblical narrative, entailing the interdependence of Old Testament and New Testament;

---

30. Levering, *Participatory Biblical Exegesis*, 6.

31. Christopher R. Seitz, *Word without End: The Old Testament as Abiding Theological Witness* (Grand Rapids, MI: Eerdmans, 1998), 4.

32. Christopher R. Seitz, *Figured Out: Typology and Providence in Christian Scripture* (Louisville, KY: Westminster John Knox, 2001), 4.

33. Seitz, *Figured Out*, 6.

recognition of multiple senses of Scripture rather than restricting meaning to authorial intent; the Gospels as the true locus of Jesus' identity; the church as location of biblical interpretation; seeing the communion of saints through time as the history of interpretation we need to read Scripture faithfully; inviting dialogue from those outside the church; and finally the eschatological nature of interpretation, which requires ongoing reading and appropriation of Scripture in concert with the Spirit's ministry.[34] Contributors go on not only to explore these theses theoretically, but also through the ecclesial and theological practice of sermonizing.

The Brazos and Two Horizons commentary series are efforts to bring theological interpretation into practice via the commentary genre. R. R. Reno, general editor of the Brazos commentaries, says his series' point of departure is "the conviction that dogma clarifies rather than obscures."[35] Reno's is an audacious claim, given the fragmentation of academic disciplines, as well as the divisions between academy and church. Nevertheless, Reno (and by extension, the commentators in the series) argues that "you shall know the truth of doctrine by its interpretive fruits,"[36] and therefore Brazos is distinctive for choosing primarily commentators known for their expertise in Christian doctrine, rather than exegetes as conventionally understood in biblical studies.[37] Reno argues that alongside Scripture has arisen a rule of faith that encompasses, or is encompassed by, the creedal, confessional, and baptismal traditions of the church, but that also exists as an internalized sensibility that guides Christian theological interpretation of the Bible. This is the exegetical touchstone for much of the church's history of interpretation, and it is the programme that defines the Brazos series.

The Two Horizons New Testament series, edited by Joel B. Green and Max Turner, has similar goals in mind but goes about them somewhat differently. The Two Horizons series is introduced by a programmatic text, *Between Two Horizons*, with the same editors, bringing together contributions from primarily practitioners in biblical studies.[38] In their opening essay, Turner and Green note the lack of theological fruit borne of modern commentaries, as well as an approach that locks the text commented upon in the world of the author. In response, Two Horizons seeks to understand biblical texts both within the ancient world of their production, and the modern world of their present

---

34. See "Nine Theses on the Interpretation of Scripture," in *The Art of Reading Scripture* (ed. Ellen F. Davis and Richard B. Hays; Grand Rapids, MI: Eerdmans, 2003), 1-5.

35. R. R. Reno, "Series Preface," in Jaroslav Pelikan, *Acts* (Grand Rapids, MI: Brazos, 2005), 13.

36. Reno, "Preface," 15.

37. Two Brazos contributors, Fowl and Seitz, are biblical scholars however. Yet their theological commitments are not representative of the biblical studies guild.

38. Trevor Hart appears to be the sole systematic theologian among the contributors.

interpretation.[39] For the Two Horizons series, this approach is possible due to a shift from a methodological monopoly held by historical criticism, to a methodological pluralism; a move from "behind the text issues" to "in the text" and "in front of the text" ones; and finally a renewed interest in potential connections between biblical studies and systematic theology.[40]

The *Dictionary for Theological Interpretation of the Bible* is yet another kind of collaborative project in theological hermeneutics. The purpose of the dictionary, as stated by editor Kevin Vanhoozer, is "to provide biblical interpreters with a tool that would help make sense of the diverse interpretive approaches and evaluate these approaches as to their contribution toward a theological interpretation of the Bible."[41] This purpose will be fulfilled if it helps readers successfully cross the gaps between both academic disciplines, and the academy and church. Most of all, Vanhoozer sees theological hermeneutics as "biblical interpretation oriented to the knowledge of God,"[42] and attempts to aid in the acquisition of this knowledge through articles based on biblical texts, hermeneutics, interpreters and interpretive communities, and doctrines and themes.

Finally, theological hermeneutics as an academic subject of study in its own right has grown to the point that two recent introductions to it have appeared. In *Introducing Theological Interpretation of Scripture*, Daniel Treier gives a comprehensive survey of many of the main issues that define theological hermeneutics.[43] He traces the watershed influence of Karl Barth to the methodological pluralism of contemporary interpreters, and highlights the major trends, such as recovering past interpretive practices, the ecclesial location of interpretation, and interdisciplinarity.

Stephen Fowl has also published an introduction (or more precisely, a "companion") to theological interpretation.[44] Fowl's book is not as in-depth as Treier's but he proceeds in a similar manner, drawing on general trends and formulating his own proposal, which in many ways looks like his earlier *Engaging Scripture*. His own agenda for students of theological interpretation is centered on learning the ecclesial practices essential to reading the Bible theologically, especially confession, forgiveness, reconciliation, truth telling, admonition, friendship, and conversation.[45] Fowl supports continued curricular reform to accommodate the blurring of disciplinary lines in theological hermeneutics, greater involvement of churches in forming interpreters,

---

39. Max Turner and Joel B. Green, "New Testament Commentary and Systematic Theology: Strangers or Friends?" in Green and Turner, eds., *Between Two Horizons*, 2-3.
40. Turner and Green, "New Testament Commentary and Systematic Theology," 4.
41. Vanhoozer, "Introduction," in *Dictionary for Theological Interpretation*, 20.
42. Vanhoozer, "Introduction," 22.
43. Treier, *Introducing Theological Interpretation of Scripture*.
44. Fowl, *Theological Interpretation*.
45. See Fowl, *Theological Interpretation*, Part Three.

promoting the sermon as the exemplary genre of theological hermeneutics, and recognizing the prevalence of confessional differences among the more regularly acknowledged methodological ones.[46]

Treier's and Fowl's books bear passing resemblance to this study, but it is little more than that. Treier paints his picture of theological interpretation with broad strokes, and what constructive proposals he makes come from that general standpoint. Fowl is more particular in his commitments, but both deal with theological hermeneutics in general. If anything, I follow Fowl's recommendation to give more attention to confessional particularities by exploring and proposing a Wesleyan theological hermeneutic of Scripture. But I cannot do in a single introductory chapter what these two scholars have done in whole books; their contributions are both unique and valuable.

Theological Hermeneutics: Summary of the Issues

Treier and Fowl both correctly proceed from the recognition that, among the numerous differences between participants in theological hermeneutics, there are common themes that all more or less take up. Having surveyed some of the major voices in contemporary theological interpretation, the following themes present themselves as integral to the conversation.

The Aftermath of Modernist Criticism
The current flurry of proposals and forays into theological hermeneutics is possible because of the critique of interpretative methodologies that have defined modernism. These modernist approaches (usually glossed as "historical criticism") have dominated academic study of the Bible since at least the eighteenth century.[47] In this milieu, the Bible became an object to be acted upon using critical, scientific methodologies in a secularized intellectual atmosphere. Moving away from these assumptions and practices has opened the conversation to addressing divisions within academe, rethinking the dominance of modern ideas of "history," as well as recognizing interpretive pluralism and the role of the engaged reader in connection with meaning. Given the association of "criticism" with the problems of modernism, some scholars have called contemporary methodologies *postcritical*.[48]

Division, Academic and Ecclesial
That modernism has led to over-specialization within academe, and a gap between academe and church, many recognize. How to deal with this situation is

---

46. See Fowl, *Theological Interpretation*, Part Four.
47. See Hans W. Frei, *The Eclipse of Biblical Narrative: A Study in Eighteenth and Nineteenth Century Hermeneutics* (New Haven, CT: Yale University Press, 1974).
48. E.g., Peter Ochs, ed., *The Return to Scripture in Judaism and Christianity: Essays in Postcritical Scriptural Interpretation* (New York: Paulist, 1993).

hardly agreed upon. Francis Watson, as noted above, seeks an interdisciplinary solution, essentially affirming the integrity of the various academic disciplines. Joel Green, however, sees theological interpretation as offering a way out of disciplinary divisions, leading to a wholesale rethinking of what we understand theology and biblical studies to be.[49] Fowl has strongly criticized the "professionalization" of biblical studies.[50] The Brazos commentary series, by assuming Christian doctrine as its interpretive framework, is trying to produce commentaries by scholars that can serve ministers in the pulpit.

The Centrality of Scripture in the Church
The role of the Bible as the book that shapes the life and faith of the church is paramount, but so too is the church as the native context of the Bible read as Christian Scripture. Scholars now recognize that many of the working assumptions of modern criticism abstracted the Bible from the church by making it an object of scientific study. The move to more postcritical methodologies results in less attention to the process of the biblical texts' formation, and more attention on its reception in its final form within the church. Although critical study of the Bible is favored by the scholars mentioned above, Christian doctrine and practices are being seen more and more as essential for biblical interpretation within an ecclesial context. This is obvious in the turn to practical wisdom, or *phronesis*, or even "virtuous" or "participatory" readings.[51] This has also led to a rethinking of the interconnectedness of Scripture and tradition, the role of the sacraments in theological interpretation, and even the sacramental nature of reading Scripture itself. But it also raises issues about the interplay of Christian living and theological interpretation in the formation of Christian identity. In other words, Christian theological interpretation is impossible apart from Christian life, which has its locus in the church.

Doctrine and Bible
The reintroduction of Christian doctrine to hermeneutics is also a major development, as it acknowledges the impossibility that anyone could be neutral in theological exegesis. It also opens the door to engage anew the history of Christian interpretation—especially premodern interpreters—as both formal guides, and material contributors to contemporary hermeneutics.[52] From this

---

49. Joel B. Green, "Scripture and Theology: Uniting the Two So Long Divided," in Green and Turner, *Between Two Horizons*, 37-43; also, idem, *Seized by Truth: Reading the Bible as Scripture* (Nashville, TN: Abingdon, 2007).

50. Fowl, "Introduction," xiii.

51. As already noted, these themes are prominent in Fowl (*Engaging Scripture*) and Levering (*Participatory Exegesis*). See also Daniel J. Treier, *Virtue and the Voice of God: Toward Theology as Wisdom* (Grand Rapids, MI: Eerdmans, 2006).

52. David C. Steinmetz, "The Superiority of Pre-Critical Exegesis," in *The Theological Interpretation of Scripture*, ed. Fowl, 26-38; also, John J. O'Keefe and R. R.

ressourcement has come a new appreciation for the richness and indispensability of the rule of faith. Looking particularly to early interpreters like Irenaeus, contemporary theological hermeneuts have probed how the rule of faith—both in the proto-creedal form of Irenaeus and in the more confessionally crystallized form of the Nicene Creed—can guide the interpretive sensibilities of Christian readers.[53]

Literal Sense, Figural Reading, and the Biblical Canon
The critique of modernist ideas of history and the reintroduction of Christian doctrine have permitted a reevaluation of Scripture's literal sense and the unity of the biblical canon. No longer necessarily confined to authorial intent, the literal sense of Scripture has become a more formal concept, accommodating interpretive pluralism, yet disciplined by the rule of faith, which sets parameters on what is "Christian" about Christian theological hermeneutics.[54] Through renewed interest in figural or typological reading, which allows Christians to read the Old Testament as the Old Testament, and not as the "Hebrew Bible,"[55] a Christian literal sense reading can affirm that the God of the Old Testament is also the God of the New Testament, repairing the fragmentation of the canon by modernism.[56] Figural reading has a further dimension, allowing readers to have their identities shaped by Scripture's stories and personalities, through re-imagining the world in which they live as the world of Scripture.[57]

Reno, *Sanctified Vision: An Introduction to Early Christian Interpretation of the Bible* (Baltimore, MD: Johns Hopkins University Press, 2005).

53. See Robert W. Wall, "Reading the Bible from within Our Traditions: The 'Rule of Faith' in Theological Hermeneutics," in *Between Two Horizons*, ed. Green and Turner, 88-107; also, Christopher R. Seitz, ed., *Nicene Christianity: The Future of a New Ecumenism* (Grand Rapids, MI: Brazos, 2001); and O'Keefe and Reno, *Sanctified Vision*, esp. ch. 6.

54. See K. E. Greene-McCreight, *Ad Litteram: How Augustine, Calvin, and Barth Read the "Plain Sense" of Genesis 1-3* (Issues in Systematic Theology 5; New York: Peter Lang, 1999). Watson takes an exception to this in *Text and Truth*, pressing for a literal sense that is tied to authorial intent, while Vanhoozer appears to attempt a middle way in *The Drama of Doctrine*.

55. As Francis Watson puts it, "The current tendency to rename [Old Testament scholars'] object of study the 'Hebrew Bible' is the result not only of sensitivity to the presence of Jewish scholars in the field but also of a long-standing unease about the encroachment of 'anachronistic' Christian theological concerns and conceptuality" (*Text and Truth*, 5).

56. Along with Seitz's work, noted above, see R. W. L. Moberly, *The Bible, Theology, and Faith: A Study of Abraham and Jesus* (Cambridge Companions in Christian Doctrine; Cambridge: Cambridge University Press, 2000).

57. This idea in a postmodern context was most compellingly presented by Hans Frei, *The Eclipse of Biblical Narrative*. For a more recent treatment of figural reading and its soteriological impact on readers, see John David Dawson, *Christian Figural Reading and the Fashioning of Identity* (Berkeley: University of California Press, 2002).

Karl Barth and Theological Hermeneutics

In his recent introduction to theological hermeneutics, Treier has rightly pointed to the significance of Karl Barth as the forerunner of the present conversation.[58] Although much has rightly been made about the preface to the second edition of Barth's commentary on Romans, all the basic concerns are already laid out in his original preface.[59] The opening of the first edition immediately flies in the face of the historicism of Barth's day: "Paul, as a child of his age, addressed his contemporaries. It is, however, far more important that, as Prophet and Apostle of the Kingdom of God, he veritably speaks to all men of every age." Barth is well aware of the milieu in which he writes: "The historical-critical method of Biblical investigation has its rightful place: it is concerned with the preparation of the intelligence—and this can never be superfluous." This preparatory method is subsidiary to a doctrine of inspiration that makes as one the concerns of Paul and of those reading Paul today, "and if we be enlightened by the brightness of his answers, those answers must be ours."[60]

Barth's words were taken by critics to be an assault on historical criticism, but in the preface to the second edition, Barth clarifies that he is only pointing out the limits of modernist methodology: "I have nothing whatever to say against historical criticism. I recognize it, and once more state quite definitely that it is both necessary and justified. My complaint is that recent commentaries confine themselves to an interpretation of the text which seems to me to be no commentary at all, but merely the first step towards a commentary."[61] The delimitation of historical criticism opened a contemporaneity between text and reader, but this insight is only part of Barth's contribution.

As Richard Burnett has shown, Barth's central discovery was that the subject matter of the Bible was God.[62] This "theological conversion" set up the

---

58. Treier, *Introducing Theological Interpretation*, 14-21.

59. I am not occupied here with tracing the development of Barth's theological exegesis throughout his career, only to acknowledge his significance as a watershed figure, a significance most often associated with the Romans commentary. For more on Barth's hermeneutics in his later work, especially in *Church Dogmatics*, see, e.g., Werner G. Jeanrond, "Karl Barth's Hermeneutics," in *Reckoning with Barth* (ed. Nigel Biggar; Oxford: Mowbray, 1988), 80-97; also Francis Watson, "The Bible," in *The Cambridge Companion to Karl Barth* (ed. John Webster; Cambridge Companions to Religion; Cambridge: Cambridge University Press, 2000), 57-71.

60. Karl Barth, *The Epistle to the Romans* (London: Oxford University Press, 1977), 1.

61. Barth, *Romans*, 6.

62. Richard E. Burnett, *Karl Barth's Theological Exegesis: The Hermeneutical Principals of the Römerbrief Period* (Wissenschaftliche Untersuchungen zum Neuen Testament 145; Tübingen: Mohr Siebeck, 2001), 74. Expressing the converse of this same point, Bruce McCormack calls Barth's commentary a "revolution" because Barth "shows the limits of historical-critical study of the Bible in the interests of a more nearly

hermeneutical process for Barth, "a dialectical relation between a specific, holy, transcendent God and a specific human creature."[63] As he famously stated in an early essay, "within the Bible there is a strange, new world, the world of God."[64] As opposed to the historical criticism of the day, which interpreted the Bible according to secularized canons of truth, Barth claimed that God invites us into the reality of Scripture—on God's own terms.[65] Entailed in this was a different view of "scientific objectivity." In Barth's time, theology was able to claim a historical object and methodology, sanctioning its status as a science (or *Wissenschaft*) within the university.[66] For many scholars of the day, to be scientific, or properly critical, of the biblical text meant to distance oneself, searching for the meaning through neutrally applied tools. Barth found this unacceptable. Since God is the subject matter of Scripture, real critical interpretation is participatory, as the interpreter "entered the meaning of Scripture."[67] To do anything else in the name of science was to not be critical enough, for historical reconstruction merely resulted in preliminaries, not actual interpretation.[68] His belief in the necessary act of surrender to the truth of Scripture set Barth against the prevailing *Zeitgeist* in which he wrote, but it essentially defined his theological project for the rest of his life.[69]

Barth's hermeneutics was theological through and through. His starting point was that Scripture witnesses to the God revealed in his Word, Jesus Christ.[70] Humanity cannot attain this knowledge of revelation, but must instead receive it as God communicates it. This unified witness licensed Barth's recovery of Scripture's wholeness. Moreover, the old movement between part and whole was again conceivable, meaning particular passages were to be read

---

theological exegesis" ("Historical-Criticism and Dogmatic Interest in Karl Barth's Theological Exegesis of the New Testament," *Lutheran Quarterly* 5 [1991]: 211).

63. Burnett, *Barth's Theological Exegesis*, 76.

64. Karl Barth, "The Strange New World within the Bible," in *The Word of God and the Word of Man* (New York: Harper Torchbooks, 1957), 33.

65. "The being of God is the truth and...the being of God precedes all human questioning" (Burnett, *Barth's Theological Exegesis*, 91).

66. McCormack, "Historical-Criticism," 212. For more on *Wissenschaft* and theology in the German university, see Hans Frei, *Types of Christian Theology* (New Haven, CT: Yale University Press, 1992); also Edward Farley, *Theologia: The Fragmentation and Unity of Theology Education* (Minneapolis: Fortress, 1983).

67. See esp. Burnett, *Barth's Theological Exegesis*, ch. 4.

68. Barth, *Romans*, 6-7.

69. For a strong argument for continuity between Barth's earlier and later theological methodology, see Bruce McCormack, *Karl Barth's Critically Realistic Dialectical Theology: Its Genesis and Development, 1909-1936* (Oxford: Clarendon, 1995).

70. As Watson explains, "For Barth, the Bible *is* 'the Word of God' in that the Word that God spoke once for all continues to address us in the word or testimony of the biblical writers" ("The Bible," 61).

in light of the overarching theme of the Bible. Barth also reforged language and content; the biblical interpreter was no longer to try to get "behind" the text, into its past, to retrieve meaning. The text as it comes to the interpreter *in its final form* is what is interpreted, not the process of the text's formation. As a result, the text could again be taken at face value, unified by the one God's address to created humanity. This hermeneutical conviction is famously laid down with Barth's recourse to Calvin:

> How energetically Calvin, having first established what stands in the text, sets himself to re-think the whole material and to wrestle with it, till the walls which separate the sixteenth century from the first become transparent! Paul speaks, and the man of the sixteenth century hears. The conversation between the original record and the reader moves round the subject-matter, until a distinction between yesterday and to-day becomes impossible.[71]

Ironically, much of what Barth argued for (or tried to assume in his exegesis) is still being debated. The ubiquity of his influence is hardly controversial; several contemporary practitioners in theological hermeneutics are indebted to him.[72] Of those surveyed above, Watson is the most deeply indebted to Barth.[73] But Barth's fingerprint is detectable in Vanhoozer, and it shows up somewhat indirectly in Seitz due to his dependence on Childs. In some cases Barth's influence is not obvious, but his significance is acknowledged, either outright or implicitly by looking to him for examples.[74]

In noting Barth's place today, I want to recall a point made earlier, in slightly different ways, by Watson and Fowl. Watson states that theological hermeneutics means doctrinal decisions can inform hermeneutical moves. Fowl is more open than most about the prominence of one's confessional background in how one interprets Scripture.[75] Both of these scholars affirm that one's doctrinal tradition can and does make material contributions to one's hermeneutics. Given Barth's Reformed theology, and his influence on many, it is important to recognize that Barth is working out of a particular tradition. In fact, as Burnett points out, Barth rarely discussed hermeneutics per se, focusing on dogmatic reflection and exegesis.[76] Insofar as many of the voices today draw from Barth for inspiration, they draw from his Reformed perspective. This may or may not be an issue for a given scholar, but since the Reformed tradition is

---

71. Barth, *Romans*, 7.
72. As Treier demonstrates (*Introducing Theological Interpretation*, 19-20).
73. This is most obvious in Watson's *Text, Church, and World*.
74. E.g., Fowl, *Theological Interpretation*, 3.
75. The point is also made quite thoroughly by John Webster, "Hermeneutics in Modern Theology: Some Doctrinal Reflections," *Scottish Journal of Theology* (1998): 307-41.
76. Burnett, *Barth's Theological Exegesis*, 14-23.

but one tradition among many, it raises the question: what might another tradition have to add?

Toward a Wesleyan Theological Hermeneutic of Scripture: A Preview

There is a place at the table for a Wesleyan theological hermeneutic of Scripture. As I will show in the next chapter, assorted themes and problems have been treated in an almost preliminary way in articles, but there is as yet no full-length study that proposes one. In chapter two, therefore, I will survey what has so far been done to advance that front, then turn to the issues one must address if one is to proceed from a Wesleyan perspective. A particular problem for modern Wesleyan studies has simply been how to appropriate Wesley's writings. Drawing on Alasdair MacIntyre and others I will indicate a way forward.

Chapter three develops an approach for appropriating Wesley, drawing on postliberal thought, particularly as that has developed from the work of Hans Frei. Given Barth's influence on Frei in particular and postliberalism generally, this may seem a problematic way forward, one that introduces through the back door a Reformed influence in the Wesleyan hermeneutical house. However, I draw mainly on the formal elements of Frei and postliberalism; Wesleyan theology will be allowed to directly inform and shape how that methodology is used. In the end, Frei's insights on the literal sense and the internal grammar of the faith will help illumine a postcritical appropriation of Wesley's writings in the service of a constructive proposal.

Chapter four looks at Wesley's theological hermeneutics. Taking the view that Wesley's hermeneutics are soteriological, I will survey the role of Scripture in the divine economy of salvation as a means of grace, then examine the relevant elements in Wesley's hermeneutics. The soteriological context will be divided into two aspects: the economy of salvation and the means of grace. I will also examine the analogy of faith as the grammar that rules both theological interpretation of Scripture and Christian life in Wesley's theology.

Chapter five continues this descriptive work, giving examples of the literal sense of Wesley's hermeneutics. Since the literal sense, in Frei's and others' work, eludes theoretical explanation, it is best understood through examples. I will therefore examine four instances of the literal sense in Wesley's use, before offering a characterization of it.

Chapter six begins to appropriate this description of Wesley's hermeneutics into my own proposal, focusing on the church as Spirit-formed context. I look at both the significance of Wesley's belief in Scripture as a means of grace the Holy Spirit uses to sanctify the interpreter, while also trying to rectify the ecclesiological deficit in Wesley's theology. This is especially important in light of contemporary theological hermeneutics' focus on context. Using my findings from Frei and postliberalism, I begin to explore what a communally authorized Wesleyan literal sense might look like today.

Chapter seven continues my appropriation, developing an understanding of the unity of Scripture, literal sense, and the role of figural reading in shaping Wesleyan identity. Drawing on the work of Umberto Eco, I examine the dynamic nature of meaning, and combine his concept of the model reader with a soteriological account of figural reading. The rest of the chapter sets out to answer the question, what is a Wesleyan model reader? I argue that the Wesleyan generation of meaning is part of sanctification, whereby the Holy Spirit weds our identities to that of the Jesus Christ mediated to us through Scripture.

Chapter eight completes the proposal of this study, exploring how changing contexts require a changing grammar of faith that is still Wesleyan. Specifically, I offer a way beyond Wesley's analogy of faith to a ruled reading more in line with contemporary perspectives. I then demonstrate the Wesleyan theological hermeneutic I have been developing with a sermon. From there I summarize the argument and outline what from my perspective are the essential elements of the Wesleyan theological hermeneutic of Scripture explored in these pages. These elements are:

1) Wesleyan interpretation is theological in that its aim is the knowledge and love of God.
2) Wesleyan interpretation regards the literal sense of Scripture as the soteriological sense, which leads to the knowledge and love of God. The literal sense thus has a salvific effect on the interpreter, incorporating her into the economy of salvation.
3) By recognizing the Bible as Scripture, Wesleyan interpretation is sacramental, regarding the Bible as a means of grace through which the Holy Spirit works to bring us from death to life.
4) As sacramental, Wesleyan interpretation is ecclesially located (that is, it exists within communities known as "Wesleyan").
5) As ecclesially located, Wesleyan interpretation occurs within the ongoing tradition of Wesleyan theology, as a particular expression of the church catholic.
6) Being within the Wesleyan tradition, Wesleyan interpretation will tend to pattern its reading of Scripture according to its concerns with holiness. It grammatically structures the life of sanctification Scripture facilitates through figural reading. Wesleyan readers enter the world of Scripture and embark on the Christian way of life as children of God, a way of life whose end is the Father, Son, and Holy Spirit—an end also known as *entire sanctification*, or *Christian perfection*.

2. The Wesleyan Conversation[1]

In Search of a Wesleyan Theological Hermeneutic of Scripture

John Wesley and Scripture
In the background of much of the conversation in Wesleyan hermeneutics has been John Wesley's own hermeneutical practice. Certainly, it would seem, if one wanted to be Wesleyan in theological interpretation, grasping John Wesley's interpretation of Scripture would be fundamental. In some cases Wesley's hermeneutics have been treated on their own, without direct connection to a constructive proposal.[2] Typically, however, there is at least a desire to say more. The most significant study along these lines remains Scott J. Jones' *John Wesley's Conception and Use of Scripture*, which gives a thorough analysis of Wesley's hermeneutics while also attempting to be more constructive.[3] Jones wants to articulate Wesley's doctrine of Scripture—or rather, sift his unsystematic writings to allow Wesley's own articulation of his doctrine of Scripture to come through—in the service of filling an apparent need in the history of interpretation (an adequate account of Wesley's hermeneutics). Due to the occasional nature of Wesley's writings, Jones sets himself the task of scrutinizing the mass of data, since "it is impossible to claim that a small group of Wesley's writings provides an adequate basis for determining Wesley's position on a given subject."[4] Jones filters out whatever in Wesley's writings

---

1. For much of what follows in this chapter, see now Steven J. Koskie, "Can We Speak of a Wesleyan Theological Hermeneutic of Scripture Today?" in *Wesley, Wesleyans, and Reading Bible as Scripture* (ed. Joel B. Green and David F. Watson; Waco, TX: Baylor University Press, 2012), 195-209.

2. E.g., Wilbur H. Mullen, "John Wesley's Method of Biblical Interpretation," *Religion in Life* (1978): 99-108; Larry Shelton, "John Wesley's Approach to Scripture in Historical Perspective," *Wesleyan Theological Journal* 16 (1981): 23-50; Timothy L. Smith, "John Wesley and the Wholeness of Scripture," *Interpretation* 39 (1985): 246-62; Troy W. Martin, "John Wesley's Exegetical Orientation: East or West," *Wesleyan Theological Journal* 26 (1991): 104-38; Geoffrey Wainwright, "The Trinitarian Hermeneutic of John Wesley," in *Reading the Bible in Wesleyan Ways: Some Constructive Proposals* (ed. Barry L. Callen and Richard P. Thompson; Kansas City, MO: Beacon Hill, 2004), 17-37; Donald A. D. Thorsen, "Interpretation in Interactive Balance: The Authority of Scripture for John Wesley," in *Reading the Bible in Wesleyan Ways*, 81-104.

3. Scott J. Jones, *John Wesley's Conception and Use of Scripture* (Nashville, TN: Kingswood, 1995).

4. Jones, *Conception and Use*, 13.

may possess too much "borrowed" material, such as his editorial work on *The Christian Library*, in order to detect Wesley's own views on Scripture.[5]

In general Jones believes Wesley's conception and use of Scripture cohere; sometimes the rules of thumb Wesley abided by—interpreting obscure texts in light of clearer ones, reading Scripture in light of its general or whole tenor, and reading according to the literal sense—are applied idiosyncratically, but this is largely accounted for by the occasional nature of the writings. Jones concludes by considering Wesley's doctrine of Scripture in light of its place as an authority in relation to other authorities, such as tradition, reason, and experience, and how these authorities coinhere with the wholeness of Scripture and the Christian life. Jones finds that Wesley's soteriology, his *ordo salutis*, was, in Wesley's mind, already present in the literal meaning of the biblical text.[6] Contemporary readers, Jones believes, do not have the luxury of such a view, thanks to modern criticism.

It is just at this point, however, that Jones' study ends on an intriguing note. Despite labeling his project a descriptive, historical endeavor, Jones wants to suggest what a Wesley*an* view of Scripture might look like. According to Jones, this would include a high view of Scripture's authority and inspiration, making room for authorities other than Scripture in the service of a unified view of truth, seeking the whole of Scripture's message, and employing "the best critical tools available"; finally, a Wesleyan view of Scripture would not be Wesleyan in a narrow sense, but appropriately ecumenical.[7]

Why these principles are suitable for Wesleyans is unclear. For instance, if certain of Wesley's positions and hermeneutical moves are not available to the contemporary hermeneut, what exactly would a "high" view of Scripture that is Wesleyan look like? What constitutes "the best critical tools available" and how would they be deployed? Considering how historical criticism has taken biblical interpretation so far from Wesley's interpretive assumptions and practices—given the presuppositions of history that have been associated with historical criticism since the eighteenth century and its general aversion to there being a "unified message" to the Bible—why is this principle Wesleyan? And with all these questions, who decides which are the "right" answers?

Jones' inductive study is not designed to answer such questions, though the questions are begged by his suggestions. In the end, his inductive approach to Wesley limits what he can accomplish constructively. Moreover, his methodology is not unlike what we find in modern searches for the historical

---

5. "Borrowed" is Jones' term (*Conception and Use*, 13). Two exceptions are *Explanatory Notes upon the New Testament* and the "Articles of Religion," given their prominence in early Methodism for Wesley.

6. Wesley's *ordo salutis* is his soteriology, generally explicated in steps, which vary: one example would be original sin, justification by faith, new birth, and entire sanctification. This will be discussed in greater detail in chapter four.

7. See Jones, *Conception and Use*, 222-23.

Jesus. In this case, Jones is looking for the historical Wesley, as demonstrated by his distrust of whatever Wesley heavily borrows from other sources, since these borrowings are not "Wesley's own views."[8] Drawing out a picture of the "real Wesley" is the goal. The degree to which this approach is helpful to my proposal will be weighed shortly. Be that as it may, considering how at odds Wesley's unsystematic writings would seem to be to Jones' synthetic project, Jones' account of Wesley's conception and use of Scripture is the most substantial on offer.

Wesleyan Hermeneutics
If Jones' book is the acme of attempts to describe Wesley's hermeneutics, other scholars have ventured what would comprise a Wesleyan theological hermeneutic of Scripture. The most substantive proposals have come from Robert W. Wall and Joel B. Green.[9]

Wall argues that Wesleyan biblical scholars—like biblical scholars in general—have been too occupied with descriptive tasks to provide anything useful for Wesleyan theologians. This of course is a peculiarly modern problem, which Wall believes can be transcended by the concept of "canon." Drawing from Brevard Childs, Wall uses canon to mean both the final literary form of Scripture, and its function within the church.[10] In its final form, Scripture draws attention to its subject matter, God's Word, which then "helps draw the church's theological boundaries and supply the language and grammar of normative Christian faith."[11] Important though this is, it does not yet account for how Scripture is received in the community of faith, and it is here Wall's proposal makes its Wesleyan turn. Because biblical texts are "gapped," as Wall puts it, the church contributes to the meaning of Scripture by the very nature of reading

---

8. Jones, *Conception and Use*, 13.

9. Other contributions include J. Kenneth Grider, "Wesleyanism and the Inerrancy Issue," *Wesleyan Theological Journal* 19 (1984): 51-61; Frank A. Spina, "Wesleyan Faith Seeking Biblical Understanding," *Wesleyan Theological Journal* 30 (1995): 26-49; Russell Morton, "Studying Text in a Wesleyan 'Context': A Response to Robert Wall and Joel Green," *Wesleyan Theological Journal* 34 (1999): 243-57; Thomas E. Phillips, "Reading Theory and Biblical Interpretation," *Wesleyan Theological Journal* 35 (2000): 32-48; Richard P. Thompson, "Inspired Imagination: John Wesley's Concept of Biblical Inspiration and Literary-Critical Studies," in *Reading the Bible in Wesleyan Ways*, 57-79. In virtually all cases, these texts are somewhat ambiguous in their constructive proposals, while the texts to be considered in detail lay out a more well-defined programme for a Wesleyan theological hermeneutic of Scripture.

10. For Wall's extended discussion of canon, see Robert W. Wall, "Reading the New Testament in Canonical Context," in *Hearing the New Testament: Strategies for Interpretation* (ed. Joel B. Green; Grand Rapids, MI: Eerdmans, 1995), 370-93.

11. Robert W. Wall, "Toward a Wesleyan Hermeneutic of Scripture," in *Reading the Bible in Wesleyan Ways: Some Constructive Proposals* (ed. Barry L. Callen and Richard P. Thompson; Kansas City, MO: Beacon Hill, 2004), 40.

it.[12] The biblical interpreter is also a tradent, or someone who belongs to a particular tradition of interpretation, and holds to a tradition's methodological and theological interests.[13] Since this theological location is key to interpretation, a specifically Wesleyan interpretation is one interested in "rendering the (especially soteriological) accents of the Wesleyan theological tradition."[14] The outcome of this approach is both the transformation of Wesleyan belief and the preservation of the Wesleyan perspective. Wesleyan interpreters should not read to the exclusion of non-Wesleyan traditions, as these will have "accents" also supported by Scripture's plain sense; and this openness is also ecclesiologically responsible, accounting as it does for the whole church.[15]

Wall's analysis is very helpful. He does struggle somewhat with bridging his analysis with actual Wesleyan interpretive practice today—though he is clearly concerned with it. In another essay, "Facilitating Scripture's Future Role among Wesleyans," Wall gives much space to general hermeneutical issues, before making two suggestive statements for Wesleyan interpreters. First, in an already familiar vein from his essay noted above he writes, "the self-critical Wesleyan interpreter seeks after meaning in biblical texts and stories that congrues around the distinguishing themes and *deeper logic* of a Wesleyan typology of God's Word."[16] Wall does not explain what this "deeper logic" is, but I believe it provides an important hermeneutical key to a problem Wall does not address, as I will point out momentarily. Second, Wall states that Wesleyans cannot "simply adopt as normative Wesley's particular reading of Scripture."[17] Why this is so is not spelled out, but given Wall's sensitivity to one's socio-theological location in interpretation, it appears he says this because modern-day Wesleyans live in a different context from Wesley. This difference must be held in tension with the "conservative assumption" Wall makes, that Wesleyans stand in a history of interpretation whose font is John Wesley.[18]

Wall advances the discussion in that he moves beyond those who focus solely on Wesley's hermeneutics, and begins to move toward appropriating Wesley's hermeneutics for contemporary Wesleyans. Wall is well versed in the academic roadblocks that stand in the way of his project, and makes suggestions

---

12. By "gapped," Wall means that 1) biblical texts reference and allude to other texts that a "talented interpreter" (apparently an interpreter knowledgeable of these references and allusions) will detect, and 2) the changing context of interpretation over time requires the talented interpreter to interpret for her particular community in its particular time, making the plain sense of Scripture context-specific ("Wesleyan Hermeneutic," 42).

13. Wall, "Wesleyan Hermeneutic," 43, 45.

14. Wall, "Wesleyan Hermeneutic," 43.

15. Wall, "Wesleyan Hermeneutic," 43-44.

16. Robert W. Wall, "Facilitating Scripture's Future Role among Wesleyans," in *Reading the Bible in Wesleyan Ways*, 118 (italics added).

17. Wall, "Scripture's Future Role," 119.

18. Wall, "Wesleyan Hermeneutic," 45.

of how to progress; but they are only suggestions. His pointing out that Wesleyan interpreters, as tradents, are beholden to a tradition, and that this tradition both illumines Scripture and is illumined (and therefore transformed) by that same Scripture is valuable. Also helpful is Wall's belief that Wesleyans are unable to merely repeat Wesley's hermeneutics. Here, however, Wall could certainly make a major contribution by saying more. The issue is that of appropriation: How do Wesleyans appropriate Wesley's hermeneutics; or put differently, how do Wesleyans learn interpretation from Wesley, given the differing contexts Wall notes?[19]

Joel B. Green has also contributed significantly to a constructive Wesleyan theological hermeneutic of Scripture. Green takes his point of departure from a deceptively crucial point that "much of what characterizes a Wesleyan hermeneutic must be that Wesleyans do it."[20] Though apparently obvious, Green's statement runs against modernist sensibilities that look for methods to solve every theological conundrum: "a Wesleyan mode of interpretation cannot be reduced to a particular set of techniques; there is no Wesleyan apparatus into which biblical texts can be dumped, the handle cranked, and a Wesleyan result guaranteed on the other side. What is needed, rather, is involvement in biblical interpretation by persons formed in Wesleyan communities."[21] This is essentially the same as Wall's point that context matters, and as with Wall, directs Green's attention to how that context should translate into contemporary Wesleyan interpretation.

Green, who frames his thoughts in terms of what would qualify as a valid Wesleyan interpretation, offers four theses toward a contemporary Wesleyan hermeneutic: Wesleyan interpretation is critical in a way consistent with the Bible's status as Scripture; Wesleyan interpretation must take a view of the literal sense of Scripture that is informed by contemporary hermeneutics, therefore allowing Scripture to both address contemporary readers and allow for multiple readings; Wesleyan interpretation is soteriological; Wesleyan interpretation must be holistic, overcoming disciplinary boundaries as well as the barrier between Old and New Testament studies.[22]

In these recommendations, Green argues that interpretation is more about the production of meaning than achieving understanding, and that the postmodern turn to the reader opens the door to seeing how a Wesleyan context would bestow Wesleyan themes to Wesleyan interpreters, who would in turn

---

19. Wall has flirted with the issue elsewhere. See Robert W. Wall, "Wesley as Biblical Interpreter," in *The Cambridge Companion to John Wesley* (ed. Randy L. Maddox and Jason E. Vickers; Cambridge Companions to Religion; Cambridge: Cambridge University Press, 2009), 124.

20. Joel B. Green, "Is There a Contemporary Wesleyan Hermeneutic?" in *Reading the Bible in Wesleyan Ways*, 124.

21. Green, "Contemporary Wesleyan Hermeneutic," 124.

22. Green, "Contemporary Wesleyan Hermeneutic," 125-32.

read Scripture in Wesleyan ways. Green does not see this as in any way jeopardizing Scripture's ability to speak into the life of the church; this kind of hermeneutical formation allows Scripture to be heard in the first place. Given the Wesleyan context of Wesleyan hermeneutics, a soteriological reading unites Scripture by seeing its overarching subject matter as God. Under this unity, Wesleyans would go on to pursue scriptural holiness in a way that respects Scripture's unity in accordance with a literal sense normed by the rule of faith.

As with Wall, Green helpfully sheds light on the way forward; the main problem is that more needs to be said.[23] Green introduces some of the potential fruits of interacting with contemporary hermeneutical theory by beginning to broaden the literal sense beyond a simple correspondence with authorial intent. Like Wall, he recognizes the place of context, and gives great store to the Wesleyan identity as something formed within a Wesleyan context, which cannot be created or maintained apart from biblical interpretation. He moves casually between his own knowledge of contemporary hermeneutics and Wesley's hermeneutics—though as with Wall we can ask how exactly this transaction works. How does the modern Wesleyan interpreter relate to Wesley?

In fact, we can draw out from Wall and Green two interlocking issues that a Wesleyan theological hermeneutic must address. First is what we might call the genetic relation of Wesleyan interpreters to Wesley himself. As Wall assumes (and Green does as well, judging by his frequent nods to Wesley in aspects of his work), Wesleyan hermeneuts stand in a history of interpretation traceable back to Wesley. That said, Wesleyans today live in a different milieu, with over two hundred years of hermeneutical changes making simple mimicry of Wesley's hermeneutics out of the question. This continuity and difference must be addressed. Second, recalling Green's point that no Wesleyan techniques exist to circumvent formation in a Wesleyan community, a Wesleyan theological hermeneutic must take seriously its being rooted in a tradition-constituted context. To say that Wesleyans perform Wesleyan hermeneutics is to acknowledge an ongoing community of faith through time that is identifiable by its assumptions, themes, and practices as "Wesleyan."

Wall concludes his essay, "Toward a Wesleyan Hermeneutic of Scripture," by indicating many of the key issues that must be confronted, but also a general sense of loss about how to move ahead:

> I conclude feeling even more tentative about the project of Wesleyan hermeneutics than when I began. Am I correct, however, to presume that we possess from Wesley a particular perspective on Scripture,

---

23. See also Joel B. Green, "Scripture in the Church: Reconstructing the Authority of Scripture for Christian Formation and Mission," in *The Wesleyan Tradition: A Paradigm for Renewal* (ed. Paul W. Chilcote; Nashville, TN: Abingdon, 2002), 38-51; and Joel B. Green, "Contribute or Capitulate? Wesleyans, Pentecostals and Reading the Bible in a Post-Colonial Mode," *Wesleyan Theological Journal* 39 (2004): 74-90.

and that this perspective forges in turn those presuppositions of biblical interpretation that help to shape in a decisive way what it means for Wesleyans to be the church and to act like the church should for the glory of God? Am I right to sponsor a hermeneutics whose agenda is to "retribalize" Wesleyanism in order to nurture, even to reform the theological understanding and praxis of the whole church? I think so. Moreover, the Wesleyan interpreter has primary loyalty to Wesleyan communions of believers, as prophet or priest. In this regard, the Wesleyan interpreter should cast biblical meaning/theology in a way that enables our particular cloud of Christian witnesses to understand and embody more fully a distinctively Wesleyan form of saving faith and holy life. What I am less certain of is how best to do this.[24]

How are these assumptions, themes, and practices—the "presuppositions" he refers to—transferred in the Wesleyan tradition? And how does one learn these from Wesley? If time and change makes it impossible merely to adopt Wesley's hermeneutics, what does a contemporary Wesleyan theological hermeneutic look like? These are the questions that will occupy the remainder of this study. To raise them, however, is to indicate that our procedure will have to differ from what have become common ways of doing Wesleyan theology: systematizing Wesley's thought and searching for the historical Wesley. It is in the midst of this situation that voices like Wall's and Green's speak, and perhaps it is because of the inadequacy of the predominant approaches that more has not been done to develop a Wesleyan theological hermeneutic. To further set up my proposal, then, I will briefly examine systematic and historical modes of Wesleyan theology.

The Historical Wesley and Wesleyan Systematic Theology
As William J. Abraham, Albert Cook Outler Professor of Wesley Studies at Perkins School of Theology, recently observed, much of modern Wesleyan theology is indebted to Albert Outler.[25] In fact, in Abraham's view, modern

---

24. Wall, "Wesleyan Hermeneutic," 55.
25. William J. Abraham, "The End of Wesleyan Theology," *Wesleyan Theological Journal* 40 (2005): 7-25. Abraham is not the only one to observe this. In their introduction to a 1991 volume of Outler's essays, Thomas C. Oden and Leicester R. Longden remark, "A vast reappraisal of the theological heritage of John Wesley is already proceeding apace. Wesleyan theology is currently undergoing a major recrudescence. Outler is central to it. The Wesleyan doctrinal standards are being more carefully attended in the last quarter of this century than any previous quarter. Outler is an important part of that discovery. Those who wonder why this is happening do well to attend to Outler's work" ("Introduction," in *The Wesleyan Theological Heritage: Essays of Albert C. Outler* [ed. Thomas C. Oden and Leicester R. Longden; Grand Rapids, MI: Zondervan, 1991], 11). Outler's essays in the volume make their case. Aside from Oden and Longden's collection, Outler's virtuosity is on display in the introduction to the first

Wesleyan theology is the outworking of Outler's personal project that has now run its course. Whether this is true, Abraham helpfully discerns that the driving motivation of contemporary Wesleyan theology since Outler has been to present John Wesley—and by extension the tradition that springs from him—as being a theological voice worth reckoning with.[26] As Outler writes in *Theology in the Wesleyan Spirit*,

> Now, I'm concerned...to propose [an] interpretive sketch of Wesley ...*as a significant theologian* whose importance as theologian...has been sadly underestimated by both his devotées and critics. He was, I have come to believe, the most important Anglican theologian of his century. He is, I also believe, a very considerable resource in our own time for *our* theological reflections...My aim and hope is to help rescue Wesley from his status as cult-hero to the Methodists...and to exhibit him as a creative Christian thinker with a special word for *these* parlous times and for us....[27]

The resultant program, then, is twofold—to recover this Wesley (establishing his theological proficiency by demonstrating his deft integration of multifarious strands of the Christian tradition, East and West), then adapting his ideas from the occasional genres in which Wesley wrote as a "folk theologian" to those more amenable to the modern academy and ecumenically minded church.[28] This adaptation has typically taken the form of systematization, and the formulation of a distinctly Wesleyan theological method, the Wesleyan Quadrilateral.[29] The

---

volume of the Bicentennial Edition of Wesley's *Works*, a series he inaugurated ("Introduction," in *The Works of John Wesley* [Bicentennial Edition; ed. Frank Baker and Richard P. Heitzenrater; Nashville, TN: Abingdon, 1984-], 1:1-100.

26. Abraham, "The End," 8-13. See also Randy L. Maddox, "Respected Founder / Neglected Guide: The Role of Wesley in American Methodist Theology," *Methodist History* 37 (1999): 71-88.

27. Albert C. Outler, *Theology in the Wesleyan Spirit* (Nashville, TN: Discipleship Resources, 1975), 1-2 (italics original).

28. "Folk theologian" is Outler's term to describe Wesley, as a way of defending him against academics who did not take Wesley seriously as a theologian ("Preface," *Works* 1:xi).

29. See, e.g., Thomas C. Oden, *John Wesley's Scriptural Christianity: A Plain Exposition of His Teaching on Christian Doctrine* (Grand Rapids, MI: Zondervan, 1994). As Maddox shows, the impulse for systematization came early on in Methodism for mostly apologetic reasons. The difference between systematization in the nineteenth and early twentieth centuries and that of more recent times is that the earlier efforts usually marginalized Wesley, whereas Wesleyan systematics since Outler has focused on Wesley ("Respected Founder / Neglected Guide," esp. 71-84). For a seminal essay on the Quadrilateral, see Albert C. Outler, "The Wesleyan Quadrilateral—in John Wesley," in *The Wesleyan Theological Heritage*, 21-37. Also Donald A. D. Thorsen, *The Wesleyan*

Quadrilateral, a matrix of Scripture, tradition, reason, and experience, has been embraced, criticized, and defended since its introduction by Outler.[30] Instead of entering directly into that debate, my primary reservation is not with the Quadrilateral per se, but with the larger venture of systematization. Wesleyan theologians, even when they have been critical of the theological divisions of labor,[31] have nonetheless worked to adapt Wesley's thought to the academic arena in a way that results in a theological practice different from Wesley's. Put differently, they have created a theology that is more at home among the divisions of the modern academy—divisions, for example, between biblical exegesis and systematic theology—than what Wesley, writing in the eighteenth century, would have understood. More to the point, by assuming the need to create an academically viable methodology and system, Wesleyan theologians have perhaps neglected to ask whether Wesley's own mode of theological reflection—especially as an exegetical form of theology—has anything to offer. The argument here will be that theological hermeneutics, by seeking to move beyond the exegesis/theology impasse, opens the door to revisiting the theological practices of those early and premodern theologians who did not live within contemporary academic strictures, such as John Wesley.

Before developing that idea more, the other facet to the modern Wesleyan theological approach, the search for the historical Wesley, should be addressed. In searching for the historical Wesley, Wesley's writings are seen as windows to look through to reconstruct the socio-historical background of their composition.[32] Typically, this orientation seeks to catalogue the various sources of Wesley's thought, such as in the Bicentennial Edition of Wesley's *Works*.

Quadrilateral: Scripture, Tradition, Reason and Experience as a Model of Evangelical Theology (Grand Rapids, MI: Zondervan, 1990).

30. *Embraced* by Thorsen, *Quadrilateral*; *criticized* by William J. Abraham, *Waking from Doctrinal Amnesia: The Healing of Doctrine in the United Methodist Church* (Nashville, TN: Abingdon, 1995) (and again in Abraham, "Wesleyan Theology," 12, n. 18. See also Philip R. Meadows, "The 'Discipline' of Theology: Making Methodism Less Methodological," *Wesleyan Theological Journal* 36 [2001]: 50-87); *defended* by W. Stephen Gunter, et al., *Wesley and the Quadrilateral: Renewing the Conversation* (Nashville, TN: Abingdon, 1997).

31. Randy L. Maddox particularly has written on the division of theology into practical and systematic forms. However, his own attempts at developing a Wesleyan theology, though by no means slavishly following Outler, are indebted enough to Outler's agenda that they tend to result in a form of theological reflection quite different from Wesley's (Randy L. Maddox, "The Recovery of Theology as a Practical Discipline," *Theological Studies* 51 [1990]: 650-72).

32. Among contemporary scholars, Richard Heitzenrater is surely preeminent in this approach. See his introductory musings on finding "The Elusive Mr. Wesley" in Richard P. Heitzenrater, *The Elusive Mr. Wesley: John Wesley His Own Biographer* (vol. 1; Nashville, TN: Abingdon, 1984), esp. 15-32. The influence of Heitzenrater can be seen in Jones, *Conception and Use*, 12.

The reasoning for doing so is ideological, as Abraham argues.[33] If Wesley can be shown to be a significant theological voice in the tradition through his encyclopedic and skillful use of diverse sources, credibility is transferred to the tradition he founded. As Outler writes in his introduction to Wesley's *Works*, "The credibility of any such perspective [of Wesley as a theologian worthy of serious scholarly attention]...depends upon an adequate display of Wesley's sources, and a demonstration of his way with the diverse traditions that converged in him."[34]

The Bicentennial Edition is an important scholarly accomplishment, but it perhaps does not accomplish all that Outler and others might have hoped. Certainly, as Abraham shows, it does not result in *the* historical Wesley, only in historical Wesleys.[35] Of greater interest here is its use of Wesley's texts. In its quest to establish Wesley's theological credentials, the editors of the Bicentennial Edition have sought to fashion a critical version of Wesley's writings. In a fascinating discussion of the textual work that went into the Bicentennial Edition, Frank Baker recounts the process:

> For the copy-text in the present edition...we turn in almost every instance to the first edition of each item, the only one printed directly from Wesley's manuscript and therefore the one most likely to reproduce faithfully his original intentions and to contain the freshness of his creative writing...The final edited text...is composite in character rather than a simple facsimile of the first edition, though it is a composite strongly favouring Wesley's original idiosyncrasies of style.[36]

The goal is a "critical text," hewn from the extant texts that have been retrieved. This critical text is a (re)construction created masterfully at the hands of the editors of the Bicentennial Edition. And yet, it is *this* text that is ostensibly most reflective of Wesley's "original intentions" and "contain the freshness of his creative writing." But would Wesley concur? Strictly speaking, we cannot know, but it must be noted that it is the editors who discern what the original intent of Wesley must have been, not Wesley. Required therefore is the judgment of the editor standing over the past, her studied eye making approximations, ultimately fashioning a text based on scholarly judgments which, as shown above, are steered by a particular ideological bent. A diffidence with the past is imperative; Wesley's idiosyncrasies are to be kept, though idiosyncrasies that endure the editorial process throughout Wesley's life are sifted to conform to the editors' expectations. In *The Past Is a Foreign Country*, David Lowenthal comments on such an approach:

---

33. Abraham, "The End," 8-9.
34. Outler, "Introduction," in *Works*, 1:xi.
35. Abraham, "The End," 13-14.
36. Frank Baker, Appendix A, *Works*, 4:21-22.

Recognizing the impact of the present on the past, we confront anew the paradox implicit in preservation. Vestiges are saved to stave off decay, destruction, and replacement and to keep an unspoiled heritage. Yet preservation itself reveals that permanence is an illusion. The more we save, the more aware we become that such remains are continually altered and reinterpreted. We suspend their erosion only to transform them in other ways. And saviours of the past change it no less than iconoclasts bent on its destruction.[37]

The composite critical text is not actually Wesley's text in that he never wrote it.

This elicits a second point: Wesley left his sermons for pedagogical and apologetic reasons; Baker himself observes this.[38] If properly preserved by the Methodist movement, these are living texts—a formative dynamic between Wesleyans and their spiritual founder's writings continues. When contrasted with the Bicentennial Edition, it is not clear that this dynamic is sustained by virtue of this project. Consistent with Lowenthal's comments about how we attempt to preserve the past, Baker contends that an important aspect of this task of preparing a critical text was "to secure and record any significant changes in Wesley's thought and its expression."[39] Lowenthal's view is therefore vindicated, for the result of this cataloguing is indeed an altered text.

These critical remarks are not made to claim the Bicentennial Edition is somehow *wrong* (it is uncertain what such a judgment would mean), but only to demonstrate the kind of reading found in the Bicentennial Edition has limits. It is not omnicompetent for every way of reading Wesley.[40] What the kind of analysis we find in the Bicentennial Edition is not, apparently, is the kind of reading for which we have these writings in the first place.

But even if the Bicentennial Edition is a departure from earlier receptions of Wesley's writings in the Wesleyan tradition, it is not entirely inappropriate. For surely within Wesleyanism there is a place for scholarly investigation of this kind, whether Wesley foresaw it or would have approved of it. In fact, this reinforces an essential hermeneutical point, that the future meanings of a text are no more determined by the author's intentions than is the past of the text faithfully preserved by the scholar.[41] Wesley himself was not necessarily concerned to crystallize his writings within the amber of his original intentions, as we might conclude from his own re-situating of his sermons into the *Sermons*

---

37. David Lowenthal, *The Past Is a Foreign Country* (Cambridge: Cambridge University Press, 1985), 410.

38. Baker, Appendix A, *Works*, 4:422.

39. Baker, Appendix A, *Works* 4:422.

40. Abraham would seem to concur when he observes that scholarly versions of the standard sermons, at home in the seminary or university, are inadequate as "spiritual nourishment" in the church ("The End," 24, n. 45).

41. Though this does not leave the text at the mercy of a reader's arbitrariness, as the discussion of "text intent" in chapter seven will argue.

on Several Occasions. These sermons written for particular occasions have now become trans-occasional, having a polyphonic capability that transcends the primordial reason for composition. With the Bicentennial Edition, we have different needs on the part of the interpreters, different questions, indicative of *any textual analysis*. "There is no such thing as an 'objective' analysis of a text," writes Norman Fairclough, "if by that we mean an analysis which simply describes what is 'there' in the text without being 'biased' by the 'subjectivity' of the analyst."[42]

The point of this discussion is to show that the Bicentennial Edition—as a prime example of that other facet of modern Wesleyan theology, the search for the historical Wesley—is not what it imagines itself to be. It is a certain kind of hermeneutical analysis of texts written by John Wesley; it is not Wesley himself. And as one kind of textual analysis, there are boundaries on what it can and cannot accomplish. There is a difference, in other words, between reading a text as a window into the past, and reading it for formative purposes for the present.[43] It may be helpful, therefore, to recontextualize Wesley's writings away from the questions and concerns that have animated scholarship formed within Outler's agenda, and toward the questions and concerns of this study, for they are different.[44]

To this point I have looked at what have become trademark approaches in Wesleyan theology in recent decades, and have attempted to point out their limits. In light of my readings of Wall and Green, the concerns of a Wesleyan theological hermeneutic of Scripture are not necessarily aided by what has become the status quo agenda. I am occupied here neither with bolstering Wesley's nor his tradition's status within the academy or ecumenism. Nor am I seeking to systematize his thinking or develop a method or technique for reading Scripture theologically. Finally, I am not searching for the historical Wesley, though I am interested in how his writings—the texts themselves—help shape a Wesleyan theological hermeneutic of Scripture now. To begin moving in that direction, I will close out this chapter by looking briefly at two key concepts of Alasdair MacIntyre's, tradition and craft.

---

42. Norman Fairclough, *Analysing Discourse: Textual Analysis for Social Research* (London: Routledge, 2003), 14-15.

43. Of course, theologically and morally formative readings can also be historically informed. The point is that a historical reading is neither the only nor necessarily the most important or appropriate reading of a text, depending largely on the situation.

44. A similar perspective to what I am building up to here is found in Ellen T. Charry, *By the Renewing of Your Minds: The Pastoral Function of Christian Doctrine* (New York: Oxford University Press, 1997). Charry moves away from historical analysis of major voices in the tradition, opting instead for what she calls "aretegenic" readings—pastoral readings that result in virtuous living.

MacIntyre and Reading Wesley in the Wesleyan Tradition

Wall and Green both indicate the Wesleyan tradition embodied in the Wesleyan community of faith is the incubator for a Wesleyan theological hermeneutic of Scripture, that is, a way of reading the Bible somehow based on or learned from John Wesley. Few scholars have done more to provide concepts to help understand what this could look like than Alasdair MacIntyre.[45]

MacIntyre argues that a tradition exists within a community and extends through time; said differently, tradition-constituted knowledge is historical knowledge. What this means is that every tradition over time changes, and these changes are the result of needed adaptations to novel situations, which often are beyond what could have possibly been envisioned by the progenitors of that tradition. According to MacIntyre, there are three stages to a tradition:

> A first in which the relevant beliefs, texts, and authorities have not yet been put in question; a second in which inadequacies of various types have been identified, but not yet remedied; and a third in which response to those inadequacies has resulted in a set of reformulations, reevaluations, and new formulations and evaluations, designed to remedy inadequacies and overcome limitations.[46]

New situations create problems for the interpretation of authoritative texts, authorities, practices, and beliefs. For a tradition to survive these crises requires skilled adherents who can address past inadequacies and keep intact, through every "rupture" as MacIntyre puts it, "Some core of shared belief, constitutive of allegiance to the tradition."[47] Therefore, what is

> central to a tradition-constituted enquiry at each stage in its development will be its current problematic, that agenda of unsolved problems and unresolved issues by reference to which its success or lack of it in making rational progress toward some further stage of development will be evaluated. At any point it may happen to any tradition-constituted enquiry that by its own standards of progress it ceases to make progress...[48]

It is interesting to compare MacIntyre's stages of a tradition with Abraham's critique of Wesleyan theology, referenced above ("The End of

---

45. For my purposes, the primary texts are Alasdair C. MacIntyre, *Whose Justice? Which Rationality?* (Notre Dame, IN: University of Notre Dame Press, 1988); and idem, *Three Rival Versions of Moral Enquiry: Encyclopaedia, Genealogy, and Tradition* (Notre Dame, IN: University of Notre Dame Press, 1989).

46 .MacIntyre, *Whose Justice*, 355.

47. MacIntyre, *Whose Justice*, 356.

48. MacIntyre, *Whose Justice*, 362.

Wesleyan Theology"). Whereas Abraham judges the failure of Outler's agenda to be the end of Wesleyan theology, we might on a MacIntyrean analysis say that Abraham is participating in the second stage of the Wesleyan tradition, and this study is part of stage three. In fact, Abraham's own admission that Wesleyan communities of faith will continue on is the best argument against the idea that Wesleyan theology has ended, since it is from such communities that theology should come—or so goes the argument here. Additionally, Abraham makes a distinction between reading Wesley for constructive theological reasons, and reading Wesley for personal devotion. In Abraham's opinion, what is needed in Wesleyan scholarship is a revised historical agenda. Meanwhile, Wesleyan churches should begin to venerate Wesley as a church father whose rich spirituality is a defining bequest for his ecclesial progeny.[49] In part, Abraham argues that this is necessary because appealing to Wesley as an authority in theology is a category mistake; Wesley himself only ever appealed to Scripture in the final balance of things.

If MacIntyre is correct, however, Abraham's criticism that a Wesleyan appeal to Wesley is not a move Wesley would have made is irrelevant, since the tradition issuing from Wesley has moved into territory he could not have imagined.[50] Additionally, Abraham's suggestion that Wesley be venerated as a church father does not preclude reading Wesley for constructive theological purposes; it should instead be the basis for it.

To unpack this point, consider MacIntyre's idea of learning a craft for the purposes of moral enquiry. In order to become a skilled practitioner, a person must submit to an authority, as this authority is someone who knows how to initiate a student into the craft to be learned. As MacIntyre frames the matter:

> The authority of a master within a craft is both more and other than a matter of exemplifying the best standards so far. It is also and most importantly a matter of knowing how to go further and especially how to direct others towards going further, using what can be learned from the tradition afforded by the past to move towards the *telos* of fully perfected work. It is thus knowing how to link past and future that those with authority are able to draw upon tradition, to interpret and reinterpret it, so that its directedness towards the *telos* of that particular craft becomes apparent in new and characteristically unexpected ways.[51]

---

49. Abraham, "The End," 24-25.

50. Abraham's own critique of Protestant biblicism is a primary case in point. If sola scriptura as Wesley practiced it is no longer viable, adherents to the Wesleyan tradition must find the resources to innovate in the face of these new challenges. In fact, this seems to be what Abraham is attempting to do, though his own remarks on the failure of his tradition are at times confusing.

51. MacIntyre, *Rival Versions*, 65-66.

Moreover, "we shall have to learn from that teacher and initially accept on the basis of his or her authority within the community of a craft precisely what intellectual and moral habits it is which we must cultivate and acquire if we are to become effective self-moved participants in such enquiry."[52]

What MacIntyre provides here is a reorientation away from modes of reading Wesley derived from Outler, but also a different solution—even a different way of understanding the problem—than what Abraham provides. First, MacIntyre helps us see that the frustrations both Wall and Abraham express (essentially both are frustrations with how Wesleyan theology moves forward, though they have somewhat different ideas of the future in mind) are a natural part of the lifespan of a tradition. The question is whether the Wesleyan tradition has the resources to survive. Second, MacIntyre gives more substance to the intimations of both Wall and Green that a Wesleyan theological hermeneutic of Scripture is by definition rooted in the Wesleyan tradition, which is embodied in Wesleyan communities. On this account, the way to transmit the assumptions, practices, and so on that comprise Wesleyan theological interpretation is to see theological interpretation as a craft that we can learn from Wesley (thus tying in Abraham's call to venerate Wesley as a church father; no doubt a major component of Wesley's "spirituality" was biblical interpretation).

Set in these terms, theological interpretation, if learned from Wesley, is indeed a craft in the moral sense MacIntyre endorses since, as will be seen in later chapters, interpretation for Wesley both presupposes and results in holiness. This implies departing from the academic divisions so many writing in theological hermeneutics have critiqued, and reenvisioning theological reflection as an exegetical activity within the life of the church. This second point blends with a third, that Wesley's writings are authoritative texts within the Wesleyan tradition, and have subsequently been the object of interpretive conflict, making their interpretation and reinterpretation a major resource in extending the tradition. Thus, although the texts found in the Bicentennial Edition of Wesley's *Works* are helpful to a certain kind of scholarship, its hermeneutic is not adequate for learning the craft of theological interpretation from Wesley.

---

52. MacIntyre, *Rival Versions*, 63. This also means there are ways of conceiving authority besides the narrowly epistemological conception Abraham criticizes.

3. A Postliberal Contribution

In this chapter I will develop an approach for appropriating Wesley's writings that avoids the problems of what have become the conventional approaches of Wesleyan theology, neither of which are adequate in developing a Wesleyan theological hermeneutic of Scripture. The road I will travel to reach this approach is a postliberal one, especially as that has been laid down by Hans Frei. Frei offers three important contributions to my agenda. First, Frei's project developed against the backdrop of modern theology, at least as regards certain (though central) aspects: christology, revelation, biblical criticism, and history. For this reason, Frei is uniquely situated at the other end of an era of which Wesley stands at the threshold, and does so as someone interested in recovering at least some aspects of premodern interpretation.[1] The distances that appear to separate Wesley from modern-day Wesleyans (obviously historical, but perhaps also theological and hermeneutical) may be bridgeable by following Frei's lead.

Second, Frei is worth attention due to his considerable import for contemporary theological hermeneutics. His *magnum opus*, *The Eclipse of Biblical Narrative*, is a watershed for biblical hermeneutics, and is now a standard genealogy of modernist interpretation of the Bible. His work has inspired a whole generation of inquiry into various features of theological hermeneutics, and it is easy to see, when one examines this body of material, that much of it is either directly or indirectly indebted to him.[2]

The third and most pertinent contribution is Frei's reorientation of theology as a communally located skill concerned with identity and biblical interpretation. Although in his turn to the communal site of theology Frei

---

1. Frei's desire to recover a reading of Scripture that asserted the literal ascriptive identity of Jesus in the Gospels, something he claims defined Christian interpretation of the Bible until beginning in the eighteenth century, is the most significant practice he sought to recover. A relatively concise version of his work toward this end is Hans W. Frei, "Theological Reflections on the Accounts of Jesus' Death and Resurrection," in *The Identity of Jesus Christ: The Hermeneutical Bases of Dogmatic Theology* (Eugene, OR: Wipf and Stock, 1997), 1-49. This edition also has the longer collection of essays that originally comprised *Identity*, which elaborates on the argument of "Theological Reflections." "Theological Reflections" is also reprinted in *Theology and Narrative: Selected Essays* (ed. George Hunsinger and William C. Placher; New York: Oxford University Press, 1993), 45-93. Frei's cursory evaluation of premodern hermeneutics that supported the literal ascription of Jesus' identity in the Gospels is in the first two chapters of *Eclipse*, 1-50.

2. Examples that will appear in this and/or subsequent chapters include Dawson, *Christian Figural Reading and the Fashioning of Identity*; Garrett Green, ed., *Scriptural Authority and Narrative Interpretation* (Eugene, OR: Wipf & Stock, 2000); Wood, *The Formation of Christian Understanding*.

follows George Lindbeck,³ his study of narrative, the literal sense, the grammar of faith, and figural reading, when combined with the reconception of theology after modernity as communal skill, is a seminal contribution.⁴ Frei tries to restore integrity to Christian theology as a critical practice in its own right, freeing it from the modernist tendency to subordinate theology to overarching philosophical explanations. Theology under Frei now becomes Christian self-description, more akin to social scientific ethnography than philosophy. The hermeneutical focus remains, however, as his later investigations into theology attend to the question, "What kind of theology is most nearly hospitable to the literal sense of Scripture?"⁵ Frei calls attention to Scripture's narratival nature and its deep connection to the grammar, or internal logic, of the faith.

As I intend to show, this is a conception of theology and interpretation that is friendly to the reorientation of Wesleyan theology within a tradition-constituted framework and theological hermeneutics as a craft to be learned. Frei opens up the complex interaction of reader, text, and context in a manner that will help guide my appropriation of Wesley's hermeneutics in later chapters. Frei's work is sometimes considered difficult to follow, both due to the unsystematic nature of his thought, and the fact that at his death much important work from throughout his career was not yet published. Moreover, there is what is sometimes considered a major shift in his thought, which is perhaps more of a shift of emphasis than a major reworking of earlier concepts.⁶ As a result, my

---

3. George A. Lindbeck, *The Nature of Doctrine: Religion and Theology in a Postliberal Age* (Philadelphia: Westminster, 1984).

4. Many of these themes also appear in Lindbeck, as the two influenced one another. See George A. Lindbeck, "The Story-Shaped Church: Critical Exegesis and Theological Interpretation," in Green, *Scriptural Authority*, 161-78. For consideration of the differences between Frei and Lindbeck, see Mike Higton, "Frei's Christology and Lindbeck's Cultural-Linguistic Theory," *Scottish Journal of Theology* 50 (1997): 92-94; also George Hunsinger, "Postliberal Theology," in *The Cambridge Companion to Postmodern Theology* (Cambridge Companions to Religion; ed. Kevin Vanhoozer; Cambridge: Cambridge University Press, 2003), 42-57.

5. Frei, *Types*, 2, 18. The motivating force behind the question for Frei is christological, as will be seen below.

6. Frei himself acknowledged a development in his thought, though many commentators have considered it a serious departure from earlier views. At the very least, a shift does appear to occur between his earlier writings, *The Eclipse of Biblical Narrative* and *The Identity of Jesus Christ*, with their indebtedness to New Criticism and emphasis on "realistic narrative," and his subsequent "sociological turn" that focuses on self-description and the rule-governed communal consensus of the literal sense, as displayed in *Theology and Narrative* and *Types of Christian Theology*. See Frei, "The 'Literal Reading' of Biblical Narrative in the Christian Tradition: Does It Stretch or Will It Break?" in *Theology and Narrative: Selected Essays* (ed. George Hunsinger and William C. Placher; New York: Oxford University Press, 1993), 142-43. Cf. David Lee, *Luke's Stories of Jesus: Theological Reading of Gospel Narrative and the Legacy of Hans Frei* (Journal for the Study of the New Testament Supplement Series 185;

interaction with Frei will proceed in two parts. First I will give an overview of Frei's theological hermeneutics. This will not be a comprehensive survey of Frei's corpus, but more of an exposition of the main themes that are relevant to this study, ordered roughly according to how they appear in publication. Second, where some of these themes require development to set up my appropriation of Wesley's hermeneutics in subsequent chapters, I will bring other voices into dialogue with Frei, many of whom have done work associated in some way with Frei's.[7]

Hans Frei's Theological Hermeneutics

Identity and Narrative
According to George Hunsinger, Frei's theological intent was "to break with the entire modern liberal tradition in theology, while still remaining within the purview of that tradition to the extent that he [did] not wish merely to relapse into the pitfalls of the older orthodoxy."[8] Frei's thesis in *Eclipse* is that a realistic interpretation of the Bible as a coherent narrative had characterized premodern Western Christianity, where the world was interpreted from within the vision of Scripture. But with the eighteenth century the procedure was turned inside out, as the subject matter and meaning of the biblical text were segregated, and explanations of reality that were "external" to Scripture prevailed.[9] The result was an apologetically motivated modern theology, as theologians sought to demonstrate the Bible's accord with the canons of

---

Sheffield: Sheffield Academic Press, 1999), 18-42; Gerard Loughlin, *Telling God's Story: Bible, Church and Narrative Theology* (Cambridge: Cambridge University Press, 1999), 78; Mike Higton, *Christ, Providence and History: Hans W. Frei's Public Theology* (London: T & T Clark, 2004), esp. ch. 8. A recent attempt to stress continuity in Frei's thought is Jason A. Springs, "Between Barth and Wittgenstein: On the Availability of Hans Frei's Later Theology," *Modern Theology* 23 (2007): 393-413.

7. E.g., Kathryn Tanner's essay on the plain sense (Kathryn E. Tanner, "Theology and the Plain Sense," in *Scriptural Authority and Narrative Interpretation*, 59-78) appears in a volume dedicated to Frei. Charles Wood was a doctoral student of Frei's, and Frei credits Wood's dissertation with influencing him (*Eclipse*, 342, n. 1). Frei likewise credits his Yale colleague, David Kelsey, as an influence (*Eclipse*, ix). Kelsey's *The Uses of Scripture in Modern Theology*, originally published in 1975, evinces an intellectual kinship with Frei's thought, and will be consulted below (reprinted as David H. Kelsey, *Proving Doctrine: The Uses of Scripture in Modern Theology* [Harrisburg, PA: Trinity Press International, 1999]).

8. George Hunsinger, "Afterword: Hans Frei as Theologian," in *Theology and Narrative*, 236.

9. An excellent complementary view on this discussion, focusing on the Bible's relationship to science, is Kenneth J. Howell, *God's Two Books: Copernican Cosmology and Biblical Interpretation in Early Modern Science* (Notre Dame, IN: University of Notre Dame Press, 2002).

modernist criticism, particularly its historical consciousness. Revelation became the predominant category of the period, and its form was decidedly christological.[10]

Once the biblical narrative was demoted from its status as *the* interpretation of history, the identity of Jesus Christ was similarly affected. Jesus became a mythic symbol whose content was essentially anthropological, the fulfillment of an abstraction.[11] Between *Eclipse* and his second published book, *The Identity of Jesus Christ*, Frei attempts to recover both the identity of Jesus as the one present to the church, and the Bible as realistic narrative, arguing that in Jesus, identity and presence were uniquely allied, such that Jesus could not be envisaged as not being present. In Frei's opinion, once a distrust opened up between scholars and the biblical text, the intention communicated in the events was no longer found in the words on the page, but in something else, such as a reconstruction of historical events. When this happened, the Gospels no longer meant what they said, leading scholars to circumvent them in some way to get to a "real" meaning. Thus, what Jesus says and does in the Gospels is no longer to be trusted, divorcing who Jesus is from what he does in the text. The true Jesus is located somewhere other than the biblical narrative.[12]

Yet Frei believes "that it is perfectly proper to describe *what* a person is by what he *does*, and *who* he is by what he is and does," because "the strong link between a person's centeredness in himself on the one hand and his personal qualities, changing bodily structure, and overt activity in both physical and social contexts on the other is so tough and organic."[13] With Jesus, this can only be found in the Gospels, his predicates uniquely ascribed to him by virtue of his relationship with God. To treat this fact correctly, we must be content to *describe* the narrative of Jesus, not *explain* it by resorting to an extrabiblical rationale. With Frei, Jesus' intentions and actions coalesce most powerfully in his passion, making that the point at which he is most himself. Jesus is the ascriptive subject of the Bible, whose intentions and actions are always his own, and who becomes ever more himself as the Gospels progress, especially in his passion.[14]

Frei thinks of the biblical narrative as "history-like," comparing it with the modern novel with its ability to render identity to the reader: "Realistic narrative is that kind in which subject and social setting belong together, and characters and external circumstances fitly render each other. Neither character nor circumstances separately, nor yet their interaction, is a shadow of something else

---

10. Frei, *Eclipse*, 52-54.
11. Hunsinger, "Afterword," 239.
12. This is essentially the argument of *Eclipse*. Frei revisits the themes very briefly in the preface to *Identity*, originally written the year *Eclipse* was published (*Identity*, 59-63).
13. Frei, *Identity*, 18.
14. For more, see *Identity*, esp. ch. 4.

more real or more significant. Nor is the one more important than the other in the story."[15] To protect the Jesus of this history-like narrative, Frei separates meaning and truth, claiming that, while questions of factuality are probably inevitable, the meaning of Jesus for salvation is not determined by historical referent but by *intratextuality*, which is how the biblical text contains meaning within itself, irreducible to extra-narratival account. It is by intratextuality that the Bible figurally "absorbs" the extrabiblical world, as opposed to the hermeneutical direction indicative of modernist criticism. Intratextuality is therefore germane to "realistic narrative." This move underlines a fundamental commitment for Frei, that dogmatic theology be kept separate from apologetics.[16] Apologetics, as it developed in modern theology, became the way theologians appealed to the world "outside" the biblical text's realism in order to justify the conditions of belief.[17]

At the same time, intratextual figural reading is what allows the two testaments of Scripture to be held together as a coherent whole as well as cite Jesus as ascriptive subject. In *Eclipse*, figural reading is a forward movement from type to antitype, an extension of the Bible's literal sense.[18] The benefit of this characterization is threefold: it prevents Christian supersessionism as a "reading back" over the Hebrew Bible; it sets figural readers under the narrative, instead of allowing them to impose meaning on the text; Jesus as antitype of the older types found in Scripture, along with a resistance to readers' being able to contribute meaningfully to interpretation,[19] secures his standing as ascriptive subject. Jesus' identity is unsubstitutable and uniquely his own by virtue of his relation to the Father.

The Literal Sense and the Community of Interpretation
Frei repeats much of the above in his later essay, "The 'Literal Reading' of Biblical Narrative in the Christian Tradition."[20] He had consistently claimed up

---

15. Frei, *Eclipse*, 13-14.
16. Frei, *Identity*, 56-57. In doing so, theology is shielded from public criteria, and becomes a communal practice of conceptual description that examines the language of the church. This will be examined below.
17. Cf. *Eclipse*, esp. ch. 6.
18. Frei draws heavily from Eric Auerbach for this conception, though not uncritically (*Eclipse*, 2-4).
19. Frei approvingly construes Calvin and "the large majority of the Western Christian tradition up to his time" as holding that, "Interpretation or the gathering of meaning is in no sense a material contribution on the part of the interpreter or a unique perspective he might represent" (*Eclipse*, 34). Meaning was located within "realistic narrative," irrespective of the reader. In *Eclipse* Frei believed the subjective element introduced in modern hermeneutics contributed to the problems he saw (*Eclipse*, 322-23). Although he later allowed for the community to contribute to the literal sense, he remained ambivalent about what this meant for Jesus' identity, as will be seen below.
20. Frei, "Literal Reading," 117-52.

to that point that the literal sense was the governing sense of biblical interpretation, and that its recovery was imperative for a realistic reading of the Bible to be feasible. Frei eventually grew bothered that "realistic narrative" had assumed the status of an overarching category into which the Bible was made to fit, in part due to his earlier view's indebtedness to New Criticism.[21]

In "Literal Reading," Frei has not surrendered the priority of the literal sense, but, under the influence of George Lindbeck's cultural-linguistic theory, repositions it within the community of interpretation. Lindbeck states that doctrines act as rules, as opposed to either propositions or expressions of religious experience, which serve a regulative function within religious communities.[22] Within their native communities, doctrines are the second-order "grammar" that norm first-order language and behavior. Frei does not adopt Lindbeck's theoretical proposal wholesale; his concerns are more properly christological.[23] He is ambivalent about a strict first- and second-order division, compared with Lindbeck, and does not commit to a "purely" regulatory approach to doctrine.[24] Nevertheless, "Literal Reading" finds Frei musing on Scripture and christology in a manner that is clearly influenced by his Yale colleague.[25]

The literal sense for Frei is now that which is the consensus of the church, set within a tradition, and not an element intrinsic to the text itself. The literal sense ought not to be analyzed by general theories; rather, "the theoretical task compatible with the literal reading of the Gospel narratives is that of describing how and in what context it functions."[26] The indigenous site, so to speak, of the literal sense is the community of interpretation—the church—and it therefore should be described by the ground rules of that same community:

---

21. Frei, "Literal Reading," 141-43, 148.

22. Lindbeck, *Nature*, 74. My cursory remarks on Lindbeck are due to my focus on Frei. *The Nature of Doctrine* has been so influential it is impossible to give a concise survey of the scholarship it has catalyzed, both in its favor and against it. Recent Lindbeck-inspired efforts include Charry, *By the Renewing of Your Minds*; Reinhard Hütter, *Suffering Divine Things: Theology as Church Practice* (Grand Rapids, MI: Eerdmans, 2000); Vanhoozer, *The Drama of Doctrine*. For a critique, see Alister E. McGrath, *The Genesis of Doctrine: A Study in the Foundation of Doctrinal Criticism* (Grand Rapids, MI: Eerdmans, 1990). A defense is Bruce Marshall, "Aquinas as Postliberal Theologian," *The Thomist* 53 (1989): 353-406.

23. Higton, "Frei's Christology and Lindbeck's Cultural-Linguistic Theory," 92-94.

24. For these reasons Hunsinger argues Frei is actually "postliberal," while Lindbeck is better characterized as "neoliberal" ("Postliberal Theology," 44).

25. A detailed comparison of these two "founders" of postliberalism is outside my interests. The kinship of Frei's and Lindbeck's projects are important only to the degree they allow me to effectively sketch the significant features of Frei's theological hermeneutics.

26. Frei, "Literal Reading," 144.

> The descriptive context, then, for the *sensus literalis* is the religion of which it is part, understood at once as a determinate code in which beliefs, rituals, and behavior patterns, ethos as well as narrative, come together as a common semiotic system, and also as the community which is that system in use—apart from which the very term ("semiotic system") is in this case no more than a misplaced metaphor.[27]

In this same essay Frei disputes general hermeneutical theory, believing it perpetuates the fallacy of modern theology of making the subject matter of Scripture something other than realistic, narrative meaning.[28] If set within this kind of theory, Frei says, the literal sense will "break" due to the strain placed upon it always to ensure that the meaning of the text is the general ontology shared by all readers.[29] In response, Frei advocates an *ad hoc* approach to hermeneutics, where the Christian interpreter operates according to a set of rules to which the church has traditionally held: do not deny the literal ascription to Jesus, nor should it be ascribed to any other person, event or thing; do not deny the unity of the testaments or their congruence with the ascriptive literalism of the Gospels; any readings not in principle contradicting the first two rules are permissible.[30] If these are observed, the literal reading can "stretch" in different contexts, but fundamentally Scripture can once again intratextually interpret, or "absorb," the extratextual universe, as per its right use within the Christian community.[31] Frei is able to tie all of this together into a coherent later position:

> The literal ascription to Jesus of Nazareth of the stories connected with him is of such far-reaching import that it serves not only as focus for inner-canonical typology but reshapes extratextual language in its manifold descriptive uses into a typological relation to these stories. The reason why the intratextual universe of this Christian symbol system is a narrative one is that a specific set of texts, which happen to be narrative, has become primary, even within scripture, and has been assigned a literal reading as their primary or "plain" sense. They have become the paradigm for the construal not only of what is inside that system but for all that is outside. They provide the interpretive pattern in terms of which *all* of reality is experienced and read in this religion.[32]

---

27. Frei, "Literal Reading," 146.

28. Frei elaborates on his critique in "Theology and the Interpretation of Narrative: Some Hermeneutical Considerations," in *Theology and Narrative*, 94-116. This makes way for his view of theology as communal self-description, to be taken up shortly.

29. Frei, "Literal Reading," 124-139.

30. Frei lists historical-criticism and literary readings as "the two obvious candidates" for compliance to this last rule ("Literal Reading," 144-45).

31. Frei, "Literal Reading," 147.

32. Frei, "Literal Reading," 147-48.

"Narrative" is still present in Frei's thought, but its standing is altered as it is no longer the defining property of the Bible. It is now representative of the whole of Scripture because the community gives primacy to a certain set of narrative texts (the Gospels) read according to the literal sense.[33]

The question that persists, however, is what exactly *is* the literal sense? Frei admits a specific definition is impossible. The rules he culls from the tradition—Scripture's literal ascription is reserved for Jesus alone; respect the unity of Scripture in compliance with the ascriptive literalism of the Gospels; readings not in violation of these two rules are permissible—are formal, and Frei acknowledges the literal sense changes greatly.[34] What he gives instead are a few "rough rules," namely, that the literal sense is the result of communal consensus about how to use Scripture; that we cannot get "behind" the text to ask what the author meant in writing, for intention and enactment are united in the literal sense; and the sense of Scripture and its subject matter are to be taken together.[35]

Frei's apparent ambivalence about these rules may be better regarded as a sign of the unfinished character of these late reflections. What emerges, however, is Frei's maintenance of the primacy of the literal sense in the tradition, only now as something the content of which is contributed to by the community. But in light of modern theology's repeated lapses into intellectual habits that dislocated the literal sense from the community of faith, fractured biblical unity, and denied Jesus as the Bible's literally ascriptive subject, Frei sought to develop an account of theology most amenable to the literal sense as he had come to understand it.

Theology as Christian Self-Description

In discussing the literal sense in his later work, Frei introduces the community of faith into the conversation and locates theology there. For Frei, this inevitably invites a critique of the academy, since in modernism the academy has become the home for theology as a professional discipline that has fostered some of the worst intellectual habits. Modern academic theology tends, in Frei's opinion, to make theology an instance in a general class—of religious experience, for instance. When this occurs, theology is typically co-opted by philosophy as an academic discipline that may or may not have any connection with the Christian

---

33. Thus, the sociological turn in Frei's thought, while it does result in his critiquing "realistic narrative" as a general category, does not dispense with his earlier concerns with narrative (or identity) altogether. If anything, they are retained and refined. In this sense Springs' argument for scholars recognizing a stronger sense of continuity in Frei's thought would seem to be validated (Springs, "Between Barth and Wittgenstein").

34. See Frei, *Types*, 15. Though he does not state it, this admission is presumably an observation based on the history of interpretation.

35. Frei, *Types*, 15-16.

community.³⁶ Moreover, Jesus as the literal ascriptive subject of the Bible tends to dissolve into a general anthropology.

Frei's answer to this is to relocate theology within the Christian community as a communal skill of self-description. "Theology," writes Frei, "is the grammar of the religion, understood as a faith and as an ordered community life";³⁷ it is "an inquiry into the specific language peculiar to, in fact constitutive of, the specific semiotic community called the Christian Church or churches";³⁸ likewise, "Communal Christian self-description is a matter of being able to use words like faith, hope, and love in the context of the Christian community…on the basis of how you learned it there in worship and the formation of Christian identity."³⁹ Here Christianity is cast as a religion as Frei finds that detailed in cultural anthropologist Clifford Geertz, a religion with a sacred text and a semiotic system of beliefs and practices that are governed by communally constituted rules into which adherents are socialized. For Frei, what the theologian on this definition of theology is trying to achieve is what Geertz calls "thick description," which is akin to an ethnographic survey of the inner workings of a community.⁴⁰

Frei unpacks his definition of theology by distinguishing between three intermingled aspects. *First-order* theology is the Christian witness itself, exemplified in the comprehensive life of the church. *Second-order* theology, which is in fact what Frei has in mind when he defines theology in the first place, is "the Christian community's second-order appraisal of its own language and actions under a norm or norms internal to the community itself."⁴¹ More precisely, the "appraisal" to which he refers has both descriptive and critical tasks. Descriptively, theology articulates the grammar or internal logic of the Christian faith in its first-order expressions. Critically, it determines whether given articulations of first-order language adhere to the norm or norms regulating that language. Theology of this stripe is "an explanation not usually of (first-order statements') truth, but of their meaning; it is *re-description* in technical concepts rather than their *explanation*. It is conceptual analysis."⁴² Lastly, *third-order* theology is more apologetic, "a kind of quasi-philosophical or philosophical activity," with the theologian trying to relate the Christian grammar to those outside the community.⁴³

---

36. As Frei shows, this is due to the academy—beginning in nineteenth-century Germany—using *Wissenschaft* as the standard for all viable academic inquiry (Frei, *Types*, 95-116).

37. Frei, *Types*, 20.
38. Frei, *Types*, 78.
39. Frei, *Types*, 92.
40. Frei, *Types*, 12-13; cf. "Literal Reading," 146-47.
41. Frei, *Types*, 2.
42. Frei, *Types*, 81 (italics original).
43. Frei, *Types*, 21.

This permutation of theology's dimensions accepts that there is something called academic theology, but it attempts to protect Christian faith from modernism's generalizing propensities. Frei does not intend his depiction of the levels of theology to be taken rigidly, but they are useful insofar as they help him research how and why theology and the literal sense have often been taken captive in modernism by alien explanatory schemes. Frei believes that, as Christian self-description, theology is not insulated within the community, but it does have its own logic that takes precedence over other, alternative logics.

The question then is how these logics relate. Looking to Karl Barth, Frei argues that alternative logics are necessary to read Scripture at all, but that these must be subordinated to the faith through *ad hoc correlation*.[44] Granting second-order theology's technical nature, it must look to general theories for conceptual tools, because it does not have its own. However, unlike so much modern theology, Barth teaches Frei not to systematically implement general theory, which would in fact subordinate the Christian grammar to an abstract explanatory framework. Instead, the theologian's use of theories should be ruled by the Christian semiotic network and adapted unsystematically. This Frei sets forth as the "always *ad hoc performance* of subordinating explanatory theory and philosophy more generally, as a tool in Christian communal self-description, so that in effect a conceptual scheme that may function *explanatorily* in a general or philosophical context functions only interpretively or descriptively in a Christian context."[45] The general is thus domesticated by the particular; the internal logic of Christianity thus governs the external, alternative logics of the academy. This brings us back to the matter of the literal sense and why this portrayal of theology is most agreeable to it.

Recalling what Frei takes to be the traditional hermeneutical rules of Christianity, theology as self-description respects the integrity of Christian faith and theological discourse, but not at the expense of a sort of intellectual realism. That is, theologians do often have to draw from other areas of knowledge in the service of theology. Frei wants to ensure this arrangement continues, without theology being conscripted into a foreign intellectual programme. By privileging the internal logic of the Christian faith, the church maintains ownership of Scripture, affirming its narrative unity, as well as securing the priority of the literal sense and its unsubstitutable ascription of identity to Jesus Christ. The academy is relativized, but by no means dismissed, in deference to the church as the natural environment of Christian theology.

Preliminary Evaluation of Frei's Contribution
Frei's work certainly appears valuable because it touches on so many of the issues that chapters one and two named as essential to a proposal such as the one being developed presently: the unity and role of Scripture within the Christian

---

44. Frei, *Types*, 70-91.
45. Frei, *Types*, 81 (italics original).

community, the primacy of the literal sense, ruled reading—all of these are topics that occupy scholars writing in theological interpretation today. Moreover, Frei's "sociological" take on how the theologian operates within the community of faith is helpful in light of MacIntyre's argument that traditions are extended by adherents who make skilled reinterpretations of authoritative material. Frei seems to give greater clarity to how that might look. Having surveyed these themes, an evaluation of their contribution is in order.

First, although Frei's turn to narrative has drawn much attention due to his corresponding ambivalence about history and truth,[46] the most important contributions coming from this turn for a Wesleyan theological hermeneutic are a renewed emphasis on the final form of Scripture, as well as its identity-rendering power.[47] Among other things, the fracturing of biblical narrative has marked modernist criticism, so that a basic assumption most premodern Christians could make about the wholeness of Scripture was undermined.[48] Frei's use of narrative serves as a contemporary recovery of that assumption. Moreover, in Frei's theological hermeneutics Bible has the power to render identity, both divine and human. In other words, from the biblical narrative the church learns who God is through the Bible's ascriptive subject, Jesus of Nazareth, while also having its own identity shaped as God's people through that same narrative. This shaping occurs through figural interpretation, the use of which both holds together the Old and New Testaments, and allows Christians to "enter" into the world of Scripture. As a result, the modernist phenomenon Frei decries is reversed; the Bible once again absorbs the world, instead of the other way around.

Second, Frei in his later writings begins to appreciate biblical interpretation as a dynamic interaction of reader, text, and context.[49] This complication of interpretation is peculiarly postmodern, for now interpretation is not solely located in either the text or in something "behind" the text, whether authorial intent or the conditions of the text's formation. The literal sense remains the privileged sense of Scripture, but it is now more of a formal element of interpretation whose content varies in communities as part of each group's indigenous semiotic network.

---

46. Cf. Frei's remarks, "Response to 'Narrative Theology: An Evangelical Appraisal," in *Theology and Narrative*, 207-12. For criticism, see Watson's, *Text, Church and World*, ch. 1. Stephen Fowl offers a critique of Watson's critique in *Engaging Scripture*, 21-24.

47. Cf. Gary L. Comstock, "Two Types of Narrative Theology," *Journal of the American Academy of Religion* 55 (1987): 690.

48. Wesley shared this assumption, as the following chapter will show.

49. As David Lee argues, "One of Frei's *formal* contributions to the discussion of theological interpretation is the recognition that Gospel interpretation is no longer a function of the text alone" (*Luke's Stories*, 102).

Finally, by tying together theology as communal self-description with a privileged literal sense, Frei points beyond the impasse between systematic theology and biblical studies by making theology more exegetical, as an intrinsic part of the semiotic system of ecclesial life. Interpreting the biblical narrative is now the church's means of making sense of its life in the world. Furthermore, the church as the community of interpretation reclaims its place as the foremost "site" of theology. The first and second-order distinction keeps the language and practices of the ecclesial community as the proper object of theological investigation even if that investigation is carried out largely in academic circles. Along these lines, Frei's principle of ad hoc correlation protects the church's priority by keeping the act of communal self-description from captivity to academic explanation.[50] Moreover, the sociological emphasis allows for particular communities to have their own legitimate customs, language, and criteria, opening the door for a specifically *Wesleyan* theological hermeneutic.

Some criticisms of Frei's work can be leveled, however. For instance, once Frei's use of narrative, identity, and figural reading are brought together, limitations in his conception of these appear. Frei's examples of how his own proposal effects a theological interpretation of Scripture are severely limited, focusing primarily on the Gospels and christology.[51] And despite his later view opening the way for meaning as a dynamic, emergent product of the interplay of reader, text, and context, Frei remains vague about how this works. Frei is wont to avoid lapsing into a method for reading, but his own phenomenology of reading is not rigorous enough in exploring the generation of meaning out of these constitutive hermeneutical elements.[52]

How it is that Scripture is capable of shaping the identities of its readers is similarly ambiguous. The issue revolves around the christological core of Frei's hermeneutics. In his regard for Jesus as the unsubstitutable ascriptive subject of the Bible, Frei creates a distance between Christ and reader that threatens the transformative power of the biblical text. The tension appears in the contrast between earlier and later positions in Frei's thought. In the earlier phase, Jesus' unsubstitutability is correlated with realistic narrative, where the literal sense is identified with the text. Later, realistic narrative, with its New Criticism roots, is dismissed in favor of the contribution of the reading community to a now

---

50. However, this should not negate the importance of such a theoretical endeavor, only set it in its proper place. For a nuanced discussion of description and explanation, see Comstock, "Two Types." Though he acknowledges the third-order level for theology, Frei gives little attention to it, since it is concerned primarily with apologetics. Since that level is irrelevant to my project, I too will set third-level theological inquiry aside.

51. See Frei, *Identity*, esp. part 4.

52. Whether this is due to the unfinished character of his work or an apparently characteristic reticence toward certain matters is debatable. See Paul Schwartzentruber, "The Modesty of Hermeneutics: The Theological Reserves of Hans Frei," *Modern Theology* 8 (1992): 181-95.

polysemous literal sense. Yet the distance between Jesus and his followers apparently remains. If the community of interpretation now contributes to the substance of what is called the literal sense of Scripture, and if the literal sense is both the sense that ascribes to Jesus his identity and serves as the doorway the world enters into the world of Scripture, how can Jesus' identity not be in some way tied to the identities of the readers?

What is at stake in this distance is the soteriological ability of Scripture, or its power to transform readers into a form whose content is Christ himself, as his identity is communicated in the biblical narrative. Combined with Frei's later hermeneutical insights into how the community participates in the meaning of the text, readerly subjectivity as a constitutive element in ascribing to Jesus his unsubstitutable identity would seem to require acknowledgement and development. Frei realizes he has introduced something that was once impermissible to his hermeneutics on theological grounds, but he contends in his later writings that, theologically though not existentially, "Christian subjectivity, or how to become a Christian, must be…subordinate to the *what* of Christianity."[53] Theologically, the logic of faith takes "pragmatic priority" over the existential aspect, although in truth "the two belong fully together—that is part of the logic or grammar of faith."[54] Frei is approvingly commenting here on Barth's theology, and though he has moved away from the problems of his earlier views in *The Eclipse of Biblical Narrative* and *The Identity of Jesus*, the gap that seems to remain between Jesus and the interpreting community validates John David Dawson's criticism that Frei's hermeneutics do not sufficiently account for discipleship and transformation.[55]

This points to a final critique of Frei, the inadequacy of his conception of figural reading. Frei rightly notes the crucial role of figural reading for theological interpretation, but his version of it, combined with the problem of how Jesus' identity relates to the church's, appears to limit figural reading to maintaining the unity of Scripture. If this is not addressed, it remains unclear how exactly the community of interpretation is able to enter into the world of the Bible after all, despite Frei's intentions.

Frei's work points to the interconnectedness of communal identity and biblical text, with the literal sense as the hermeneutical linchpin holding them together. Within this matrix, the places of figural reading and theology as self-description can be located. In the next section I will look beyond Frei to scholarship that develops this hermeneutical complex to gain direction in how I might appropriate Wesley in the service of a Wesleyan theological hermeneutic of Scripture.

---

53. Frei, *Types*, 43.
54. Frei, *Types*, 43.
55. Dawson, *Figural Reading*, 213.

In Dialogue with Frei

The result of integrating the above themes—especially communal identity, literal sense, biblical narrative, and theology as self-description—is perhaps best captured by Kathryn Tanner when she writes, "Questions of faithfulness to one's communal identity become questions of textual interpretation, broadly construed."[56] The questioning Tanner refers to is the theological task, and the text interpreted is the Bible according to its literal (or as Tanner calls it, its *plain*) sense.[57]

How is such a congruence between text and identity imaginable? The answer is to be found in how the literal sense of Scripture is conceived. According to Charles Wood, the literal sense is the "meaning which the community of faith has normally acknowledged as basic, regardless of whatever other constructions might also properly be put upon the text—[it] is grounded in the community's own experience with the text...it is the sense whose discernment has become second nature to the members of the community."[58] Similar to Frei's later work, Wood moves us away from the literal sense as a property of the Bible (as it was with realistic narrative), to becoming a result of a certain type of interaction between the community of interpretation and the biblical text.

In other words, what begins to emerge from the above interaction with Frei is an understanding of theological hermeneutics as the interworkings of reader, text, and context. Those who read Scripture within the life of the church read it in a certain way, which they have learned by virtue of that life.

Frei's survey of modernist hermeneutics showed that the Bible can be read in various ways, some of which lead to its fragmentation, undercutting its formative power. In recovering the Bible's narrative character, however, Frei indicates that narrative refers also to the function of the Bible in the life of the church. Narrative is not the unity of the Bible as an inherent property of the text, but a way of perceiving its sixty-six books that allows it to render the identity of Jesus Christ such that it presents to the reading community an inhabitable world rooted in who Jesus is.[59] This is not to suggest the church fabricates or invents

---

56. Tanner, "Plain Sense," 69. Due to the soteriological import of figural reading for the hermeneutic argued for in these pages, I will treat that topic in chapter seven.

57. Tanner takes an even broader sociological, and therefore less christological, approach than does Frei, but her treatment of these topics is by no means unfriendly to Frei's theological commitments.

58. Wood, *Christian Understanding*, 43. Tanner gives much the same quote, but omits the phrase "is grounded in the community's own experience with the text." As I will contend in this and subsequent chapters, Wood gives an indispensable proviso for how the modifier *Wesleyan* can remain attached to both a certain perception of the literal sense and those communities of interpretation that practice that perception. For Tanner's quotation of Wood, see "Plain Sense," 63.

59. Cf. Frei's remarks on Barth and the world projected by the Bible, *Types*, 160-61.

the unity of biblical narrative. As James Phelan argues, narrative "is not just story but also action, *the telling of a story by someone to someone on some occasion for some purpose.*"[60] The church receives the Bible as part of the continuation of its life as the *church*. In concert with the rest of the semiotic network that makes the church what it is as a community existing in time, the very fact that *these* sixty-six books as opposed to others have been handed down in the church indicates a broadly conceived idea of unity.

Grasping this unity is a matter of figural reading, Frei's version of which is limited soteriologically. A more soteriologically fruitful depiction of figural reading can be found in John David Dawson:

> Figural reading in the Christian tradition seeks to express the dynamic process of spiritual transformation in ways that respect the practitioners' commitment to both past and future, both old identity and newly refashioned identity. Imbedded in figural practice is all the drama of discerning the point of existence and identifying one's place in it, figured as a journey from a former mode of existence through various states of transformation toward some ultimate end.[61]

Following Dawson's understanding keeps figural reading from being simply about interpreting the text, and particularly about holding together the Old Testament and New Testament. "What is always ultimately at stake is the reality and the proper characterization of a divine performance in the material world of space and time, a performance that defines the personal, social, ethical, and political obligations of Christians in the present, as well as their stance toward past and future."[62] Figural reading is not only about prophecies and their fulfillment, types and their antitypes within the text. It is about what God has done and is continuing to do in the economy of salvation, and particularly in the lives of those who read the Bible as Christian Scripture. Figural reading as soteriological reading opens the door to a theological hermeneutic that allows Jesus' identity in Scripture to transform the identities of readers in the Wesleyan community. For the moment, Dawson's definition of figural reading indicates that the literal sense as the soteriological sense unifies the biblical texts into one Scripture, while at the same time unifying the life of the community of faith with the world Scripture presents to it.

The life of the community—those beliefs and practices that comprise its identity—is thus interwoven with what it is that community understands the literal sense to be. Wood makes this point when he asserts that, although the literal sense is the second-nature, or the obvious, unreflective reading of

---

60. James Phelan, *Narrative as Rhetoric: Technique, Audiences, Ethics, Ideology* (The Theory and Interpretation of Narrative Series; Columbus: Ohio State University Press, 1996), 8 (italics original).

61. Dawson, *Figural Reading*, 216.

62. Dawson, *Figural Reading*, 216.

Scripture, "what is obvious to a reader depends a great deal on how the reader has been schooled to approach the text." The literal sense is therefore "intimately bound up with the conventions of reading, with the capacities and dispositions, linguistic and personal, which the reader brings to the text, by virtue of having been formed in a community with a fairly secure style of interaction with this material."[63] Biblical interpretation cannot be abstracted from the "interpretive aims, interests, and practices," of the community.[64] Bible and church are therefore "dialectically related," as David Kelsey says.[65] What Frei referred to as the grammar of faith, or the internal logic, embedded in communal life regulates this dialectical relation.

Both the life of the church and the biblical narrative are ordered to particular ends. For the church to incorporate this narrative in seeking to achieve those ends is to accord it a certain authority that is analytic to what it means to call the Bible "Scripture."[66] In this vein, Kelsey rightly defines "scripture" as a way of reading a text that allows it to "shape persons' identities so decisively as to transform them."[67] To read the Bible narratively according to the grammar or rule of faith is therefore to read it scripturally. *This* narrative has a purpose consonant with the aims, interests, and practices that define the church, and the church uses this narrative accordingly, a use fittingly called *scriptural*. Similarly, to perceive the narrative of the Bible is to interpret it according to the literal sense, for this is the normative, second nature way Christians have been "schooled" to read.[68]

Tanner helpfully summarizes why and how the literal sense becomes bound to a community's self-perception by noting three characteristics. First, the literal sense is *functional*. The literal sense is the result of how a community conventionally uses a text. As conventional, the literal sense is also the *consensual* reading of the text. It is truly the community's reading; to depart from it would be a minority and perhaps even deviant interpretation. Finally, the literal sense is the *traditional* sense. This is the standard or normative way of taking the text, so that "all other senses, as both new and nonobvious senses, require some additional warrant."[69] This traditional aspect preserves the historical quality of the community's reading, so that in tandem with the literal sense community identity is extended through time.

---

63. Wood, *Christian Understanding*, 40.
64. Fowl, *Engaging Scripture*, 55-56. See also Tanner, "Plain Sense," 70.
65. Kelsey, *Proving Doctrine*, 92.
66. For more on Scripture and authority see Kelsey, *Proving Doctrine*, 97-100.
67. Kelsey, *Proving Doctrine*, 90.
68. Cf. Frei, "'Narrative' in Christian and Modern Reading," in *Theology and Dialogue: Essays in Conversation with George Lindbeck* (ed. Bruce D. Marshall; Notre Dame, IN: University of Notre Dame Press, 1990), 160. For more on the rhetorical power of narrative to achieve a certain end, see Phelan, *Narrative as Rhetoric*.
69. Tanner, "Plain Sense," 63.

These three characteristics reinforce what Wood says about the literal sense, that it is "a fairly secure *style* of interaction" with the text. There is a distinctive way the whole community uses the Bible that is scriptural, a way that can be called *literal*.[70] Parsing Wood's phrase is telling. As "fairly *secure*," the literal sense is a traditional sense, in that it must accompany a community over time. It possesses the quality of identity preservation because it is fused with other communal practices that make up a common life. Otherwise the literal sense cannot serve as a standard for identity. However, in saying the literal sense is only "*fairly* secure," Wood allows that what those aims, interests, and practices into which members are schooled may change over time. Because the literal sense is "style" (formal) rather than "substance" (material) a gap exists between the biblical text itself and the literal sense, and this gap, combined with changing circumstances over time, creates the need for communal self-reflection and self-criticism.

It is within this need that room exists for the theologian to do her work. The gap between sense and text makes material judgments about interpretation an empirical matter to be taken on a case-by-case basis. Even so, there must be some standard for making such judgments; they cannot be completely disjointed, despite their being unpredictable a priori, or talk of a community identity at all is nonsense. In addition, the fact that a community's situation, aims, interests, and practices can change over time creates—if not crises—questions about whether and to what extent the continuity of a community's identity is being maintained. This is a basic issue for fashioning a Wesleyan theological hermeneutic, as I discussed in chapter two.

The theologian operates here, carrying out the descriptive and critical tasks Frei defines in *Types of Christian Theology*. Specifically, it is in discovering and examining the grammar of the faith, the internal logic that norms communal language and practice (including the practice of biblical interpretation), that the theologian can serve the church. As Paul L. Holmer describes it,

> The grammar of a language is that set of rules that describes how people speak who are doing it well and with efficacy. A logical schematism is also that set of criteria and lawlike remarks that describe how people think when they make sense. For those of us who are just learning to speak and to think, these rules are like prescriptions and even onerous requirements. But with the practices once mastered, the rules are no longer alien and become part of the "how," the way, we behave. Theology is also dependent upon a consensus of belief and practice, that of Jesus and the Apostles, of the Scripture's teachings and the lives limned by its pages. Theology answers the question—what is Christianity? But it tells us the answer by giving us the order and priorities, the structure and morphology, of

---

70. "Literal," therefore, is not the opposite of nonliteral or figurative. It is instead a term that simply denotes how the community typically takes the Bible in its reading.

the Christian faith. It does this by placing the big words, like *man*, *God*, *Jesus*, *world*, in such a sequence and context that their use becomes ruled for us.[71]

Hermeneutically, the grammar functions as a rule or canon that authoritatively measures, not only interpretation, but communal life as a whole.[72] As Frei writes, "The creed, or 'rule of faith' or 'rule of truth' which governed the Gospels' use in the church asserted the primacy of the literal sense."[73] According to its typical use in premodern interpretation, the rule of faith was considered a hypothesis about the substance of the biblical narrative.[74] But as Frei sees, the grammar of faith is not confined to the Bible alone, but is the governing logic of the community's way of life. As John O'Keefe and R. R. Reno have observed, "The rule of faith was a rule for life as well as a rule for reading scripture and teaching its meaning. It was a spiritual rule that guided the whole person toward fellowship with God."[75] Granting the interconnectedness of literal sense and communal practice already established in this chapter, the scope of the grammar to encompass not only a ruled reading but also, as it were, a ruled life where that reading is most at home, should not be surprising.

The theologian approaches her charge in a way akin to a sociologist or anthropologist, except the theologian is a member of the community. To detect the grammar of the faith requires the theologian to map the various conventions that constitute the community's semiotic network, including of course the interpretation of Scripture according to the literal sense. Within this complex of

---

71. Paul L. Holmer, *The Grammar of Faith* (San Francisco: Harper and Row, 1978), 20.

72. The word we translate "rule" is the Greek κανών. Although "canon" has recently been defined rather pedestrianly as "list," as a *rule* canon has traditionally functioned as a standard or measure of truth. For more on canon as list, see William J. Abraham, *Canon and Criteria in Christian Theology* (Oxford: Oxford University Press, 1998), ch. 1. For reflections on canon as standard of truth in antiquity, see John Behr, *The Way to Nicaea* (Formation of Christian Theology 1; Crestwood, NY: St. Vladimir's Seminary Press, 2001), esp. ch. 1. For more on the relationship of canon and Scripture, see Kelsey, *Proving Doctrine*, 104-08.

73. Frei, "Literal Reading," 122. Although Behr argues that, historically, creeds and rules of faith or truth possessed different functions in the faith, in contemporary theological hermeneutics the ability of creeds to "rule" theological interpretation is being stressed. See, e.g., Wall, "Reading the Bible from within Our Traditions," 88-107; also Ephraim Radner and George Sumner, eds., *The Rule of Faith: Scripture, Canon, and Creed in a Critical Age* (Harrisburg, PA: Morehouse, 1998). Of course, given that the assembly confesses a creed, it might be more appropriate to call this an *internalized* grammar rather than an internal one. In other words, the church is socialized into its grammar so that, even if it assumes a second nature familiarity, the grammar is not "hidden" to the church.

74. Behr, *The Way to Nicaea*, 32-33.

75. O'Keefe and Reno, *Sanctified Vision*, 128.

language and practice a person who has learned the communal skill of theological reflection should be able to both distill the grammar of the faith (the descriptive task) and discern whether and to what extent the community continues to adhere to that grammar (the critical task). Among other attributes, awareness of the tradition is a requirement, since without this awareness it is impossible for the theologian to judge the degree of consistency or change in the community's identity over time.

This discussion of themes from Frei may appear too one-sided. As with Frei's later position, one could argue Kelsey, Tanner, Wood, and those with similar views give too much weight to the life of the community, and not enough to the text itself.[76] And when one brings to the interpretation of Scripture a familiarity with the history of reception, especially in one's own tradition where the question of tradition-constituted identity is in view, insisting on a formal definition of the literal sense can seem inadequate, if not question-begging. In the present undertaking, to claim that the difference in interpretation of a single biblical passage between Wesley in the eighteenth century and Wesleyans today can be accounted for in terms of different aims, interests, and practices, might leave something to be desired. We are left to wonder not only how it is that a text has the ability to support different meanings, but also how to adjudicate between them. The variance of meanings that result in the history of reception seems to make it necessary to give a more rigorous account of textuality and meaning than what Frei and others here are willing to provide. I give this further attention in chapter seven.

---

76. Although in fairness, Tanner, to take one example, is more concerned with a sociological account of theology than she is with hermeneutics per se. See her cursory comments on the "critical force" of a text and the plain sense "over contemporary forms of communal life" ("Plain Sense," 70). Nevertheless, she does refer to her account of theology as an "interpretive approach."

4. Wesley's Theological Hermeneutics

In this chapter I will begin my appropriation of Wesley's hermeneutics in the service of a contemporary Wesleyan theological hermeneutic of Scripture, building on the surveys in the previous two chapters of Alasdair MacIntyre and Hans Frei. In what follows I will first depict the way of life Wesley envisioned for his Methodist followers, which he understood as a participation in the economy of salvation. With this way of life sketched, I will, second, map the semiotic system that, in Wesley's thought, gives meaning to the life of a "real Christian." In Wesley's Anglican theology, this system is known as the means of grace. My particular focus here will be on the place and role of Scripture as a means, which Wesley calls "the way to heaven."

Finally, I will discuss the grammar or internal logic of the faith for Wesley, crystallized in the analogy of faith. The analogy of faith regulates both the way Wesley reads the literal sense of Scripture, and how the semiotic system of the means of grace generates meaning in a Wesleyan context. It rules both interpretation and life, in other words. Thus, I will further develop my discussion of the analogy of faith discussing Wesley's rules for his bands and societies, where a ruled "reading" of Methodist Scripture and life come together. Since it will prove impossible to do this without giving some attention to the literal sense, some preliminary comments on it will be in order, but this will not detract from the need for a more comprehensive analysis of the literal sense in Wesley's hermeneutics in chapter five.

John Wesley's Soteriological Vision

The Economy of Salvation
Grace is, in Wesley's vision, what undergirds all of life. As Thomas Langford says about Wesley's theology, "Grace is God's active and continuous presence. Definitively expressed in Jesus Christ, grace covers the entirety of life: It creates, redeems, sustains, sanctifies, and glorifies."[1] Because of grace, Wesley can conceive of the Christian faith as having a certain purpose, or end, toward which everything points: "True religion is right tempers towards God and man. It is...gratitude and benevolence; gratitude to our Creator and supreme Benefactor, and benevolence to our fellow-creatures. In other words, it is the loving God with all our heart, and our neighbour as ourselves."[2] He continues:

> It is in consequence of our knowing God loves us that we love him,
> and love our neighbour as ourselves. Gratitude toward our Creator

---

1. Thomas A. Langford, *Practical Divinity: Theology in the Wesleyan Tradition* (vol. 1; rev. ed.; Nashville, TN: Abingdon, 1998), 20. If anything is lacking in this otherwise pithy and accurate statement, it is mention of the Holy Spirit.
2. "The Unity of the Divine Being," §16, *Works*, 4:66-67.

cannot but produce benevolence to our fellow-creatures. The love of Christ constrains us, not only to be harmless, to do no ill to our neighbour, but to be useful, to be "zealous of good works," "as we have time to do good unto all men," and be patterns to all of true genuine morality, of justice, mercy, and truth. This is religion, and this is happiness, the happiness for which we were made.[3]

For Wesley, *happiness* is the state wherein the human person as creature is united with God in full communion—a communion for which humanity was created. Of entering into that state of happiness, "for which we were made," Wesley goes on to say,

This begins when we begin to know God, by the teaching of his own Spirit. As soon as the Father of spirits reveals his Son in our hearts, and the Son reveals his Father, the love of God is shed abroad in our hearts; then, and not till then, we are happy. We are happy, first, in the consciousness of his favor, which indeed is better than the life itself; next, in the constant communion with the Father, and with his Son, Jesus Christ; then in all the heavenly tempers which he hath wrought in us by his Spirit; again, in the testimony of his Spirit that all our works please him; and, lastly, in the testimony of our own spirit that "in simplicity and godly sincerity we have had our conversation in the world." Standing fast in this liberty from sin and sorrow, wherewith Christ hath made them free, real Christians "rejoice evermore, pray without ceasing, and in everything give thanks." And their happiness still increases as they "grow up into the measure of the stature of the fullness of Christ."[4]

Since growing up "into the measure of the stature of the fullness of Christ" is what we were made for, the soteriological thrust of Christianity in Wesley's theology is rooted in God's creative purpose. Wesley describes this in more detail in his sermon, "Justification by Faith":

In the image of God was man made; holy as he that created him is holy, merciful as the author of all is merciful, perfect as his Father in heaven is perfect. As God is love, so man dwelling in love dwelt in God, and God in him. God made him to be "an image of his own eternity," an incorruptible picture of the God of glory. He was accordingly pure, as God is pure, from every spot of sin. He knew not evil in any kind or degree, but was inwardly and outwardly sinless and undefiled. He "loved the Lord his God with all his heart, and with all his mind, and soul, and strength."[5]

---

3. "The Unity of the Divine Being," §17, *Works*, 4:67.
4. "The Unity of the Divine Being," §17, *Works*, 4:67.
5. "Justification by Faith," §I.1, *Works*, 1:184.

Wesley goes on to speak of the "law of love" imprinted on humanity's heart, allowing a grace-given freedom for humanity to obey God joyfully. This is the state of paradise—a state of holiness and happiness because humanity lived fully as God's image in the world.[6]

When this perfect state was corrupted by the sin of disobedience, death entered the creation and the image of God was marred. This is the state of original sin into which all humanity after Adam is born.[7] Yet even at this moment God's redemption begins in his giving of prevenient (or preventing) grace.[8] According to Kenneth J. Collins, there are no less than five benefits to prevenient grace in Wesley's thought. It restores 1) a basic knowledge of God, 2) the moral law in the hearts of believers, 3) conscience, 4) a degree of free will, and 5) restraint against wickedness.[9] Humanity is therefore made able once again to enter communion with God, but only as a response to God's gracious invitation

That gracious invitation culminates in God sending his Son to save humanity from death through the cross. Through faith in Christ's death and resurrection, God gives the grace to justify believers and regenerate them, so that the Holy Spirit adopts the newborn believer as a child of God, filling the heart again with love. In Wesley's soteriology, these are two aspects on one divine movement: justification is what God does for us, removing the guilt of sin; whereas new birth, or regeneration, is what God does in us, renewing our fallen nature.[10] Salvation for Wesley is thus a recovery of the divine image within the heart, also known for him as the kingdom of God,[11] allowing humanity to again experience the knowledge and love of God, which leads to love of neighbor.

Redeemed humanity is therefore set on the path of sanctification, as God's grace continually renews persons who repent and do good works. For Wesley, participation in this graced life is called holiness, As Langford says, in Wesley's theology "a static condition of salvation was set aside in favor of a dynamic, moment-by-moment relationship with God."[12] The culmination of this journey is Christian perfection, where the love of God is perfectly shed abroad within the

---

6. "Justification by Faith," §§I.3 and 4, *Works*, 1:184-85.
7. "Original Sin," *Works*, 2:172-85.
8. See "The Original, Nature, Properties, and Use of the Law," §I.4, *Works*, 2:7.
9. Kenneth J. Collins, *The Theology of John Wesley: Holy Love and the Shape of Grace* (Nashville, TN: Abingdon, 2007), 77-82. Collins' treatment of Wesley's soteriology is far more comprehensive than what I can offer here.
10. "Justification by Faith," II.1, *Works*, 1:187; "The New Birth," §1, *Works*, 2:187.
11. See "The Way to the Kingdom," *Works*, 1:218-232.
12. Langford, *Practical Divinity*, 45.

heart, and sanctified persons fully lay hold of the life for which they were created.[13]

The Means of Grace

Love as the essence and purpose of life is cultivated in Wesley's theology through holiness, or participating in the life of the church through the means of grace: "By 'means of grace' I understand outward signs, words, or actions ordained by God, and appointed for this end—to be the *ordinary* channels whereby he might convey to men preventing, justifying, or sanctifying grace."[14] Through these means the Holy Spirit works to conform us to Christ's image and bear spiritual fruit.[15] The divine image is thus restored within as the Christian is inducted into communion with the Father, through the Son, by the Holy Spirit.[16] Without this telos, the means of grace are nothing:

> But we allow that the whole value of the means depends on their actual subservience to the end of religion; that consequently all these means, when separate from the end, are less than nothing, and vanity; that if they do not actually conduce to the knowledge and love of God they are not acceptable in his sight…We allow likewise that all outward means whatever, if separate from the Spirit of God, cannot profit at all, cannot conduce in any degree either to the knowledge or love of God.[17]

Because Wesley's account of what exactly comprise the means of grace varies, Henry H. Knight III, building on the work of Ole E. Borgen, has created

---

13. John Wesley, *A Plain Account of Christian Perfection* (Kansas City, MO: Beacon Hill, 1966).

14. "The Means of Grace," §II.1, *Works*, 1:381. This definition is rooted in *The Book of Common Prayer*'s definition of a sacrament, which Wesley quotes, "a sacrament is 'an outward sign of inward *grace*, and a *means* whereby we receive the same'" ("Means," I.1, 1:381). The means of grace are also referred to elsewhere by Wesley as "ordinances of God" ("The Nature, Design, and General Rules of the United Societies," §6, *Works*, 9:73), a term that indicates a larger berth for the concept of means of grace than "sacraments" (Ted A. Campbell, "The Means of Grace and Forms of Piety," in *Oxford Handbook of Methodist Studies*, 281).

15. See "The Means of Grace," *Works*, 1: 378-97.

16. As he writes in his sermon, "On the Trinity," "The knowledge of the Three-One God is interwoven with all true Christian faith" (§17, *Works*, 2:385). For more on the Trinity in Wesley's hermeneutics, see Wainwright, "Trinitarian Hermeneutic," 17-37; also, idem, "Trinitarian Theology and Wesleyan Holiness," in *Orthodox and Wesleyan Spirituality* (ed. S. T. Kimbrough Jr.; Crestwood, NY: St. Vladimir's Seminary Press, 2002), 59-80.

17. "The Means of Grace," §§II.2 and II.3, *Works*, 1:381-82.

a single typology of three categories.[18] There are the "General" (universal obedience, keeping all the commandments, watching, denying self, taking up one's cross daily, exercise of God's presence); "Instituted" or "Particular" (prayer, searching the Scriptures, Lord's Supper, fasting or abstinence, Christian conference); and "Prudential" (particular rules or acts of holy living, class or band meetings, prayer meetings and various services, visiting the sick, doing all the good one can with no harm, reading devotional classics and the like). Furthermore, Wesley at times speaks of "works of piety" (instituted means) and "works of mercy" (prudential means), the former being those practices that lead one to the love of God, and the latter leading to love of neighbor.[19]

These practices come together to form the "semiotic system" of Methodism within which persons could seek out their created purpose as children of God.[20] Through these means a person participates in the economy of salvation; one's life becomes meaningful traversing the path from sin to salvation, as the grace given by the Holy Spirit reshapes a person's identity from sinner to child of God.

The economy of salvation and the means of grace comprise the context of interpretation for Wesley. Without God's gracious movement toward us, we would be dead in sin. Since God has so moved, the means of grace are the channels through which we can participate in the divine life opened to us. Participation in this life includes interpreting the biblical text, to which I now turn.

The Soteriological Role of Scripture as Means
"Searching the Scriptures" for Wesley is part of the instituted means of grace. The instituted means are those means that Wesley believed to be appointed by God, mostly because they are found in Scripture and were therefore binding at all times and places.[21] As a means of grace, Scripture's role in the Christian life is to evoke belief in God and the attainment of wisdom.[22] It is, as he famously writes in his preface to *Sermons on Several Occasions*, "the way to heaven":

---

18. For what follows, see Henry H. Knight III, *The Presence of God in the Christian Life: John Wesley and the Means of Grace* (Pietist and Wesleyan Studies 3; Metuchen, NJ: Scarecrow, 1992), 5. Knight's three categories (general, instituted/particular, prudential) reflect Borgen's, though he has amended those means under the third category—the prudential—that also appear in the general. See also Ole E. Borgen, *John Wesley on the Sacraments: A Theological Study* (Grand Rapids, MI: Francis Asbury, 1972), 104-6.

19. Knight, *Presence*, 3-4.

20. They find their most coherent expression in the General Rules, published in 1743 (*Works*, 9:67-75). More attention will be given to the General Rules below.

21. Campbell, "Means," 282.

22. "The Means of Grace," §§III.7-8, *Works*, 1:387.

> I want to know one thing, the way to heaven—how to land safe on that happy shore. God himself has condescended to teach the way: for this very end he came from heaven. He hath written it down in a book. O give me that book! At any price give me the Book of God! I have it. Here is knowledge enough for me. Let me be *homo unius libri*. Here then I am, far from the busy ways of men. I sit down alone: only God is here. In his presence I open, I read his Book; for this end, to find the way to heaven.[23]

Despite the language of "the way to heaven," and landing "safe on that happy shore," Wesley is clear elsewhere that his understanding of salvation is not reduced to the soul's state after death:

> What is salvation? The salvation which is here spoken of is not what is frequently understood by that word, the going to heaven, eternal happiness. It is not the soul's going to paradise, termed by our Lord, "Abraham's bosom." It is not a blessing which lies on the other side death; or, as we usually speak, in the other world. The very words of the text itself put this beyond all question: "Ye are saved." It is not something at a distance: it is a present thing; a blessing which, through the free mercy of God, ye are now in possession of. Nay, the words may be rendered, and that with equal propriety, "Ye have been saved": so that the salvation which is here spoken of might be extended to the entire work of God, from the first dawning of grace in the soul, till it is consummated in glory.[24]

The present arrival of this state of salvation is developed as sanctification leading to Christian perfection through means of grace. As one of those means, searching the Scriptures is to occur in a threefold manner: reading, hearing, and meditating.[25] Wesley fleshes out what he means here in the Large Minutes:

---

23. "Preface," *Sermons on Several Occasions*, §5, *Works*, 1:105-6.
24. "The Scripture Way of Salvation," §I.1, *Works*, 2:156.
25. "The Means of Grace," §I.1, *Works*, 1:381. Campbell equates searching the Scriptures with "the spiritual practice of devotional biblical study" ("Means," 284). Similarly, Knight argues that this way of searching the Scriptures refers primarily to the shaping of identity and the opening of one to God's presence (*Presence*, 149, 151). The indication is that this is something other than theological reading. Knight says as much after quoting Outler on Scripture's role as the "pre-eminent norm" of theological reflection (*Presence*, 148). Given that that conversation frames Scripture's role within a theological method in the service of systematic theology, it is hard to see how this is not anachronistic, though it can be granted that what Wesley says in the Large Minutes about searching the Scriptures can be understood in the way Campbell and Knight describe it (see n. 18). Even so, Wesley likely would not have distinguished between reading for theology and reading for identity formation, anymore than he would have distinguished between biblical exegesis and theology. The point is relevant insofar as contemporary theological hermeneutics attempts to recombine the two, which modernism sundered for

(i) Reading: Constantly, some part of every day; regularly, all the Bible in order; carefully, with the Notes; seriously, with prayer before and after; fruitfully, immediately practising what you learn there?
(ii) Meditating: At set times? By any rule?
(iii) Hearing: Every morning? Carefully; with prayer before, at, after; immediately putting in practice: Have you a New Testament always about you?[26]

Two characteristics are obvious: routine and prayer. Searching the Scriptures for Wesley is a discipline that must be attended to on a regular basis. Prayer, which is also one of the other instituted means of grace, is intertwined with biblical interpretation. In fact, this threefold method for searching Scripture is combined with what might be called Wesley's "ethics of reading" in the preface to his *Explanatory Notes upon the Old Testament*.

If you desire to read the scripture in such a manner as may most effectually answer this end, would it not be advisable, 1. To set apart a little time, if you can, every morning and evening for that purpose? 2. At each time if you have leisure, to read a chapter out of the Old, and one out of the New Testament: if you cannot do this, to take a single chapter, or a part of one? 3. To read this with a single eye, to know the whole will of God, and a fixt resolution to do it? In order to know his will, you should, 4. Have a constant eye to the analogy of faith; the connexion and harmony there is between those grand, fundamental doctrines, Original Sin, Justification by Faith, the New Birth, Inward and Outward Holiness. 5. Serious and earnest prayer should be constantly used, before we consult the oracles of God, seeing "scripture can only be understood thro' the same Spirit whereby it was given." Our reading should likewise be closed with prayer, that what we read may be written on our hearts. 6. It might also be of use, if while we read, we were frequently to pause, and examine ourselves by what we read, both with regard to our hearts, and lives. This would furnish us with matter of praise, where we found God had enabled us to conform to his blessed will, and matter of humiliation and prayer, where we were conscious of having fallen short. And whatever light you then receive, should be used to the uttermost, and that immediately. Let there be no delay. Whatever you resolve, begin to execute the first moment you can. So shall you find this word to be indeed the power of God unto present and eternal salvation.[27]

"scientific" reasons. As a result, reading Wesley with a mind to see theology and spiritual formation as inseparable is more sympathetic to his texts, and opens the possibility to learn more for the sake of the present.

26. "Large Minutes," (Q.48), n. p., *Works on CD-ROM*.

27. "Preface," *Explanatory Notes upon the Old Testament*, §18, n. p., *Works on CD-ROM*.

This litany of practices and dispositions gives content to the headings and questions from the Large Minutes. When Wesley prescribes "set times" and regular reading, he means daily, perhaps even twice a day (points 1 and 2 from the Old Testament preface). The very idea of doing these things as a means of grace is reflected in his comments about reading with a "single eye" (point 3), meaning to combine understanding and will; we are to read the words, then put them into action. Additionally, since it is the Holy Spirit who, being the author of both Scripture and life, works through the means, Wesley has the theological tools to tie together more deeply interpretation and holiness. Interpreting Scripture aids our happy restoration as God's creatures in his image (point 5). Likewise, prayer undergirds the interpretation of Scripture and drives reflection on the state of one's heart in light of what is learned (points 5 and 6).

This brings up a key insight. It is *searching* the Scriptures, and not merely the Bible itself, that appears to be a means of grace for Wesley. Whether through reading, meditating, or hearing, interpretation is the means, and the Bible, though eminently venerated, is apparently only connected with "the end of religion" insofar as it is a meeting point between the person who interprets and the Spirit who works through the biblical channel. Of course, with his soteriological reading and his famous commitment to be *homo unius libri*, it is obvious that only the Bible is appropriate to be interpreted as that instituted means of grace alongside, for example, the Lord's Supper and prayer. And while it is the act of interpretation that is needed for Scripture to be activated as an ordinary channel of grace, this act is a response to the work of the Spirit already attested to in both Scripture itself,[28] and the tradition.[29] As the author of Scripture, it is God who has ordained "his Book" to be that set of writings that shows "the way to heaven."

But what about point 4 above, on the analogy of faith? If the economy of salvation is the ultimate context for the Christian life in Wesley's theology, and the means of grace are the semiotic system of the community whereby the life of faith is made intelligible, and if biblical interpretation is properly contextualized within those spheres, then the analogy of faith is that internal logic or grammar that governs the whole. It is to that I now turn.

---

28. See Wesley's reference to 2 Tim 3:15 as Paul's endorsement of Scripture's designation as ordained by God for its role in the economy of salvation ("Means of Grace," III.8, *Works*, 1:388).

29. In introducing the concept of means of grace, Wesley sets it within the life of "the Christian church for many ages" ("Means of Grace," §II.1, *Works*, 1:381). Wesley also alludes to the assistance of tradition in understanding the salvific message of the Bible at the end of the well-known paragraph excerpted above on the Bible as showing the way to heaven: "If any doubt still remains (about the meaning of a biblical text), I consult those who are experienced in the things of God, and then the writings whereby, being dead, they yet speak" ("Preface," §5, *Works,* 1:106).

Hermeneutics and Holiness

The Analogy of Faith and the Grammar of Faith
Traditionally, the *analogia fidei*, the analogy of faith, was directly tied to the Protestant doctrine that Scripture was its own interpreter.[30] The analogy of faith provided an overall coherence to Scripture, a message, in which interpretations of particular texts could be set and compared. Though the details of the analogy could vary among interpreters in the centuries just prior to Wesley, basic characteristics were discernable. As Richard A. Muller puts it, it was because of the analogy of faith that "the fundamental articles of faith enunciated in the basic catechetical topics of Creed, Lord's Prayer, and Decalogue [could] operate as interpretive safeguards upon the interpretation of particularly difficult texts."[31] This meant that Scripture could not contradict Scripture and that, were one to come across an obscure passage, the analogy of faith made it possible to interpret that passage via comparison with a clearer one.[32]

This is all true as far as it goes, but on my analysis of the analogy of faith as the grammar of Wesley's theology, the analogy does more than simply operate as a hermeneutical principle. Building on Hans Frei's concepts of theology and grammar in the last chapter, I turned to Paul Holmer, who argued, "Theology answers the question—what is Christianity? But it tells us the answer by giving us the order and priorities, the structure and morphology, of the Christian faith. It does this by placing the big words, like *man, God, Jesus, world*, in such a sequence and context that their use becomes ruled for us."[33] This is what we find in the analogy of faith. It shows us "the big words" for Wesley, and sets them in a certain order. Using that order teaches us what it means to think theologically as Wesley did and provides "the structure and morphology" of Christian living.

This Christian living includes, of course, theological interpretation, so that the analogy of faith functions for Wesley as his hermeneutical rule for reading Scripture's literal sense. Its function as an internal logic of faith is actually predicated upon a theological principle: in the same way God is author of both

---

30. Muller, Richard A., *Prolegomena to Theology* (vol. 1; Post-Reformation Reformed Dogmatics: The Rise and Development of Reformed Orthodoxy, ca. 1520 to ca. 1725; Grand Rapids, MI: Baker Academic, 2003), 120.

31. Muller, Richard A., *Holy Scripture: The Cognitive Foundation of Theology* (vol. 2; Post-Reformation Reformed Dogmatics: The Rise and Development of Reformed Orthodoxy, ca. 1520 to ca. 1725; Grand Rapids, MI: Baker Academic, 2003), 493.

32. Of the analogy of faith in the sixteenth and seventeenth centuries, Jones writes, "The various writers generally take it to refer to a system of doctrines which represent the wholeness of Scripture, although they disagree on whether any such system genuinely represents the message of the whole Bible" (*Conception and Use*, 46-47). Jones is unsure how Wesley learned his version of the analogy of faith, speculating it could have come during his education at Oxford. He does note a letter addressed to Wesley from his mother, dated August 18, 1725, where she mentions it.

33. Holmer, *The Grammar of Faith*, 20.

Scripture and life, so too the analogy of faith is the grammar of both Scripture and life, giving a narratival coherence to both within one soteriological context. Wesley provides a detailed explication of the analogy of faith in his note on Rom 12:6, "Having then gifts differing according to the grace which is given us, whether it *be* prophecy, *let us prophesy* according to the analogy of faith" (italics original):

> St. Peter expresses it [the analogy of faith], as the oracles of God: according to the general tenor of them; according to that grand scheme of doctrine which is delivered therein, touching original sin, justification by faith, and present, inward salvation. There is a wonderful analogy between all these; and a close and intimate connection between the chief heads of that faith "which was once delivered to the saints." Every article, therefore, concerning which there is any question, should be determined by this rule: every doubtful scripture interpreted, according to the grand truths which run through the whole.[34]

Although this quotation deals more with the analogy of faith and Scripture, it alludes to 1 Pet 4:11, which deals more with the analogy and life. For the moment, two elements of the above quotation stand out: the content of the analogy of faith and its relation to biblical interpretation. I will treat these before turning to the analogy's role in Christian living. These strands will then be brought back together with a look at the General Rules.

The Analogy of Faith and Scripture
The content of the analogy of faith varies somewhat in Wesley's corpus. In the Rom 12:6 note, it is "original sin, justification by faith, and present, inward salvation." In the Old Testament notes preface, quoted earlier, the list is original sin, justification by faith, the new birth, and inward and outward holiness." In "Causes of the Inefficacy of Christianity," Wesley speaks of "the connected chain of Scripture truths.... Namely, the natural corruption of man, justification by faith, the new birth, inward and outward holiness."[35] In *Principles of a Methodist Farther Explained*, Wesley declares, "Our main doctrines, which include all the rest, are three, that of repentance, of faith, and of holiness."[36]

---

34. *Explanatory Notes upon the New Testament* (New York: Lane & Tippett, 1847), 397, n. 6. Although Wesley is commenting on a Pauline verse, it is interesting that he immediately links it to 1 Pet 4:11 (hence his mention of Peter at the comment's opening). How the analogy of faith helps Wesley read the whole of Scripture will be discussed below.

35. "The Causes of the Inefficacy of Christianity," §6, *Works*, 4:89.

36. §VI.4, *Works*, 9:226-27. Jones notes that Wesley could identify doctrines as essential that otherwise never appear in a summary of the analogy of faith. Wesley stipulated that some beliefs were essential, others were "opinions," and ought not to stand

Although there is some variation here, none of it is theologically contradictory. What is most obvious is the clear soteriological content of the analogy of faith. Perhaps less obvious on an initial reading is that the analogy of faith is neither a systematic theology, nor a doctrinal scheme laid over Scripture—a point that might be obscured by Wesley's calling it "that grand scheme of doctrine." This should be balanced with a phrase at the quotation's end, that unclear Scripture should be interpreted "according to the grand truths which run through the whole." These are not doctrines arranged systematically like beads on a string. Instead, they are a précis of the whole of Scripture, which is sometimes referred to as the "whole" or "general tenor" of the Bible.

The concept of the general tenor combines naturally with the analogy of faith for Wesley. In the quotation above, from Rom 12:6, the general tenor and the analogy of faith are mentioned in parallel ways to elaborate a point about Scripture's message. Scott Jones, drawing from David Kelsey's notions of unity (consistency and coherence of parts) and wholeness (a pattern in Scripture discernible by the theologian), states, "In these terms, Wesley holds Scripture to be both whole and unitary. It not only functions toward a single end, but it is throughout consistent and coherent."[37] Worded differently, Scripture has a singular soteriological message consistent with its function as a means of grace in the economy of salvation.

The dynamic at play here is a circular one. On the one hand, the analogy of faith makes it possible to interpret Scripture as having one soteriological message. The analogy of faith is not a narrative (a list is hardly a narrative), but it is narratival. There is a sense of a beginning moving through to an end with the very ordering of the "grand scheme," and it is this sense—which when one is inducted into the Methodist way of life becomes a sensibility—that gives the analogy its grammatical force. The analogy of faith is a pattern for seeing how all of Scripture fits together as a whole in the economy of salvation. On the other hand, reading Scripture is a way of elaborating upon, or even exegeting, the analogy of faith, which is a summation of the gospel message everywhere attested to in Scripture.

An example of the analogy of faith in action is the sermon "Justification by Faith." Wesley begins by lamenting the ignorance of so many Christians regarding the doctrine of justification, considering "it contains the foundation of all our hope inasmuch as while we are at enmity with God there can be no true peace, no solid joy, either in time or in eternity."[38] But not only ignorance; many ideas about justification are "utterly false, contrary to the truth as light to

---

in the way of Christian fellowship (*Conception and Use*, 48). For a critique of Wesley's segregation of doctrine into essentials and opinions, see D. Stephen Long, *John Wesley's Moral Theology: The Quest for God and Goodness* (Nashville, TN: Kingswood, 2005), 39-43.

37. Jones, *Conception and Use*, 44.
38. "Justification by Faith," §1, *Works*, 1:182.

darkness; notions absolutely inconsistent with the oracles of God, and with the analogy of faith."[39]

The initial task Wesley sets for himself is to give the "general ground" of justification by faith. To do this, he begins with "the state of man in paradise"[40]: that humanity was made in God's image, holy as God is holy, "merciful as the author of all is merciful, perfect as his Father in heaven is perfect." Between his opening statement about humanity made in God's image and his summation of this opening, "such then was the state of man in paradise," Wesley incorporates references or allusions to Gen 1:25 and 9:6, Matt 5:48, 1 John 4:16, Wis 2:23, Mark 12:30 and/or Luke 10:27, 2 Tim 3:17 and/or 2 Thess 2:17, and Gen 3:3. What is interesting is that all of this Scripture is focused on the state of created humanity in the garden. Today a biblical scholar might balk at bringing 1 John to bear on the Genesis narrative for fear of doing violence to the voice of Genesis, at least not without qualification, but Wesley assumes a natural connection. Reference to Matthew while considering a point in Genesis creates no problems for Wesley precisely because they are all part of the same gospel. To be even more specific, the analogy of faith dictates that all of these verses can be brought to bear on the image of God in humanity because all—Genesis, Matthew, 1 John and so on— together witness to the truth of justification by faith. Why? Because God has authored both the Scripture that teaches justification as well as the lives whose need for salvation Scripture reveals by its teaching on justification.

Wesley goes on from there to recount God's command not to eat of the tree, the sin that followed, as well as its consequence, spiritual death, which through Adam has beset all humanity. Wesley can carry the narrative seamlessly through Scripture, touching on the incarnation and atonement, and then recap his summary treatment of the biblical story in even more compact form:

> This therefore is the general ground of the whole doctrine of justification. By the sin of the first Adam, who was not only the father but likewise the representative of us all, we all "fell short of the favour of God," we all became "children of wrath"; or, as the Apostle expresses it, "Judgment came upon all men to condemnation." Even so by the sacrifice for sin made by the second Adam, as the representative of us all, God is so far reconciled to all the world that he hath given them a new covenant. The plain condition whereof being once fulfilled, "there is no more condemnation for us," but we are "justified freely by his grace through the redemption that is in Jesus Christ."[41]

---

39. "Justification by Faith," §2 *Works*, 1:182-83.
40. "Justification by Faith," §I.4, *Works*, 1:184.
41. "Justification by Faith," I.9, *Works*, 1:187.

The entire narrative of salvation alluded to here can be told because the analogy of faith makes it intelligible. Old Testament and New Testament are held together as a single witness to one salvific message. At the same time, it is by pulling together across the books and testaments of the Bible that the gospel message summed up in the analogy of faith can be understood.

This is so not only when Wesley begins with a New Testament text; he does not simplistically read "backwards" from New Testament to Old Testament, as two brief examples demonstrate—Wesley's treatments of Gen 3:15 and Isa 7:14 in his *Notes upon the Old Testament*. In the Genesis comments he ponders the multifarious nature of the words, "And I will put enmity between thee and the woman," which he parses out into a threefold effect. First, the serpent himself receives "a perpetual reproach," meaning 1) he is accursed by God; 2) he is detested by humanity; 3) he is destined for destruction by the future "great Redeemer."

Second, a "perpetual quarrel" between the kingdoms of God and the devil is commenced, with Wesley citing Rev 12:7 to more precisely articulate the nature of the battle, which he claims will be a "war proclaimed between the seed of the woman, and the seed of the serpent." This battle shall wage between the people of God and Satan, between "the wicked and the good," "while there is a godly man on this side heaven, and a wicked man on this side hell."

Finally, Wesley sees in this verse a promise of Christ to eventually deliver humanity from Satan's grasp. The passage reads,

> By faith in this promise, our first parents, and the patriarchs before the flood, were justified and saved; and to this promise, and the benefit of it, instantly serving God day and night they hoped to come. Notice is here given them of three things concerning Christ. (1.) His incarnation, that he should be the seed of the woman. (2.) His sufferings and death, pointed at in Satan's bruising his heel, that is, his human nature. (3.) His victory over Satan thereby. Satan had now trampled upon the woman, and insulted over her; but the seed of the woman should be raised up in the fulness of time to avenge her quarrel, and to trample upon him, to spoil him, to lead him captive, and to triumph over him, *Col 2:15*.[42]

Of interest here is not simply the presence of a christological prophecy on Wesley's reading (which was typical in premodern interpretation), but how Wesley spells the prophecy out. In all three subpoints, terminology and phraseology are lifted from Genesis to describe the nature of Christ's person and work. Wesley is not indulging in a departure from the text to enter into an abstract dogmatic exposition. There is instead what we would call intertextuality taking place. Wesley incorporates Col 2:15 (also recall Rev 12:7, cited above) to

---

42. *Notes upon the Old Testament*, n. p., Wesley Center Online; http://wesley.nnu.edu/john_wesley/notes/genesis.htm#Chapter+III; accessed July 2006.

further explicate the Christological import of the verse. Here Old and New Testament play off each other, as Gen 3:15 is illumined by Col 2:15, even as the Colossians verse is essentially rooted in the Genesis prophecy. Colossians is not merely an elaboration upon Gen 3:15, but the former's prophetic fulfillment.

A second example is Isa 7:14, "Therefore the Lord himself shall give you a sign; Behold, a virgin shall conceive, and bear a son, and shall call his name Immanuel." This verse Wesley interprets as a sign for Israel's deliverance.

> But how was this birth, which was not to happen 'till many ages after, a sign of their deliverance from present danger? This promised birth supposed the preservation of that city, and nation and tribe, in and of which the Messiah was to be born; and therefore there was no cause to fear that ruin which their enemies now threatened. Immanuel - God with us; God dwelling among us, in our nature, *John 1:14*. God and man meeting in one person, and being a mediator between God and men. For the design of these words is not so much to relate the name by which Christ should commonly he called, as to describe his nature and office.[43]

Wesley invokes John 1:14 to expound upon the prophecy's meaning, and specifies that "Immanuel" is a name designating Christ's "nature and office," not the moniker by which he would be known. The same logic is in operation as was in Genesis and Colossians: Isaiah and John have the same subject matter, Christ, which allows Wesley to use John 1:14 to unpack the full significance of Isaiah's claim. At the same time, John 1:14 is the fulfillment of Isa 7:14, for it is in the prologue of John's Gospel that the Word becomes flesh and dwells among us.

This internal logic that Wesley assumes when reading Scripture also governs his thinking on the Christian life as an extension of what he finds in the text. An entry point here is Wesley's comment on 1 Pet 4:11, mentioned above in his comments on Rom 12:6.

> *If any man speak, let him*—In his whole conversation, public and private. *Speak as the oracles of God*—Let all his words be according to this pattern, both as to matter and manner, more especially in public. By this mark we may always know who are, so far, the true or false prophets. *The oracles of God* teach that men should repent, believe, obey. He that treats of faith and leaves out repentance, or does not enjoin practical holiness to believers, does not speak as the oracles of God: he does not preach Christ, let him think as highly of himself as he will."[44]

---

43. *Notes upon the Old Testament*, n. p., Wesley Center Online; http://wesley.nnu.edu/john_wesley/notes/isaiah.htm#Chapter+VII; accessed July 2006.

44. *Notes upon the New Testament*, 616, n. 11.

Wesley here connects how the analogy directs Christian speech about God by the Christian taking on the scriptural idiom as her own. Words and phrases from Scripture should saturate Christian language in accordance with the analogy of faith. But this language is meaningless unless it connects to life that is also conformed to the logic of the gospel message. "Repent, believe, and obey," echoes depictions of the analogy of faith as sin, justification, and holiness, and Wesley admonishes his readers to not stop short of presenting the full gospel by speaking of, for instance, faith and repentance without holy living.

The analogy of faith also directs how Wesley conceives the identities of those addressed by Scripture. This is evident in his sermon, "The Spirit of Bondage and Adoption," where he speaks of the "natural," "legal" and "evangelical" person.[45] The natural person is one whose "soul is in a deep sleep." Wesley here claims such a person is completely ignorant of God, "totally a stranger to the law of God, as to its true, inward, spiritual meaning."[46] So complete is the ignorance that the natural person is existentially secure, oblivious to the presence of sin and God's wrath: "He *sees* not that he stands on the edge of the pit; therefore he *fears* it not."[47]

"By some awful providence, or by his Word applied with the demonstration of his Spirit, God touches the heart of him that lay asleep in darkness and in the shadow of death."[48] This is the state of the legal person, who is now awake and fully aware of pending judgment. The law is beginning to work in its inward, spiritual power, bringing home to the person the awful consequences of sin: "He feels that 'the wages,' the just reward, 'of sin,' of his sin above all, 'is death'; even the second death, the death which dieth not, the destruction of body and soul in hell."[49]

Recognition of the need for God's grace through Jesus Christ begets the third state, that of the evangelical person. This person has received the Spirit of adoption, the Holy Spirit reigning in the heart, and can thereby address God as "Abba, Father."[50] The love of God shed abroad in the heart, this person prevails over sin, becoming a true child of God.

This anthropology is soteriologically determined; the analogy of faith is the internal logic that gives the typology its coherence. Wesley is here taking the literal sense of the text in a twofold way, as not only a way of understanding the words on the pages of Scripture, but also as a way of understanding the life of himself and those he is addressing. Thus, whoever comes to the biblical text

---

45. The typology is Augustinian, though Outler claims the more immediate source for Wesley is Thomas Boston. See his introductory comments, *Works*, 1:248.
46. "The Spirit of Bondage and Adoption," §I.1, *Works*, 1:251. This is everywhere Wesley's view, as Outler points out (cf. *Works,*, 1:248-49).
47. "The Spirit of Bondage and Adoption," §I.2, *Works*, 1:251 (italics original).
48. "The Spirit of Bondage and Adoption," §II.1, *Works*, 1:255.
49. "The Spirit of Bondage and Adoption," §II.4, *Works*, 256.
50. "The Spirit of Bondage and Adoption," §III.1, *Works*, 260.

seeking salvation will find it, for by reading the literal sense of Scripture they will discover the literal sense of their own lives as they locate themselves within God's redemptive purposes.

In discussing the grammar of the faith last chapter, I took Frei's own arguments about grammar and context to make the point that since biblical interpretation occurs within a communal setting, the internal grammar of the faith not only governs biblical interpretation, but the entire system of beliefs and practices that go with it. Attuned to that kind of analysis, one might expect to find the elements discussed so far in this chapter to come together communally. In fact, with Wesley they do: these characteristics of the analogy of faith as the grammar of Scripture and life, as well as Scripture's role as a means of grace, converge in Wesley's General Rules.

The General Rules were created to regulate the emerging Methodist societies that formed as a result of the Wesleyan revival. They are actually a development of the Rules of the Band Societies written in 1738.[51] Wesley's opening remarks, where he recalls being approached to write what would become the Rules, already hint at the grammar of his analogy of faith shaping his recollection: "In the latter end of the year 1739 eight or ten persons came to me in London who appeared deeply convinced of sin, and earnestly groaning for redemption."[52] Wesley began meeting every Thursday with the group, which became "the rise of the United Society, first at London, and then in other places." Wesley's depiction of the groups' character is soteriological and scriptural: "Such a Society is no other than 'a company of men "having the form, and seeking the power of godliness," united in order to pray together, to receive the word of exhortation, and to watch over one another in love, that they may help each other work out their salvation.'"[53]

After laying down preliminary administrative guidelines, Wesley structures the General Rules by three principles: to do no harm, to do good, and to attend to the ordinances of God. Nearly twenty biblical quotes and allusions are woven together—in a fashion that can only be depicted as "speaking as the oracles of God"—to regulate speech, dress, commerce, loans, and other behaviors and attitudes as members "continue to evidence their desire for salvation."[54] Those who wish to join must admit to "a desire to flee from the wrath to come, to be saved from their sins."[55] Holiness in all aspects of life will bear out the sincerity

---

51. "Rules of the Band Societies," *Works*, 9:77-78.

52. "General Rules," §1, *Works*, 9:69.

53. "General Rules," §2, *Works*, 9:69. Wesley quotes from 2 Tim 3:5 and alludes to Phil 2:12.

54. This phrase appears three times, before each of the three sections, §§4, 5, and 60 ("General Rules," *Works*, 9:70, 72).

55. "General Rules," §4, *Works*, 9:70. Here Wesley quotes Matt 3:7 and alludes to Matt 1:21.

of this admission since "where this is really fixed in the soul it will be shown by its fruits."[56]

The third principle is to participate in the instituted means of grace, including, of course, searching the Scriptures. We see then how the means of grace are tied in to acts and dispositions that only make sense in a soteriological context, where someone is moving from sin to salvation and on to perfection. Wesley understands the General Rules to be the result of his own searching of the Scriptures, as his claim to finding them in the Bible and of the Spirit's ministry through Scripture shows: "These are the General Rules of our societies; all of which are taught of God to observe, even in his written Word, the only rule, and the sufficient rule, both of our faith and practice, and all these we know his Spirit writes on every truly awakened heart."[57] Likewise, the General Rules end with a poem by Charles Wesley, "A Prayer for Those convinced of Sin," which leads readers through a biblically saturated meditation whose steps are clearly ordered by the analogy of faith.[58]

Though less comprehensive, the Rules of the Band Societies evince the same soteriological grammar. The eleven questions that are to be "proposed to every one before *he* is admitted amongst us" are practically an elaborated form of the analogy of faith. The first five deal with sin and salvation: 1. Have you the forgiveness of your sins? 2. Have you peace with God, through our Lord Jesus Christ? 3. Have you the witness of God's Spirit with your spirit that you are a child of God? 4. Is the love of God shed abroad in your heart? 5. Has no sin, inward or outward, dominion over you?" The next six questions have to do with accountability, and no doubt are directed by the belief that salvation culminates in holiness. The expectation that these questions indicate what will be a regular part of the Methodist discipline assumes that those who undergo this kind of accountability are going on to perfection:

> 6. Do you desire to be told of your faults? 7. Do you desire to be told of all your faults, and that plan and home? 8. Do you desire that every one of us should tell you from time to time whatsoever is in *his* heart concerning you? 9. Consider! Do you desire we should tell you whatsoever we think, whatsoever we fear, whatsoever we hear, concerning you? 10. Do you desire that in doing this we should come as close as possible, that we should cut to the quick, and search your heart to the bottom? 11. Is it your desire and design to be on this and all other occasions entirely open, so as to speak everything that is in your heart, without exception, without disguise, and without reserve?"[59]

---

56. "General Rules," §4, *Works*, 9:70.
57. "General Rules," §7, *Works*, 9:73.
58. "A Prayer for Those Who Are Convinced of Sin," *Works*, 9:73-75.
59. "Rules of the Band Societies," *Works*, 9:77-78.

By participating in the means of grace known as searching the Scriptures, while guided by the analogy of faith, Wesley is able to create a way of life so people can together work out their salvation. It is here the semiotic system of the means of grace, set within a soteriological context, coheres by virtue of searching the Scriptures according to the analogy of faith.

5. Wesley's Hermeneutics in Action

In this chapter I will continue my description of Wesley's theological hermeneutics, giving close attention to the literal sense in Wesley's usage of Scripture. The importance of the literal sense came to the fore in chapter three, where examination of Hans Frei's and other scholars' work was shown to be, at least in part, a response to how the literal sense had suffered in modernity. Whereas the literal sense, history, and meaning were coterminous in premodern interpretation, in modernism they became sundered, with the result that the words of Scripture became secondary as exegetes began to seek the world "behind" the text in reconstructed events and authorial intentions, or to locate meaning in dogmatic or scientific concepts.

The work of Frei and others has largely been to give a postcritical account of the literal sense, resituating it from textual property, reconstructed past, or abstract concept to communal use. As a result, perhaps the two most important points about the literal sense that came out of chapter three is that it is context dependent, and a way of using Scripture. To understand the literal sense requires acquaintance with the aims, dispositions, and practices an interpreter has been "schooled"—to use Charles Wood's term again—to bring to the text. It is therefore a ruled reading of Scripture, a reading according to the grammar of the community's faith. Because the literal sense is a context specific use of Scripture—a style of interpretation—it is best understood through examples.

This need for examples in recognizing the literal sense coincides with my intention, following MacIntyre in chapter two, to learn theological interpretation as a craft in conversation with Wesley's hermeneutics. Having dealt with many of the contextual and grammatical aspects of Wesley's theological hermeneutics in the previous chapter, I will here turn to several examples of the literal sense in Wesley's writings. I will look at significant portions of two sermons, "The New Birth" and "Perfection," as well as two passages from Wesley's *Explanatory Notes*, his comments on Rom 9 and Ps 22. The two genres are important in the Wesleyan tradition, as the sermons and the New Testament notes are considered fundamental to Wesleyan theology.[1]

As an article of Wesley's *ordo salutis*, the new birth is one of the most important doctrines in his thought, as he himself claimed.[2] With the soteriological context and approach to Scripture for Wesley already established in chapter four, "The New Birth" is an appropriate sermon to examine. My reading of it will concentrate on the first two sections, which are the most

---

1. E.g., the largest Wesleyan ecclesiastical body in the world, The United Methodist Church, recognizes the sermons and the New Testament notes as doctrinal standards (*The Book of Discipline of the United Methodist Church* [Nashville, TN: United Methodist Publishing House, 2004], 102).

2. "The New Birth," §1, *Works*, 2:187.

exegetical. The second sermon is "Perfection," which is occupied with what is possibly the most controverted doctrine in Wesley's theology, that a person can in the present life be entirely sanctified, or perfected. The level of controversy this teaching provoked, and its prominence in Wesley's thought, makes the sermon an interesting specimen to study Wesley's use of the literal sense in support of it.

Romans 9 is, historically, a lightning rod for debate between Arminian and Calvinist theology. Wesley reads Rom 9 with this controversy in mind (as seen through certain indirect comments he makes) and offers a reading that moves away from Rom 9 as having to do with individual, eternal destinies. Traditionally within Christian theology (including the New Testament), Ps 22 is read christologically as having to do with the crucifixion. Wesley follows this tradition, making for an intriguing example of his reading the literal sense of an Old Testament text in a manner foreign to many modern approaches to the "Hebrew Bible."

In continuity with the preceding chapter, this examination will be primarily descriptive. My focus will be on how Wesley uses Scripture, not on what sources might have informed his exegesis.[3] At chapter's end I will summarize my findings and attempt to draw out the characteristics of the literal sense in Wesley's hermeneutics, toward the end of developing a Wesleyan theological hermeneutic of Scripture.

Sermons

Preaching is widely recognized as essential to John Wesley's life as a minister, and the sermon his preferred genre of theological reflection.[4] Wesley could commend his sermons as holding "in the clearest manner what those doctrines are which I embrace and teach as the essentials of true religion."[5]

Wesley's sermons uniformly follow a certain structure. As Frances Young observes, "(Wesley's) preaching is thematic and follows a prepared plan whose subdivisions are often announced in advance. Even within the subdivisions, it's easy to discern the outline."[6] The sermons are titled, with a verse (or fragment of a verse) as a heading. Young characterizes the sermons as "for the most part

---

3. As I indicated in chapter two, there is no shortage of such approaches in modern Wesleyan studies.

4. See, e.g., William J. Abraham, "Wesley as Preacher," in *The Cambridge Companion to John Wesley*, 98-112; Heitzenrater, *Wesley His Own Biographer*, 145-46; Outler, "Introduction," *Works*, 1:13-29.

5. "Preface," §1, *Works*, 1:103.

6. Frances Young, "God's Word Proclaimed: The Homiletics of Grace and Demand in John Chrysostom and John Wesley," in *Orthodox and Wesleyan Scriptural Understanding and Practice* (ed. S. T. Kimbrough Jr.; Crestwood, NY: St. Vladimir's Seminary Press, 2005), 140.

isolated expositions of congenial texts" where Wesley can argue "his stance and approach on various doctrinal and practical issues, which were at the fore in the evangelical revival."[7] In terms of the sermons to be examined here, "The New Birth" lays out Wesley's view on a doctrine that had risen in importance for him as the revival he led continued forward, and reflects his move to evangelical conversion, parsed in terms of justification and sanctification, as being central to his soteriology. "On Perfection" is a later version of a message Wesley had promulgated for most of his ministry career.[8] In the face of incredulity that perfection was possible in the present life, Wesley argues that perfection is nothing but love of God and neighbor.

These are, therefore, occasional pieces, highly structured to allow Wesley to develop whatever theme he is expounding upon through biblical texts. The relation between theme and biblical texts, as well as between different biblical texts as they are assembled into an exposition of the theme, will be of prime importance in recognizing the literal sense.

"The New Birth"

The heading verse is John 3:7, "Ye must be born again," which Wesley supplements in the opening paragraph when he describes the new birth as the phenomenon of being "born of the Spirit" (John 3:6, 8). Wesley begins the sermon claiming that there are two fundamental doctrines in Christianity, justification by faith and the new birth. Justification is "that great work which God does *for us*, in forgiving our sins," with the new birth being "the great work which God does *in us*, in renewing our fallen nature."[9] Temporally these acts are simultaneous; logically, justification is prior to new birth. Wesley therefore commences the sermon with reference to both John and Paul. Johannine verses are actually quoted, but Paul's concept of justification is granted priority. The new birth is introduced as tethered conceptually to justification by faith. The goal of the sermon for Wesley is to give a "clear account" of the new birth, which to date he finds lacking.[10] The rest of the sermon is therefore divided into three sections to answer three queries: the purpose of being born again, the nature or process of being born again, and the goal or telos of being born again.

To develop his answer to the first query—why new birth is required—Wesley backtracks to Gen 1. He gives a trinitarian reading to Gen 1:26-27 ("'And God,' the three-one God, 'said, Let us make man in our image after our likeness'"), then develops the divine image in terms of three aspects. There is

---

7. Young, "God's Word Proclaimed," 140. Though Young's point about the occasional nature of the sermons is true, their continued use in the Wesleyan tradition indicates their ongoing significance beyond the evangelical revival.

8. See, e.g., "The Circumcision of the Heart," *Works*, 1:398-414; "Christian Perfection," *Works*, 2:97-124; *A Plain Account of Christian Perfection*.

9. "The New Birth," §1, *Works*, 2:187 (italics original).

10. "The New Birth," §2, *Works* 2:187.

the natural image ("a picture of his own immortality, a spiritual being endued with understanding, freedom of will, and various affections"), the political image ("the governor of this lower world" of creation), and the moral image, which he describes with reference to "the Apostle" Paul in Eph 4:24 ("righteousness and true holiness").[11] Wesley then draws parallels between divine and human attributes, before conceding that Adam was not created immutable, leaving him "liable to fall" in the test that God was to place before him.[12]

It is the moral aspect of the divine image that is considered "chief" among the three. Thus, essentially, Adam was created to be righteous and truly holy, meaning free from sin. Moreover, Wesley quotes from another Johannine text, 1 John, that God is love, and so Adam at creation "was full of love, which was the sole principle of all his tempers, thoughts, words, and actions."[13] Again, Johannine and Pauline texts are used to set up the key points in the sermon.

In describing the fall, Wesley styles it as an act of rebellion whereby "man did not abide in honour" (Ps 49:12). He recites God's warning from Gen 2:17 that eating of the tree would result in immediate death, something that occupies Wesley for the rest of this section as he tries to show in what sense Adam died. According to Wesley, "he died to God, the most dreadful of deaths. He lost the life of God: he was separated from him in union with whom his spiritual life consisted. The body dies when it is separated from the soul, the soul when it is separated from God. But this separation from God Adam sustained in the day, the hour, he ate of the forbidden fruit."[14] At this point the human race loses the knowledge and love of God, "without which the image of God would not subsist," leading to both unholiness and unhappiness.[15]

Wesley closes out this first section by arguing for his view of spiritual death. To those who object that, "in the day that thou eatest thereof thou shalt surely die" ought to be taken temporally and bodily, Wesley responds that such a reading makes God a liar, since manifestly Adam did not die bodily at the moment of his sin. Wesley instead believes that spiritual death is the only reading that makes sense of Adam's long life.[16] He then connects Adam's state

---

11. "The New Birth," §I.1, *Works*, 2:188. Despite the trinitarian schema just outlined, Wesley does not draw a correspondence between it and the threefold image he introduces here.

12. "The New Birth," §I.2, *Works*, 2:189.

13. "The New Birth," §I.1, *Works*, 2:188. Wesley's quotation, "God is love," could derive from either 1 John 4:8 or 4:16; he does not specify.

14. "The New Birth," §I.2, *Works*, 2:189. A problem that does not occur to Wesley is that, if a soul separated from God is dead, and if a body separated from a soul is dead, *and* if Adam died in the sense that his soul was separated from God, would not his dead soul be as good to him as a separated one? In other words, even on Wesley's logic, should Adam have not died "bodily" at the moment of his rebellion?

15. "The New Birth," §I.2, *Works*, 2:189.

16. "The New Birth," §I.3, *Works*, 2:190.

to all humanity's, gesturing to 1 Cor 15:22 that "in Adam all died," that is, all are in need of new birth through the Spirit. Everyone is "wholly 'dead in sin' (cf. Eph 2:5; Col 2:13), entirely void of the life of God, void of the image of God, of all that 'righteousness and holiness' (Eph 4:24) wherein Adam was created." "This then is the foundation of the new birth—entire corruption of our nature. Hence it is that being 'born in sin' (cf. John 9:34) we 'must be born again' (John 3:7). Hence everyone that is born of a woman must be born of the Spirit of God."[17]

Bearing in mind that Wesley's objective is showing from Scripture why the new birth is necessary, three things are of note here. The first is how Wesley brings his entire soteriological vision to bear on this reading of Genesis. All of the most important concepts surveyed in the last chapter—knowledge and love of God, holiness and happiness, perfection—were lost at the fall. Second, Wesley also gives an exegetical orientation to his inward, and therefore more individualistic, soteriology by arguing that it is the moral image that is lost in the fall. This allows Wesley to overcome the exegetical problem of showing in what sense Adam "died" in Gen 3.[18] Third, Wesley, on this reading of Genesis, gives exegetical warrant to a connection he makes in the sermon's introduction between the command to be born again in John 3:7, and both the interiority of the new birth and its being part of a relief from God's wrath. In the sermon's initial paragraph, while arguing for the connection between justification and new birth, Wesley claims, "We first conceive his wrath to be turned away, and then his Spirit to work in our hearts."[19] There is nothing about wrath in John 3, but the conceptual connection Wesley makes between justification and new birth links new birth to it. Wesley is here scripturally weaving together the order of the analogy of faith, even as his reading is implicitly guided by it. The new birth takes its place within the order of salvation.

The new birth is required, therefore, because sin has been part of human life since the fall. Original sin makes "natural" birth a birth into death, as it were. The "spiritual," new birth Wesley advocates is God's way of delivering persons from eternal death to eternal life. It is the regeneration of a person that restores the divine image, making restored communion with God possible.

In the second section Wesley looks at how the new birth occurs. He returns to John 3 and considers Jesus' words to Nicodemus, that the Spirit blows where it may, outside of human expectations and control (John 3:8). Wesley uses Jesus' words as caution against expecting "any minute, philosophical account of the *manner how* this is done" from him, since he is only offering a "plain

---

17. "The New Birth," §I.4, *Works*, 2:190.

18. This is also of a piece with the definition of sacraments Wesley holds, as discussed in chapter four. In the same way the means of grace are outward, visible signs of inward, invisible grace, the death of humanity in sin is inward and invisible, as is its rebirth through the Spirit.

19. "The New Birth," §1, *Works*, 2:187.

scriptural account of the nature of the new birth."[20] He argues that Judaism prior to Jesus' conversation with Nicodemus knew of the new birth, linking it to baptism. According to Wesley, Nicodemus should have known this, being a teacher of Israel. Nevertheless, when Jesus uses the phrase "born again," he means it "in a stronger sense than (Nicodemus) was accustomed to."[21] This stronger sense is a spiritual rebirth, which Wesley argues for by utilizing John's wordplay on ἄνωθεν, which can have the sense of "again" or of "above": "'A man' cannot 'enter a second time into his mother's womb and be born.' But they may, spiritually. A man may be 'born from above' (John 3:3), 'born of God' (1 John 3:9), 'born of the Spirit' (John 3:6, 8)—in a manner which bears a very near analogy to the natural birth."[22] The rebirth humanity needs because of sin is "from above," a work of the Holy Spirit.

If the "how" of the new birth is accomplished by the Spirit, Wesley tries to develop this in §II.4 by way of the "very near analogy to the natural birth" he has just spoken of. Wesley had earlier quoted Eph 4:24, that humanity was created in "righteousness and true holiness." In this same chapter Paul argues that all believers are to "grow up into (Christ) in all things" (Eph 4:15), so that they reach "the full measure of the stature of Christ" (Eph 4:13).[23] There commences then an entire discussion in §II.4 on how the natural birth is like the spiritual. After enumerating elements of natural birth and development—how an unborn child has eyes but does not see; ears, but does not hear; and so on—Wesley describes the parallel between this and how a person is who needs a spiritual new birth: Spiritually, such a person has eyes but no sight, and ears with no hearing. Like the unborn child whose senses are of no use prior to birth; an unregenerated person is unable to use her spiritual senses to comprehend God: "Hence," says Wesley, "he has no knowledge of God, no intercourse with him; he is not at all acquainted with him. He has no true knowledge of the things of God, either of spiritual or eternal things. Therefore, though he is a living man, he is a dead Christian."[24] At the new birth, however, everything changes. Wesley gives a collage of scriptural phrases to describe the state of a reborn person, drawing from all over the New Testament, including Ephesians, Philippians, 1 Peter, Hebrews, Colossians, Romans, and Matthew, and one Old Testament reference to Ps 94:10.[25]

Wesley closes this section by defining the new birth in light of his scriptural exposition. The new birth,

---

20. "The New Birth," §II.3, *Works*, 2:191 (italics original).
21. "The New Birth," §II.3, *Works*, 2:191.
22. "The New Birth," §II.3, *Works*, 2:191-92.
23. Wesley took Paul to be the author of Ephesians. See *Notes upon the New Testament*, 488.
24. "The New Birth," §II.4, *Works*, 2:192.
25. "The New Birth," §II.4, *Works*, 2:192-93.

is that great change which God works in the soul when he brings it into life: when he raises it from the death of sin to the life of righteousness. It is the change wrought in the whole soul by the almighty Spirit of God when it is "created anew in Christ Jesus" (cf. Eph 2:10), when it is "renewed after the image of God" (cf. Col 3:10), "in righteousness and true holiness" (Eph 4:24), when the love of the world is changed into the love of God...In a word, it is that change whereby the "earthly, sensual, devilish" mind (Jas 3:15) is turned into "the mind which was in Christ" (cf. Phil 2:5). This is the nature of the new birth. "So is everyone that is born of the Spirit" (John 3:8).[26]

In answering the question of the second section, how the new birth occurs, Wesley shows that new birth is a work of the Spirit similar to that of natural birth. The Spirit awakens senses that were latent in the unregenerate sinner, allowing that person to grasp the God whom she was created to know.

This passage is a microcosm of how Wesley reads the literal sense of Scripture in this sermon. In the sermon, the concept to be exegeted comes from John, but the Scripture used to perform that exegesis comes primarily from Paul. So it is here: most of the citations come from Paul, but John is given a prime place at paragraph's end, consistent with the thematic heading at the sermon's beginning. John provides the, in this case, culminating thought, but its significance is as a punctuation to what Wesley takes as an essentially Pauline description of the new birth.

Having shown in sections one and two both the necessity of the new birth and how it unfolds, in the third section of the sermon Wesley deals with the goal of the new birth, that is, the reason for its occurring. For Wesley, the answer is simply holiness according to the oracles of God, by which he means "Not a bare external religion a round of outward duties, how many soever they may be, and how exactly soever performed. No; gospel holiness is no less than the image of God stamped upon the heart. It is not other than the whole mind which was in Christ Jesus" (cf. Phil 2:5).[27] This holiness is only possible once persons are renewed in the divine image. "It cannot commence in the soul till that change be wrought...till we are born again; which therefore is absolutely necessary in order to holiness."[28] Holiness is the life we are expected to live in light of the Gospel, but persons must be born again, "from above," to live the life for which they were originally created.

As an example of Wesley's use of the literal sense, "The New Birth" demonstrates how Wesley prioritizes scriptural voices around a theme. He moves through his three questions—the necessity, manner, and goal of new birth—beginning with John 3, which both heads the sermon and appears

---

26. "The New Birth," §II.5, *Works*, 2:193-94.
27. "The New Birth," §III.1, *Works*, 2:194.
28. "The New Birth," §III.1, *Works*, 2:194-95.

strategically at key points, but much of the content of new birth comes from Paul. This should be unsurprising, given how Wesley ties the new birth (an especially Johannine concept) to justification by faith (an especially Pauline concept) in the sermon's opening paragraph. Wesley does at times take a closer look at John 3, such as when he discusses Nicodemus' lack of comprehension of Jesus' teaching; he reads John 3 in light of the soteriological narrative he has been constructing around new birth, yet at the same time Scripture is being used to "read" the concept of new birth. Wesley assumes a unified soteriological perspective, and his use of Scripture shows him "thinking with," as it were, this perspective. For Wesley, the literal sense is the soteriological sense of Scripture.

"On Perfection"
The heading for the sermon is Heb 6:1, "Let us go on to perfection." At the outset Wesley places the phrase within the larger discussion in Heb 5 and 6:

> The whole sentence runs thus: "Therefore leaving the principles of the doctrine of Christ, let us go on unto perfection; not laying again the foundation of repentance from dead works, and of faith toward God"; which he had just before termed, "the first principles of the oracles of God" (Heb 5:12), and "meat fit for babes" (Heb 5:13-14), for such as have just tasted that the Lord is gracious.[29]

For Wesley, this accentuates the importance of going on to perfection; neither he nor his audience should continue with rudimentary elements of the faith, but should move toward faith's goal. He then turns to the words of "the Apostle,"[30] that perfection is mandated if a faithful life is to be lived.[31] Otherwise we risk "falling away" into a state where repentance is "'impossible' (that is, exceeding hard)."[32] In light of this mandate, Wesley structures the sermon around explaining perfection, then answering objections and offering "to expostulate a little with the opposers to it."[33]

Wesley's initial section attempts to explain perfection by first clearing away confusion about it, and arguing that he means neither angelic perfection nor the perfection of Adam. As to the former, humanity has disordered knowledge and affections, so it is impossible for humanity to aspire to what the angels possess, who are "not liable to mistake."[34] As to the latter, it is an impossibility as well since humanity is corruptible. Adam was pristine at creation, but now humanity

---

29. "On Perfection," *Works*, 3:71. The last clause appears to be a slight paraphrase of 1 Pet 2:3.
30. Wesley believed Paul to be the author of Hebrews. See his introductory comments in *Notes upon the New Testament* 563.
31. He does so quoting from Heb 6:3-6.
32. "On Perfection," *Works*, 3:72.
33. "On Perfection," *Works*, 3:72.
34. "On Perfection," §I.1, *Works*, 3:72.

after the fall "is no longer able to avoid falling into innumerable mistakes; consequently he cannot always avoid wrong affections; neither can he always think, speak, and act right."[35] This second clarification, of course, opens a possible problem for Wesley: What exactly does he mean by perfection?

Wesley is aware of the problem because he immediately begins to develop why perfection as he uses the term cannot "exclude ignorance and error, and a thousand other infirmities."[36] Instead, Wesley argues that humanity today is under the law of love, a claim he supports with a quote from Rom 13:10: "'Love is now the fulfilling of the law,' which is given to fallen man."[37] Humanity is still liable to sin, and for that reason constantly needs the blood of atonement.

To this point little Scripture has appeared, but the Romans quotation properly orients the conversation for how Wesley deals with perfection. Having conceded that humanity lives in a corruptible state, Wesley moves away from notions of perfection as doing no wrong, and instead equates it with love. There follows two quotations from Matthew: "(Perfection) is 'loving the Lord his God with all his heart, and with all his soul, and with all his mind' (Matt 22:37). This is the sum of Christian perfection: it is all comprised of that one word, love. The first branch of it is the love of God...it is inseparably connected with the second, 'Thou shalt love thy neighbour as thyself (Matt 19:19).'"[38] Wesley supplements the Matthean quotes with phrases from Proverbs and 1 John, but these commandments are central to his doctrine of perfection. Quoting Matthew again, Wesley claims, "'On these two commandments hang all the law and the prophets': these contain the whole of Christian perfection."[39] With that, Wesley slides away from perfection as errorless existence, redefining it as love of God and neighbor. Moreover, he does it complete with a warrant for his move that comes from Jesus' own words about the entire message of Scripture.

With perfection redefined, Wesley further buttresses the scriptural case for the necessity of perfection with a survey of various admonitions to it, primarily from Paul, but also 1 Peter. Wesley first expands on Phil 2:5, "Let this mind be in you, which was also in Christ Jesus." Despite the verse's reference being to Christ's humility, Wesley claims, "yet it may be taken in a far more extensive sense, so as to include the whole disposition of his mind, all his affections, all his tempers, toward God and man." This more extensive sense comes from later in the same epistle: "So that 'whatever things are holy, whatsoever things are lovely' (Phil 4:8), are included in 'the mind that was in Christ Jesus.'"[40] Wesley obviously does not consider the literal sense of the text to be limited to the

---

35. "On Perfection," §I.2, *Works*, 3:73.
36. "On Perfection," §I.3, *Works*, 3:73.
37. "On Perfection," §I.3, *Works*, 3:74.
38. This last quotation could derive from Lev 19:19 ("On Perfection," §I.4, *Works*, 3:74).
39. "On Perfection," §I.4, *Works*, 3:74.
40. "On Perfection," §I.5, *Works*, 3:74.

immediate discussion Paul is having in Philippians. He expands on it, bringing to bear on his reading the kind of comprehensive view of human nature affected by the fall that is mentioned earlier in the sermon, as well as in "The New Birth." Interestingly, this allows him to make a connection with a verse at the end of Philippians.

Wesley then turns to Galatians, where Paul "places perfection in yet another view."[41] Here he quotes Gal 5:22-23 on the fruit of the Spirit, then exclaims, "What a glorious constellation of graces is here!"[42] The dearth of direct references to perfection in Gal 5 is not a problem for Wesley, whose soteriology informs what for him is a logical understanding of this "glorious constellation of graces": "Now suppose all these to be knit together in one, to be united together in the soul of a believer—this is Christian perfection."[43]

This soteriological reading is further evident as he brings together verses from Ephesians and Colossians, in which he hears an echo of Genesis:

> Again, (Paul) writes to the Christians at Ephesus of "putting on the new man, which is created after God in righteousness and true holiness" (Eph 4:24). And to the Colossians of "the new man, renewed after the image of him that created him" (Col 3:10); plainly referring to the words in Genesis: "So God created man in his own image" (Gen 1:27). Now the moral image of God consists (as the Apostle observes) "in righteousness and true holiness." By sin this is totally destroyed. And we never can recover it till we are "created anew in Christ Jesus" (Eph 2:10). And this is perfection.[44]

Wesley finds a common theme between two Pauline passages, the latter giving rise to a quotation from Genesis, which allows him to reintroduce the moral image of God into the conversation. He then moves briskly through 1 Thess 5:23, Rom 12:1, and 1 Pet 2:5 to develop aspects of his argument, but the sum of it is that perfection is a holistic transformation of the person that leads to love of God and neighbor. Despite the bulk of this first section focusing on perfection and love, Wesley does in the end allow for perfection as "salvation from sin," citing Matt 1:21 where "an angel of the Lord" appeared to Joseph and told him to name Mary's child Jesus, because he would save his people from their sin.[45]

With his discussion of what perfection is complete, Wesley moves into the second section of the sermon. Hermeneutically, this is perhaps more interesting than how he develops his portrait of perfection, because of how he answers objections to his reading of Scripture. The first objection he considers is that no promise of perfection can be found in the Bible. Wesley finesses the problem by

---

41. "On Perfection," §I.6, *Works*, 3:75.
42. "On Perfection," §I.6, *Works*, 3:75.
43. "On Perfection," §I.6, *Works*, 3:75.
44. "On Perfection," §I.7, *Works*, 3:75.
45. "On Perfection," §I.12, *Works*, 3:76.

once again equating perfection with love: "But surely there is a very clear and full promise that we shall all love the Lord with all our hearts. So we read, 'Then will I circumcise thy heart, and the heart of thy seed, to love the Lord thy God with all thy heart and with all thy soul' (Deut 30:6)." Wesley presses through beyond the earlier citation from Matthew to the Old Testament text behind it, which does come with a promise, that God will circumcise the hearts of his people. This helps him in turn to go back and reread Matthew in a somewhat different light; or rather, it allows him to bring out a hermeneutical assumption he held all along: "Equally express is the word of our Lord, which is no less a promise, though in the form of a command: 'Thou shalt love the Lord thy God with all thy heart, and with all they soul, and with all they mind.' No words can be more strong than these, no promise more express."[46] For Wesley, a command in Scripture is a "covered promise," meaning that whatever Scripture commands a person to do, the possibility of its fulfillment is assured by the power of the Spirit.[47]

Wesley can therefore read commands in Scripture as being addressed directly to readers in his day, since God's purposes are communicated through Scripture to be effected in persons' lives. With this, he goes back in §§II.3-6 through the passages that closed out section one of the sermon—Gal 5, Eph 4 and Col 3, 1 Pet 1, 1 Thess 5—and argues that each are covered promises.[48] They not only describe perfection in all its facets, they implicitly require adherence by all who understand their meaning.

After surveying Scripture that affirms the promise that persons shall be saved from sin, Wesley turns to what he regards as a formidable objection: perfection as he reads it from Scripture is a contradiction, since it suggests a person can be saved from sin while still in a corruptible (that is, sinful) body.[49]

The objection Wesley is contesting is that it makes no sense to say one is entirely saved from sin when one is still sinful. Wesley therefore defines sin as "a voluntary transgression of the law," following 1 John 3:4, "All sin is a transgression of the law."[50] Wesley then tries to disarm the point by declaring a rather trivial stalemate. Furthermore, he dismisses the idea that persons abide in a "sinful body," since the phrase is nowhere to be found in Scripture. This is followed by a reading of "flesh" in Rom 8 as meaning unbelievers, "they that are in their natural state, they that are without God in the world."[51] Wesley then

---

46. "On Perfection," §II.1, *Works*, 3:76.
47. See Jones, *Conception and Use*, 124, 204-5.
48. These passages are concerned with the fruit of the Spirit (Gal 5); renewal of the divine image (Eph 4 and Col 3); God's call to holiness and God's willingness to empower persons to be holy (1 Pet 1); God's promise to thoroughly sanctify those called to holiness (1 Thess 5) ("On Perfection," §§II.3-6, *Works*, 3:77-78).
49. "On Perfection," §II.8, *Works*, 3:79.
50. "On Perfection," §II.9, *Works*, 3:79.
51. "On Perfection," §II.10, *Works*, 3:79.

argues that there is no reason to believe God incapable of accomplishing the work of perfection. The remainder of the section deals with the paucity of living examples of perfection. Wesley closes the sermon with a section asking his opponents why they would not want perfection as he has presented it in Scripture to be a real possibility.

Although Pauline texts remain prominent in "On Perfection," Matthew delivers the governing concept, which Wesley marries with his reading of Hebrews, that perfection is love of God and neighbor. Of greater import, however, is how this sermon pushes beyond the biblical text into the everyday lives of believers. Is perfection possible? For Wesley, the answer involves a reading of Scripture that in turn reads his interlocutors' faith in what God is indeed capable of accomplishing in the economy of salvation.

Explanatory Notes

In his preface to *Notes upon the New Testament*, Wesley characterizes Scripture in this way:

> The Scripture therefore of the *Old and New Testament*, is a most solid and precious system of Divine truth. Every part thereof is worthy of God; and all together are one entire body, wherein is no defect, no excess. It is the fountain of heavenly wisdom, which they who are able to taste, prefer to all writings of men, however wise, or learned, or holy.[52]

This hermeneutical assumption is everywhere present in the *Notes* for both New Testament and Old Testament. It explains the connections he is able to make—as will be seen—between different testaments and passages, even as he follows closely the text of whatever passage of Scripture occupies him at the time. Sometimes Wesley's comments are benign, simply rewording what is already there in the verse. Other times, more significant theological readings are given, as is the case with the two examples I will look at below.

In both Old Testament and New Testament *Notes*, Wesley is mostly abridging the work of others, as he himself acknowledges. In the New Testament *Notes*, it is Johannes Bengal; in the Old Testament *Notes*, it is Matthew Henry (with help from Matthew Pool).[53] Nevertheless, Wesley makes them his own, choosing them first for their resonance with his own theology, then appropriating them according to his own needs in educating the Methodist

---

52. "Preface," *Notes upon the New Testament*, 5.
53. He also mentions other minor contributions (*Notes upon the New Testament)*, 4; *Notes upon the Old Testament*, §§3, 14, n. p., *Works on CD-ROM*.

movement.[54] To read the *Notes*, therefore, is to get an accurate picture of how Wesley reads the literal sense of Scripture.

The first passage I will look at is Rom 9, where Paul discusses Israel's election and the inclusion of Gentiles into God's people. Given the traditional Calvinist reading of this chapter, with which Wesley knew and disagreed, his reading of Rom 9 requires him to deal with verses some of his opponents assumed thwarted his Arminianism out of hand. Yet Wesley gives no indication he is departing from the literal sense of the text, and reads Paul to be saying something, though not without tension, that accords with Wesley's theology.

The second passage is Ps 22, which the church, including the New Testament, has traditionally read as a christological psalm. Wesley, in fact, appeals to those New Testament texts to support his reading. As will be seen, what is interesting is that Wesley is quite explicit that the christological reading is true to the literal sense of the psalm, at times even at the expense of its potentially obvious reference to David.

Romans 9

Wesley gives an opening comment that hints at his disagreement with Calvinist readings of the chapter. After summarizing the chapter as one in which Paul answers opponents regarding the exclusion of Jews and inclusion of Gentiles as according with God's purposes, he claims,

> That (Paul) had not here the least thought of personal election or reprobation, is manifest: 1. Because it lay quite wide of his design, which was this: to show that God's rejecting the Jews, and receiving the Gentiles, was consistent with his word: 2. Because such a doctrine would not only have had the tendency to convince, but would have evidently tended to harden the Jews: 3. Because when he sums up his argument in the close of the chapter, he has not one word, or the least intimation about it.[55]

The first point identifies the literal sense of election language in the chapter as being corporate, not individualistic. The second works within the logic of God's love and mercy, which Wesley had just commented upon at the end of Rom 8. If God offers grace, then it is follows that his offer can be either accepted or spurned. It follows from this that, were God to communicate through Scripture that personal election or reprobation were true, it might prevent the Jews from responding to grace in Christ. Point three appears to be an argument from silence, but Wesley is ensuring that there is no confusion about what he believes Paul is arguing.

---

54. See §3 in the Old Testament *Notes* preface, where he acclaims Henry for his plainness of words and soundness according to both Scripture's general tenor and the analogy of faith (n. p., *Works on CD-ROM*).

55. *Notes upon the New Testamet*, 386.

Wesley's comments on the first three verses are fairly mundane, but with v. 4 he provides more substance. To the verse, "Who are Israelites, whose *is* the adoption, and the glory, and the covenants, and the giving of the law, and the worship *of God*, and the promises," he writes, "(Paul) enumerates six prerogatives, of which the first pair respect God the Father, the second Christ, the third the Holy Ghost."[56] Wesley divides the verse into trinitarian operations, the first two—adoption and glory—are the work of the Father; the second two—covenants and law—are the work of the Son; and the last two—worship and promises—are recognized as the Spirit's work. He does not elaborate, but this reading demonstrates Wesley's assumption that all three *hypostases* of the Trinity are involved in the economy of salvation described in Scripture.

On the phrase "the adoption and the glory," Wesley specifies that Israel is God's firstborn, and that God is Israel's glory, referring to Deut 4:7 and Ps 106:20, which reinforce the point.[57] Then, with v. 5 ("Whose *are* the fathers, and from whom, according to the flesh, Christ *came*, who is over all, God blessed for ever"), he notes that Paul adds two more "prerogatives." For the phrase "are the fathers," Wesley adds, "The patriarchs and holy men of old, yea, the Messiah himself," a reference not only to the patriarchs and holy people of the Old Testament in themselves, but also their typological significance in prefiguring Christ, who in fact comes from them. Wesley then acknowledges the theme of God's sovereignty with the phrase, "Who is over all, God blessed for ever": "The original words imply, the self-existent, independent Being, who was, is, and is to come: over all, the Supreme; as being God, and, consequently, blessed for ever. No words can more clearly express his Divine, supreme majesty, and his gracious sovereignty both over Jews and Gentiles."[58] The comment is expansive compared to the scriptural phrase, perhaps a rhetorical device on Wesley's part to increase the dramatic tension of sovereignty and freedom felt in Calvinist and Arminian debates before showing how Paul could not possibly support a Calvinist reading.

Looking to v. 6, Wesley amplifies Paul's statement that the word of God had not "fallen to the ground; for all *are* not Israel, who are of Israel." "Even now, says the apostle," writes Wesley, "some enjoy the promises; and hereafter all Israel will be saved."[59] At this point Wesley makes a distinction between what Jews believed and what Paul is arguing has always actually been the case regarding who is truly part of Israel. At the phrase in v. 6 that all are not Israel who are of it, he remarks,

---

56. *Notes upon the New Testament*, 387.

57. Deuteronomy 4:7 reads, "For what nation is there so great, who hath God so nigh unto them, as the LORD our God is in all things that we call upon him for?" Psalm 106:20 implies that God is Israel's glory through reciting Israel's idolatry at Horeb: "Thus they changed their glory into the similitude of an ox that eateth grass."

58. *Notes upon the New Testament*, 387.

59. *Notes upon the New Testament*, 387.

> The Jews vehemently maintained the contrary; namely, that all who were born Israelites, and they only, were the people of God. The former part of the assertion is refuted here, the latter, ver. 24, &c. The sum is, God accepts all believers, and them only; and this is no way contrary to his word. Nay, he hath declared his word, both by types and express testimonies, that believers are accepted as the children of the promise, while unbelievers are rejected, though they are children after the flesh.[60]

Wesley is here assuming what we have already seen in the sermons, that those of natural birth still require spiritual birth. What he is arguing is that this truth holds throughout Scripture, so that what he takes to be a more "biological" view of the Jews is in fact a misunderstanding of God's purposes.

Wesley's soteriological assumption is unpacked through vv. 7 and 8, where he argues that even through the promise of Abraham's seed, it is not enough to be "children of the flesh." Instead, looking to how God's promise is given to one son, Isaac, over another, Ishmael, Wesley argues that it is not "the lineal descendents" of Abraham that can claim the promise, but "they to whom the promise is made, that is, believers, are the children of God."[61]

The argument Wesley is building toward is that there is a difference between being in a line of descent and being part of God's people.[62] The former does not necessarily imply the latter. In his comment on v. 6 he mentions that through types God showed that it was believers who are considered children of God. He develops this in vv. 7-13, first by looking to God's choice of Isaac over Ishmael ("This is a clear type of things to come; showing us, that in all succeeding generations, not the children of the flesh," but believers are the children of God).[63] At v. 9, where Paul sets up his quotation of Gen 18:10 with the phrase, "For this *is* the word of the promise," Wesley states, "By the power of which Isaac was conceived, and not by the power of nature." Apparently, Wesley is claiming that the power that allowed Isaac to be conceived is the same power of salvation for believers. Wesley then argues that the choice of Jacob over Esau was in order to show that God's favor is not the result of merit, or works, further establishing that the promise does not extend to all of Abraham's descendents by right of natural birth.[64]

---

60. *Notes upon the New Testament*, 387.
61. *Notes upon the New Testament*, 387.
62. Of course, this argument is based on his reading of Paul according to his (Wesley's) understanding of the literal sense.
63. *Notes upon the New Testament*, 387.
64. Wesley is safeguarding his doctrine of universal atonement against Calvinism's doctrine of limited atonement. As Jason E. Vickers argues, this is the linchpin of Wesley's Arminianism ("Wesley's Theological Emphases," in *The Cambridge Companion to John Wesley*, 193).

When Paul quotes Mal 1:2-3, "I have loved Jacob, and hated Esau," Wesley reads him as talking of posterity, not the individuals Jacob and Esau. He reasons this to be so since Esau did not actually serve Jacob, as Paul's quote of Gen 25:23 would suggest (Rom 9:12). Wesley takes this reading as a cue for the following summation of Paul's argument thus far:

> I (God) have loved Jacob with a peculiar love; that is, the Israelites, the posterity of Jacob; and I have comparatively hated Esau, that is, the Edomites, the posterity of Esau. But observe, 1. This does not relate to the person of Jacob or Esau. 2. Nor does it relate to the eternal state either of them or their posterity. Thus far the apostle has been proving his proposition, namely, that the exclusion of a great part of the seed of Abraham, yea, and of Isaac, from the special promises of God, was far from being impossible, that, according to the Scriptures themselves, it had actually happened.[65]

Wesley reads Paul to be saying that the choice of Jacob over Esau is not about the individuals, but about their posterity, showing that the exclusion of some from God's people, despite birth, is not a matter of God's capriciousness, but their choice.

Verses 14-17 further develop the complicity of persons in their state before God. Wesley, who claims that God acts according to terms he has set for people, echoes Paul's argument that the situation he has described is not unjust. The quotation from Exod 33:19, after Israel's transgression, allows Wesley to argue that God can deal with rebellion however he pleases, since he sets the terms for faithfulness. Wesley's theological position would appear to be tested when Paul cites God's words to Pharaoh that he had raised up Pharaoh to rebel for a purpose. To the phrase, "For this very thing I have raised thee up" in v. 17, Wesley writes, "That is, unless thou repent, this will surely be the consequence of my raising thee up, making thee a great and glorious king, that my power will be shown upon thee, (as indeed it was by overwhelming him and his army in the sea,)." When Wesley comes to the phrase, "and my name declared through all the earth," he opines that "this may have a still farther meaning," specifically that God's smiting of Pharaoh was meant to display divine power to all persons throughout time.

Whatever the case, it is interesting that Wesley allows the possibility that Pharaoh could have repented. This is consistent with his theological position, restated in a comment on v. 18: "(God) does show mercy on his own terms; namely on them that believe." And on those whom God has hardened, Wesley clarifies that this refers to those who do not believe, so that God "Leaves [them] to the hardness of their hearts."[66] Wesley returns to the point when commenting

---

65. *Notes upon the New Testament*, 389.
66. *Notes upon the New Testament*, 389.

on v. 22; Pharaoh should have repented when calamity struck.[67] Wesley refuses to allow that Pharaoh had no choice in his fate.

This theological line concerning the possibility of repentance is carried throughout the rest of Wesley's comments. God's fixing of the terms of faithfulness gives him the right to show mercy to whomever he wishes who rebels. Paul's use of the vessels as a metaphor in v. 21—one for honor, one for dishonor—is glossed by Wesley as referring to believer and unbeliever, respectively. Wesley then offers a lengthy exposition on God as "sovereign Lord and Proprietor of all," and God as "moral Governor and Judge." In the former role, God ordains the circumstances of life "with perfect wisdom, but by rules that lie quite out of our sight"; in the latter, God makes his ways of dealing with people "clearly revealed and perfectly known."[68] When he punishes, he does so, not as "an arbitrary, capricious, or tyrannical being," but as one who "wills nothing but what is infinitely wise and good; and therefore his will is a most proper rule of judgment." God only shows wrath in response to sin.[69] The literal sense of Paul's argument is clear to Wesley: "(God) will show mercy, as he hath assured us, to none but true believers, nor harden any but such as obstinately refuse his mercy."[70]

The next several verses keep in this vein. At v. 30, where Paul appears to bring the argument to a close ("What shall we say then?"), Wesley likewise sums up his reading of Paul. That the Gentiles, who at one time cared nothing for righteousness, now possess it, Wesley interposes "justification" next to "righteousness," to emphasize that salvation has come to the Gentiles, whereas the Jews, who had the law and therefore should have attained righteousness, did not. As to why, Wesley argues:

> Is it because God eternally decreed they should not? There [sic.] is nothing like this to be met with; but agreeable to his argument, the apostle gives us this good reason for it, Because they sought it not by faith, whereby alone it could be attained; but as it were, in effect, if not professedly, by works. For they stumbled at that stumbling-stone, Christ crucified.[71]

The unfaithfulness of the Jews is not a result of God decreeing it ahead of time, but because they did not use the law "duly" toward "righteousness or justification which is one great end of the law."[72] Interestingly, though he names Christ crucified as the stumbling stone of v. 32, Paul's quotation of Isa 8:14 at v.

---

67. *Notes upon the New Testament*, 390.
68. *Notes upon the New Testament*, 389.
69. See Wesley's comment on v. 22 (*Notes upon the New Testament*, 389).
70. *Notes upon the New Testament*, 390.
71. *Notes upon the New Testament*, 391, n. 32.
72. *Notes upon the NT*, 391, n. 30.

33 ("Behold, I lay in Sion a stone of stumbling, and a rock of offence") leads Wesley to equate "Sion" with the church, which is "the only sure foundation of happiness," yet is "an occasion of ruin to many, through their obstinate unbelief."[73] Though nothing more is said of this, it seems that Wesley equates the church with the believing Gentiles, who are the "children of the promise."

Wesley's commentary on Rom 9 provides Wesley with an opportunity to make a crucial theological distinction between himself and his opponents. He mostly follows Paul's own cues for looking into the Old Testament, and his reading of these passages helps him give a more "corporate" (rather than individualistic) reading of the chapter, especially as that pertains to the language of Jacob and Esau. Wesley is convinced Paul is not writing on the eternal destinies of individuals, but is occupied instead with who is truly part of the people of God.

The commentary on Rom 9 shows how, even with a verse-by-verse reading of Scripture, the reader brings aims, dispositions, and more that inform the shape of the literal sense. Wesley's remarks often read as if he were answering certain positions; but are these positions found in the text, or in the people reading them? Wesley does not take up this question explicitly, but at the very least he seems to suggest the reading he is combating is based on a misunderstanding of key texts, and he relies mainly upon other Scripture to make his case. To that end, Wesley mainly follows where Paul takes him, discussing Abraham and his descendants, making the literal sense in this case very much a matter of going with the verbal sense of the text.

Psalm 22
Wesley's reading of Ps 22 is interesting precisely because he sees it referring to the Messiah and not David. Though it is "A psalm of David," Wesley gestures toward Jewish interpretive tradition, as well as Christ and the apostles to support his claim that David is in fact speaking of Christ all along. As he states in his opening,

> It is confessed that David was a type of Christ, and that many passages of the Psalms, though literally understood of David, yet had a further and mystical reference to Christ. But there are some other passages, which were directly, and immediately intended for, and are properly to be understood of the Messiah; though withal there may be some respect and allusion to the state of the penman himself. And this seems to be the state of this psalm, which is understood of the Messiah, by the Hebrew doctors themselves, and by Christ himself and by his apostles. And there are many passages in it, which were literally accomplished in him, and cannot be understood of any other.[74]

---

73. *Notes upon the New Testament*, 391.
74. *Notes upon the Old Testament*, n. p., Wesley Center Online; http://wesley.nnu.

Wesley does not deny that David is a type of Christ, but he does deny that David is speaking of himself. In fact, some of his comments in the course of his reading explicitly argue that a given verse or phrase cannot refer to David, but Christ only. Thus, the literal sense of Ps 22 is messianic.[75] Having noted this, it is somewhat amazing that Wesley only alludes to the crucifixion in v. 1, which is the first sentence of which appears in Matt 27:46 and Mark 15:34 ("My God, my God, why hast thou forsaken me?"). Wesley makes some general comments about God as friend and father who "now...frownest upon me." He highlights the obvious despair and pain of the speaker, then at the word "forsaken" comments that "this was in part verified in David, but much more fully in Christ" – an allusion, it would seem, both to the fallout from David's sin against Bathsheba and Uriah, and the crucifixion.[76] Wesley makes a similar interpretation favorable more to Christ than David at v. 6, when he claims that the "people" who despise and reproach are both great and common—a fact that "doth not so truly agree to David as to Christ."[77]

He says little of v. 7, and nothing directly of v. 8, other than to comment that both are "applied to Christ, *Matt 27:39, 43*."[78] As a result, even though Wesley fails to directly identify the cruciform significance of v. 1, it is clear by now that Wesley is reading this psalm in the tradition of Christ's crucifixion. Over the next several verses Wesley does little more than reword the psalm, until reaching v. 16, where the word "pierced," leads him to argue that "these words cannot with any probability be applied to David, but were properly and literally verified in Christ."[79]

But Wesley's reading of Ps 22 as referring to the crucifixion is perfectly clear at v. 17 ("I may tell all my bones: they look and stare upon me"). At the phrase, "may tell," Wesley states flatly, "By my being stretched out upon the cross."[80] On Wesley's reading, of Ps 22 *is* Jesus' lament upon the cross. Wesley sees further evidence for this reading in the next verse: "They part my garments among them, and cast lots upon my vesture." "This also cannot be applied to David," he claims, "but was literally fulfilled in Christ, *Matt 27:35 John 19:24*."[81]

---

edu/john_wesley/notes/psalms.htm#Chapter+XXII; accessed May 2010.

75. In this sense Wesley's reading is in line with his approach to the rest of the Old Testament, where Jesus Christ is central. As William M. Arnett writes, in reading the Old Testament, "again and again he calls attention to the Messianic element...For Wesley, Jesus Christ is the very center of God's revelation and man's salvation" ("A Study In John Wesley's *Explanatory Notes upon the Old Testament*," *Wesleyan Theological Journal* 8 [1973]: 21).

76. *Notes upon the Old Testament*, n. p.; Wesley Center Online; accessed May 2010.
77. *Notes upon the Old Testament*, n. p.; Wesley Center Online; accessed May 2010.
78. *Notes upon the Old Testament*, n. p.; Wesley Center Online; accessed May 2010.
79. *Notes upon the Old Testament*, n. p.; Wesley Center Online; accessed May 2010.
80. *Notes upon the Old Testament*, n. p.; Wesley Center Online; accessed May 2010.
81. *Notes upon the Old Testament*, n. p.; Wesley Center Online; accessed May 2010.

In all of this, it is plain that Wesley is reading Ps 22 in light of the New Testament's use of certain verses from it. This rules his reading of other verses. In v. 22, where the psalmist writes, "I will declare thy name unto my brethren: in the midst of the congregation will I praise thee," Wesley claims that "I declare thy name" cannot refer to David, who never gives his title to anyone but his kin, but to Christ, "who extends this name to all his disciples, *Matt 12:48, 49*, and to whom this very text is applied, *Heb 2:11, 12*."[82]

Wesley does not comment on the phrase "seed of Jacob" in v. 23, but he does mention it in his comment on v. 22. Recalling his reading of Rom 9, it is significant that, when he comes to v. 25 ("My praise shall be of thee in the great congregation: I will pay my vows before them that fear him") that he takes "great congregation" to mean "the universal church, of Jews and Gentiles."[83] Wesley's reading of Ps 22 is as soteriological as Rom 9; his argument from Romans about who is truly part of the people of God is implied in his comment on Ps 22:25.

This soteriological reading is punctuated in Wesley's comment on vv. 27-31. Wesley understands "the world" in v. 27 ("All the ends of the world shall remember and turn unto the LORD: and all the kindreds of the nations shall worship before thee") to refer to "all nations from one end of the world to the other. So this is an evident prophecy of the calling of the Gentiles, and a clear proof, that this psalm immediately speaks of Christ; to whom alone, this and divers other passages of it, belong."[84] He then gives a brief description, on the word "remember" from the same verse, of how the Gentiles will remember both their rebellion and Christ's suffering for their sake. The reference to "the LORD" Wesley takes as a moniker for both God and Christ, "to whom this name of Jehovah is often ascribed in scripture."[85] Verse 28 ("For the kingdom is the LORD's: and he is the governor among the nations") is added, Wesley says, for a reason, to explain "why the Gentiles should be converted, because God is not only God and the Lord of the Jews, but also of the Gentiles, and of all nations."[86] When v. 29 states, "All that are fat upon the earth shall eat and worship," what it is they will eat, according to Wesley, is "Christ and all his

---

82. *Notes upon the Old Testament*, n. p.; Wesley Center Online; accessed May 2010. Although Wesley does not develop it, there is an interesting implication for his soteriology grounded in his citation of Heb 2:11, 12. Verse 10 speaks of God making Christ perfect through suffering; v. 11 speaks of how God is Father of both Christ, who sanctifies, and the congregation (the church) that is sanctified, so that Christ claims the sanctified as his siblings. Then follows the quotation from Ps 22:22. Might the idea that Christ is perfected through the cross, and then declares his name to believers, be read by a Wesleyan to ponder what it means for a "perfected" Christ (that is, a sanctified Christ) to invite believers to share in his identity as children of God?

83. *Notes upon the Old Testament*, n. p.; Wesley Center Online; accessed May 2010.
84. *Notes upon the Old Testament*, n. p.; Wesley Center Online; accessed May 2010.
85. *Notes upon the Old Testament*, n. p.; Wesley Center Online; accessed May 2010.
86. *Notes upon the Old Testament*, n. p.; Wesley Center Online; accessed May 2010.

benefits," otherwise known as "the bread of life." The language of a "seed" in v. 30 invites practically a one-sentence digest of Rom 9: "Christ shall not want a seed or posterity, for though the Jewish nation will generally reject him, the Gentiles shall come in their stead."[87]

The last verse, v. 31 ("They shall come, and shall declare his righteousness unto a people that shall be born, that he hath done this"), takes an evangelical, missional turn on Wesley's reading. Where "they," the seed, come from is "Judea and Jerusalem (from whence the gospel was first to go forth) to the Gentile world, to the several parts whereof the apostles went upon this errand"; the message to be taken is "God's righteousness: his wonderful grace and mercy unto mankind, in giving them Christ and the gospel; for righteousness is often put for mercy or kindness"; the recipients of this message will be "succeeding generations."[88]

Wesley then closes with what has been his hermeneutical key for the psalm, which he believes David himself provided: "Whereby David gives us a key to understand this psalm, and teaches us that he speaks not here of himself, but of things which were to be done in after-ages, even of the spreading of the gospel among the Gentiles, in the time of the New Testament…They shall declare that this is the work of God, and not of man."[89]

Wesley's reading of Ps 22 is an example of figural, or typological, reading that has the weight of Christian tradition—beginning already with the New Testament—behind it. The literal sense here is therefore very much the traditional sense, as Kathryn Tanner argued.[90] Yet what is interesting is that Wesley does not merely read the verses that show up in the New Testament christologically; he sees the entire psalm as a consistently christological text, complete with an evangelical message. Wesley assumes the Old Testament is to be read as part of the Christian canon, without question, because even there the Gospel is plainly evident. The upshot is that without the Old Testament, the New Testament would be unintelligible for Wesley.

The Literal Sense in Wesley's Hermeneutics

I have proceeded in this chapter on the view that the literal sense is a particular use of Scripture; it is a style of reading that is better grasped through examples than definitions or theories. Having now studied four examples of Wesley's literal sense in action, I can make the following observations.

---

87. *Notes upon the Old Testament*, n. p.; Wesley Center Online; accessed May 2010.
88. *Notes upon the Old Testament*, n. p.; Wesley Center Online; accessed May 2010.
89. *Notes upon the Old Testament*, n. p.; Wesley Center Online; accessed May 2010.
90. Tanner, "Plain Sense," 63.

The Literal Sense as Soteriological Sense
First, for Wesley the literal sense of Scripture is its soteriological sense. When Wesley reads Scripture, he does so assuming that all of it contributes to the economy of salvation, as was evident in the way he could bring various texts throughout Scripture to bear on a particular theme in the sermons. This points to his assumption of the unity of the divine purpose to bring salvation to fallen humanity, so that the unity of the trinitarian missions (such as how he grouped Rom 9:4 into three sets corresponding with the Godhead) is reflected in the unity of the entire Bible. This unity is also on display in the figural reading of Ps 22, where Wesley both assumes a christological and evangelical meaning.

Scripture is therefore open to all persons seeking salvation through it because it is through Scripture that God addresses them. As a means of grace the literal sense of Scripture is the instrument by which the God who is creator of all reveals both who he is and who humanity is as well. The analogy of faith is obviously at work here, and it orients, or patterns, Wesley's attention to the text in a way that allows him to see connections of divine intent throughout the Bible. Of course, Wesley also learns to see these connections from Scripture itself, as his commentary on Rom 9 shows. This intent is to save humanity from sin and lead it on the path of sanctification. The literal sense is thus the sense of the Bible *pro nobis*.

The Moral Aims of the Literal Sense
This soteriological reading is suggestive for other ways we might think of Wesley's use of Scripture. In the middle ages there developed four biblical senses: the literal, the allegorical, the tropological (or moral), and anagogical. Exegetes read Scripture according to these senses, depending both on their aims in reading and on where they believed the text itself indicated it needed to be read, an indication ultimately given by the Spirit.[91] A well-known verse from the time illustrates the roles of the different senses:

> The letter shows us what God and our fathers did;
> The allegory shows us where our faith is hid;
> The moral meaning gives us rules of daily life;
> The anagogy shows us where we end our strife.[92]

How these senses were prioritized and navigated varied, depending on the interpreter, but eventually the literal sense began to separate from the others, which were grouped together as the "spiritual sense" of Scripture. With the Reformation the literal sense became the only sense of Scripture to read, unless

---

91. See Henri de Lubac, *Medieval Exegesis: The Four Senses of Scripture* (vol. 1; Grand Rapids, MI: Eerdmans, 1998).

92. As quoted in Robert M. Grant with David Tracy, *A Short History of the Interpretation of the Bible* (2nd ed.; Philadelphia: Fortress, 1984), 85.

one came across a contradiction or other absurdity that allowed, in a limited way, a spiritual reading.

Following Protestant tradition, Wesley adhered to the primacy of the literal sense, unless tensions in the text demanded something else; at that point he would allow a "spiritual" or allegorical, reading to circumvent the problem.[93] However, in his soteriological reading of Scripture, Wesley is constantly interpreting with an eye to how Scripture converts and sanctifies. This is perhaps most obvious in "On Perfection," which not only argues that perfection as the love of God and neighbor is possible, but strongly insinuates a moral problem on the part of those who oppose it. It is also apparent, however, in "The New Birth," where Wesley shows both what new birth is, and why it is necessary to embrace it. For Wesley, the literal sense of Scripture is not confined to the words on the page, but places a call for response upon the life of the interpreter.[94]

The view of the literal sense I have brought to this chapter is based on two concepts: that the literal sense is context dependent, and that it is a style of reading. Given the soteriological context and style of Wesley's hermeneutics, it seems that the literal sense in his reading of Scripture has a moral aim. Although I am not suggesting that Wesley conscientiously moved from the literal sense to something called the moral sense, his own use of Scripture is not merely "literal" in the sense of being descriptive, but is moral as well in its relentless move from text to life.[95] We might say, therefore, that another characteristic of Wesley's literal sense is that it is the literal-moral sense of Scripture.

The Literal Sense as Verbal Sense
The literal sense in Wesley's hands is also the verbal sense. This may seem plain enough, but for Wesley this is not a simplistic thing. Wesley does not equate the literal, verbal sense of Scripture with an "original meaning." He is not afraid, as he shows in his reading of Phil 2:5 in "On Perfection," to expand beyond what is the apparent meaning of a text. And yet he does not commit the hermeneutical heresy Frei indicts modernists with of departing from the text into a reconstructed history or a set of abstract concepts; he remains with the text in its final form, following the grammar on the page.

---

93. Jones, *Conception and Use*, 117.

94. As Robert Wall argues, for Wesley, "Interpretation is never a mere matter of linguistic analysis and meaning-making, but of rendering the manner of God's grace in real people in real places" ("Wesley as Biblical Interpreter," 125).

95. In her comparative study of Wesley and Chrysostom, one convergence Frances Young sees between the two in the history of preaching and interpretation is that both are moralizers. As she says of Wesley in particular, "Yet a great many of his sermons are moralistic, and Christian conduct is his main concern" ("God's Word Proclaimed," 143). This is also the contention throughout Thomas Langford's *Practical Divinity* (see esp. ch.2).

Even so, as I noted with Young above, Wesley's sermons are highly structured around themes, and he is fond of bringing concepts to bear on the text, such as the threefold image of God he introduces—the natural, the political, and the moral—to explain in what sense Adam died in Gen 3. Is it not the case that Scripture resists this kind of systematization and conceptualization?

The modernist form of this tendency is what Frei documents in *Eclipse*. Paul Holmer also discusses it. Holmer argues that the desire of theologians for systematic concepts that are more precise than ordinary religious language causes them to create a scientific language, a language of learning that is at a remove; it is a language "about" religious belief. Religious language, on the other hand, is a language "of"; it is the language of faith requiring self-involvement. Concepts in the scientific sense move away from lived faith into something abstract and neutral, but concepts in the religious sense help mediate faith, aiding believers in faithful living.[96]

For Wesley, concepts like the threefold divine image are religious concepts in that they are descriptive of the text itself; they are not refuges from the particularity of the text where true meaning can be found. The "moral image," for instance, helps illumine the literal sense of Genesis, thereby making the story of salvation told in the text more inviting to those inclined to respond. Consequently, Wesley's fondness for concepts and schemas is not necessarily a problem for the literal sense as the verbal sense of Scripture.

What of Wesley's approach in his sermons, of organizing biblical texts around a theme? Does this not do violence to the literal sense as the verbal sense, by extracting texts from their original settings and resituating them around a theme they may otherwise have nothing to do with? To this two things may be said. First, the literal sense is for Wesley a ruled reading of the Bible. It accords grammatically with the analogy of faith. In Rom 9, Wesley reads the same words as his Calvinist opponents; for instance both see "Jacob" and "Esau." But how they take those names in Rom 9 depends on what has been ingrained in them. Although Wesley sees where others read "Jacob" and "Esau" as referring to individuals predestined to different eternal residences, he reads them as symbolic names of two peoples within the larger story of a promise made. The words on the page are not mere data; they must be read and therefore interpreted.

With the ruled nature of the literal sense in mind we can note, secondly, that interpreting Scripture—again, a means of grace—is not something done for its own sake, but to achieve a particular end. All of Scripture for Wesley participates in a message; it has a general tenor summarized in the analogy of faith. As a result, the point of interpretation is not to understand the text itself, but to understand through the text. Charles Wood makes this point when, after quoting Gerhard Ebeling's contrast between "understanding *of* language" and "understanding *through* language," he says readers must move "from a

---

96. Holmer, *The Grammar of Faith*, 62-68, 90.

knowledge of the text to the knowledge which the text fosters. Such knowledge does not leave the text behind, but the text comes into use as the instrument rather than only the object of one's knowing."[97]

To say that for Wesley the literal sense is the verbal sense does not imply that for him the Bible is an object, and his only aim with it is linguistic analysis. Rather, it is to say that he is attentive to the words on the page. These words, arranged into sentences, sometimes easily support the literal sense, sometimes not. But they are always his point of interface with the Gospel message. Yet in a very real sense, because the Bible is an instrument in the economy of salvation, Wesley's characteristic style of interpretation—his version of the literal sense—finds him understanding the Gospel message through the text. So, for instance, when he brings John, Matthew, Romans, Genesis, and everything else together in "The New Birth," he is exegeting not so much the texts themselves as he is exegeting the theme of new birth through these texts. And as we have seen, some texts are more cooperative in that endeavor than others.[98]

The Literal Sense and the Pauline Witness
Pauline themes dominate Wesley's hermeneutics. They shape his analogy of faith, and they in turn determine his style of interpretation. Even when Wesley uses other passages in key places, such as when he invokes John 3:7 to head "The New Birth," the content of new birth comes from Paul. Although he turns to Matthew to equate perfection with love, Pauline verses still structure the argument. And when Wesley arrives at the end of Ps 22, his remarks on the "evangelical" ending of the psalm are basically a summary of Rom 9. This privileging of Paul is part of Wesley's Augustinian-Protestant heritage, and is maybe the most conspicuous characteristic of his style of interpretation to the modern reader.

This is not to discount other important voices for Wesley, however. As Robert Wall has shown, 1 John has a prominent place in Wesley's theology, even going so far as to call it Wesley's "canon within a canon."[99] Yet Wall also concedes that it is "the Pauline witness" that "underwrites [Wesley's] core belief," by which he means justification.[100] Wall rightly points out places where Wesley heavily endorses 1 John's importance, and he argues that if Pauline writings supported Wesley's "core belief" of justification, 1 John gives warrant

---

97. Wood, *Christian Understanding*, 42.
98. It is therefore a real question for a Wesleyan theological hermeneutic whether and how the biblical text is allowed to "push back" against the reader. Is the text allowed to dictate where the meaning goes, so to speak, or is it at the mercy of the reader? This will be dealt with in subsequent chapters. For now, though, the point is that for Wesley the biblical text agrees with the way he reads it to exegete themes like new birth and perfection.
99. Wall, "Wesley as Biblical Interpreter," 116-18.
100. Wall, "Wesley as Biblical Interpreter," 118.

to the subsequent expectation that all who are justified are to pursue "spiritual rebirth marked out by a life of perfect love."[101]

However, as I have shown above in Wesley's later sermon "On Perfection," Pauline writings still play a significant role in shaping Wesley's understanding of new birth and perfect love. Wesley's understanding of original sin and justification both come from a tradition that privileged Pauline writings, and the two doctrines are at least conceptually prior to entire sanctification in Wesley's soteriology. At the very least, it seems correct to claim that Wesley's reading of Paul set a trajectory for how Wesley reads the rest of Scripture.

---

101. Wall, "Wesley as Biblical Interpreter," 118. Wall bases at least some of his claim on Wesley's sermon "Christian Perfection," which preceded the sermon examined above, "On Perfection," by about forty-three years.

6. Appropriating Wesley I

In chapters four and five I began to appropriate John Wesley's hermeneutics as an initial step toward a Wesleyan theological hermeneutic of Scripture. I surveyed the context, grammar, and literal sense of Wesley's hermeneutics in the service of learning theological interpretation as a craft.

The present chapter shifts from a descriptive mode to a more critical one, and will focus on contextual issues. Specifically, I will develop an account of the church as Spirit-formed context, in which theological interpretation is understood as a means of grace, and where Wesleyan interpreters are formed. I will appropriate Wesley's idea of biblical interpretation as a means of grace through which the Spirit sanctifies us. In the economy of salvation, the Spirit adopts us, conforming us to the image of Christ, the image of God. We thus become children of God and journey in sanctification toward the transforming knowledge and love of God, from which springs love for neighbor. This sanctification is mediated, however, through the means of grace, which are the ordinary channels through which the Spirit ministers in and to the church.

In order for there to be the communal context Frei demonstrates is a must for theological hermeneutics, and in order for this context to make sense within a Wesleyan soteriology, I will argue that as a means of grace, theological interpretation's "native site" is the church, for the Spirit institutes the church in the economy of salvation, and never ceases to be the condition for the church's ongoing existence. In other words, the means of grace, including scriptural interpretation, are not only the channels through which the Spirit sanctifies individuals. They are the ways by which the Spirit constitutes the church in history.

However, this will require a critique of Wesley's soteriology insofar as it does not adequately develop the place of the church in the economy of salvation, focusing instead on salvation of the "soul" in justification by faith and the new birth. Simultaneously, this theological aspect to my argument will introduce a crucial hermeneutical aspect that is also contextual: how evolving assumptions that are brought to bear on interpretation—for instance, through historical critical research on justification by faith—changes the questions readers ask of a text. This will relativize Wesley's doctrine of justification, in the sense of characterizing it as a reading of Scripture based on the reigning assumptions of his day, rather than as a self-sufficient doctrine detached from Scripture. It will in turn open the door for a contemporary Wesleyan hermeneutic to remain Wesleyan while acknowledging how new assumptions and questions may lead to a departure from, or reconfiguring of, traditional Wesleyan themes.

Thus, my critique of justification will have two movements. First, differences in present assumptions and questions about justification by faith and its place in the biblical canon create external pressures to rethink Wesley's account of justification, moving away from its more individualistic and forensic undertones. This leads, second, to the introduction of the church as a more integral part of what salvation is than Wesley allows, though I will maintain that Wesley, especially in his earlier view of baptism, has the resources in his thought already to begin this revision of his soteriology. If successful, this chapter will therefore conclude with an account of the soteriological context of Wesleyan theological hermeneutics that includes the Spirit, church, and theological interpretation. Such a context will prove friendly to seeing holiness and discipleship as key components in a Wesleyan hermeneutic, as well as lay the groundwork for a discussion of theological interpretation of Scripture and Wesleyan identity in chapter seven.

Church as Spirit-Formed Context

The Holy Spirit as Hermeneutical Issue
A Wesleyan emphasis on the Holy Spirit is timely, not only for theological hermeneutics, but for theology more generally.[1] One recent attempt to answer the question of how the Spirit relates to hermeneutics comes from Stephen E. Fowl. In *Engaging Scripture*, Fowl sets up the problem as one of wondering how the Spirit "enables believers to understand the words of Jesus in the light of his death and resurrection," a query mandated by the conviction that "the Spirit's intervention and interpretive work is crucial if the followers of Jesus are faithfully to carry on the mission Jesus gives them." By staking a position on this, Fowl hopes to establish the cooperation of the Spirit with the Father and Son, providing a trinitarian grounding for resolving the hermeneutical problem. Otherwise, the Spirit may be seen as "a free-floating entity operating in distinction from the other persons of the Trinity."[2]

Eccesiology is not an explicit part of Fowl's argument, though the church is latently present in Fowl's reference to the "followers of Jesus," and appears elsewhere as the "Christian communities"[3] and in his comment on the need for "ecclesial practices" in discerning the Spirit's work.[4] But ecclesiology makes at best an indirect contribution to how Fowl conceives of the Spirit's participation in biblical interpretation. From a strictly hermeneutical point of view, this risks marginalizing interpretation of one of its most important elements, context.[5]

---

1. Eugene F. Rogers Jr, "The Mystery of the Spirit in Three Traditions: Calvin, Rahner, Florensky or, You Keep Wondering Where the Spirit Went," *Modern Theology* 19 (2003): 243-60 (243); also, Carl E. Braaten and Robert W. Jenson, "Introduction: Gospel, Church, and Scripture," in *Reclaiming the Bible for the Church* (ed. Carl E. Braaten and Robert W. Jenson; Grand Rapids, MI: Eerdmans, 1995), xiii.

2. Fowl, *Engaging Scripture*, 98

3. E.g., Fowl, *Engaging Scripture*, 101.

4. Fowl, *Engaging Scripture*, 119.

5. Gadamer helps establish context's hermeneutical importance through his work on tradition and bias (*Truth and Method*). For more on context at the communal level and its constitutive role in interpretation, see Stanley Fish, *Is There a Text in This Class? The*

Fowl understands the importance of context better than most,[6] but when it comes to interpretation of Scripture specifically, the church is a particular kind of context that perhaps requires more rigorous attention.

Without that attention, Fowl's discussion appears to turn the question of how the Spirit and interpretation are related into a hermeneutical conundrum that cannot resolve a primary difficulty, namely, the seemingly arbitrary interpretation that has been attributed to the Spirit. Theologically, it is debatable whether talk of the Spirit should be directly linked to the question of validity in interpretation. The problem as Fowl presents it is the result of what tends to emerge in such a linkage as the only possible options for treating the matter—either seeing the Spirit as the seal for valid interpretation or making the Spirit a component in a hermeneutical theory. The latter is unsatisfactory, as it tends to reduce the Spirit to one interpretive principle alongside others.

The former option, which Fowl chooses, also has its problems, as is evident when examined against Rowan Williams' discussion of the Holy Spirit. According to Williams, Christian theology has perennially felt the strain of achieving a description of the Spirit's role in the divine economy that does justice to the *humanum*—the historicality of human existence—without reducing the Spirit to a communicative bridge between God and us.[7] More to the point, Williams wants a pneumatology that stresses how the Spirit transforms persons, how that hypostasis identified as "Holy Spirit" is "the constitutive reality or quality of Christian existence."[8] In exchange for using the Spirit to "close the hermeneutical circle,"[9] the pneumatology Williams has in mind is very much at home in Wesleyan theology: "Thus the presence of the Spirit can be associated with 'freedom' (as in II Cor. 3.17-18)...and of course, with adoptive sonship (Rom. 8.14-17, Gal. 4.6-7), the condition of maturity, the end of servitude, sharing in the quality of Christ's own life, in the tension between suffering and glorification."[10]

Williams' proposal would allow for a comprehensive account of the Spirit's presence in the life of the church, but not at the expense of "the actual texture of

---

Authority of Interpretive Communities (Cambridge, MA: Harvard University Press, 1982).

6. See Fowl and Jones, *Reading in Communion*.

7. Rowan Williams, *On Christian Theology* (Challenges in Contemporary Theology; Oxford: Blackwell, 2000), 108-09.

8. Williams, *On Christian Theology*, 116.

9. Williams, *On Christian Theology*, 117. Williams levels this critique against Barth and Barth's own concerns with revelation, which, though Fowl does not share Barth's theological commitments, seems also to be the heart of the matter for him. For Williams' more thorough treatment of the problems of Spirit and interpretation in Barth, see Rowan D. Williams, "Barth on the Triune God," in *Karl Barth: Studies of His Theological Method* (ed. Stephen W. Sykes; Oxford: Clarendon, 1979), 147-93.

10. Biblical citations appear as they are in Williams, *On Christian Theology*, 119.

Christian life and experience."[11] The grammar of the Holy Spirit is connected to "spirituality" as a form of life in which the relation of Father and Christ is what we live into; the church exists as this Christlikeness in the world, as adopted children of God.[12]

What needs to be resisted, therefore, is any move that brings the Spirit in—even at the last possible second—as a way of obviating the work of interpretation.[13] At the same time, as Williams hints, the life of the Spirit with humanity must be concrete, something I will argue is accomplished by linking the Spirit's mission in the economy of salvation with the founding and sustaining of the church.[14] The church is the sign of the Spirit's presence in the world, and Williams paraphrases Vladimir Lossky that "the face of Spirit is…the assembly of redeemed human faces in their infinite diversity."[15]

The first step, therefore, in resolving the question Fowl poses is to change the question. What really occupies Fowl is not foremost a matter of hermeneutics, but soteriology. Or at least, the former needs to be couched within the latter in a way that allows for the kind of transformation of identity and life that Williams argues is a hallmark of the Spirit's presence in the world. This means not turning the issue of the Spirit and interpretation into a question of "mechanics" (*how* the Spirit operates hermeneutically). Borrowing an insight from Dietrich Bonhoeffer in his *Christology*,[16] the pneumatological dimension of theological hermeneutics ought primarily be a question about *who*: who the Spirit is as the Spirit of adoption that, in conforming us to Christ, makes it possible for us to identify God as "Abba, Father"; and, in the *pro nobis* tradition of theological reflection on the doctrine of God, who we are as adopted children.

---

11. Williams, *On Christian Theology*, 116.
12. Williams, *On Christian Theology*, 124.
13. The temptation is a real one for the Wesleyan tradition, not only due to its kinship to more charismatic strands of the faith, but also to what Albert Outler calls Wesley's "pneumatocentric" soteriology (*Works*, 1:81). Wesley gives a pronounced place to the Spirit in his soteriology, believing it to underlie every moment of the economy of salvation, but he rejected the formal causality of his Calvinist counterparts. Williams points out that if the Spirit is the condition and reality of the Christian life, a strictly charismatic way of conceiving the Spirit's interaction with humanity is too restrictive, and perhaps even misleading (*On Christian Theology*, 125-26).
14. Williams' contention that using the Spirit to close the hermeneutical circle renders the place of Christian *praxis* ambiguous seems to find its mark with Fowl, whose attempt to sort through the Spirit's function in theological interpretation turns to the concept of "friendship" more on the model of what Williams calls the "Spirit-filled community." Williams instead argues for the church as sign of the Spirit to the world; it is in the life of the church the Spirit is seen translating the life of Son and Father into the reality of human being together (Williams, *On Christian Theology*, 124-25).
15. Williams, *On Christian Theology*, 125.
16. Dietrich Bonhoeffer, *Christology* (London: Collins, 1966), 27-37.

To quote Williams:

> Human persons grown to the fullness of their *particular* identities, but sharing in the common divine gift of reconciled life in faith, these are the Spirit's manifestation. The Son is manifest in a single, paradigmatic figure, the Spirit is manifest in the 'translatability' of that into the contingent diversity of history. Freedom in the Spirit is uncircumscribed; and yet it always has the shape of Jesus the Son—another way of expressing Paul's paradoxes of law and liberty. It is Spirit who leads us to 'Godlessness' in order to bring out of us the cry of '*Abba*'; who emancipates us from God to bring us to the trinity.[17]

The process Williams here describes occurs in the church, where the Spirit's activity of sanctification "translates" through the means of grace. The Spirit works to adopt and sanctify persons through the church, and this takes place in part through interpretation. Interpretation, however, is a human act, making it provisional and incomplete. The presence of the Spirit through all aspects of the life of the church does not sidestep these characteristics of the human work of interpretation; the Spirit is the condition for human interpretation to occur at all.

Thematically, Williams' vision, with the place it gives to adoption by the Spirit, is very much like Wesley's. However, Williams gives a more obvious and essential role to the life of the church in the economy of salvation than Wesley, though as I noted in chapter four, this can be attributed to Wesley assuming a church more than it is to him having given thought to a "doctrine of the church" (ecclesiology). Nevertheless, ecclesiology is noticeably lacking in Wesley's thought, which tends to focus more on the salvation of the individual. This is somewhat ironic, given both the more corporate reading of Romans 9 I observed in chapter five,[18] as well as the prominence he grants the means of grace.[19] In the interest of developing the context of a Wesleyan theological hermeneutic on both the level of the divine missions in the economy of salvation and the semiotic system of the means of grace, I will now begin to expand the scope of Wesley's soteriology, and therefore tie the mission of the Spirit in with

---

17. Williams, *On Christian Theology*, 125.

18. Despite the fact that it does not resolve what may be an inconsistency in his soteriology, Wesley's reading in Romans 9 is in part explained by the rebuttal of Calvinist readings, as seen in chapter five.

19. Geoffrey Wainwright maintains that, had Wesley reflected on the theological implications for his view on the appropriation of salvation, he would have an ecclesiology "rather on the 'Catholic' side in the debates concerning the instrumentality of the Church, in which some contemporary ecumenists have located 'the basic difference' between Roman Catholics and Protestants" (*Methodists in Dialog* [Nashville, TN: Kingswood, 1995], 104).

the means of grace ecclesiologically in a way Wesley does not. In doing this I will show that Wesley's doctrine of justification is a reading of Scripture that may not be tenable for Wesleyans today.

Wesley on Justification and Paul

Justification by faith became central to Wesley's soteriology after his Aldersgate experience in 1738.[20] That evening he experienced the love of God shed abroad in his heart as he realized that Christ died for him—"that he had taken away my sins, even mine, and saved me from the law of sin and death."[21] This became both the paradigm and the impetus for his evangelical theology and preaching. The presence of original sin made all guilty before God and in need of salvation. The grace that came with justification was what Wesley called a "relative" change, one that changed our standing before God. It is a gift that cannot be earned by works. Justification removes the guilt of sin, and regeneration removes the power of sin in one's life. This is the soteriology reflected in the analogy of faith, which of course rules Wesley's reading of Scripture. He believed his Aldersgate experience was made sensible by the message of the Bible.

In his sermon "Justification by Faith" the doctrine's hermeneutical centrality is on full display, allowing one to see how this theme was undergirded by the analogy of faith so as to orientate the whole tenor of Scripture.[22] The first major section of the sermon considers "the general ground" of the doctrine, and Wesley treats this ground with a synopsis of creation, fall, and redemption whose backbone is clearly the analogy of faith. Humanity is created sinless and in God's image, loving God totally. God gave humanity "a perfect law, to which he required full and perfect obedience,"[23] a law written in the heart.[24] However, humanity disobeyed God's "one positive law," not to eat of the tree of the knowledge of good and evil, so that "he was condemned by the righteous judgment of God" and experienced death as separation of the soul from God, and susceptible to eventual bodily death.[25] With all humanity now contaminated by original sin through the first man, God sent his Son in love to die on humanity's behalf, causing God to "remit the punishment due to our sins, to

---

20. See Outler's introductory note to sermon 5, "Justification by Faith," *Works* 1:180. Wesley discusses his views on justification in *The Principles of a Methodist*, *Works* 9:47-66.

21. *Works*, 18:249-50.

22. Although I looked at this sermon in chapter four as an example of how the analogy of faith works in Wesley's hermeneutics, I revisit it here to show that Wesley's doctrine of justification is a reading of Scripture in service of my other goals in this chapter.

23. "Justification by Faith," §I.2, *Works*, 1:184.

24. "Justification by Faith," §I.3, *Works*, 1:184.

25. "Justification by Faith," §§I.3, 5, *Works*, 1:184, 185.

reinstate us in his favour, and to restore our dead souls to spiritual life, as the earnest of life eternal."[26]

It is interesting, in light of the prominence in this sermon given to the Bible's wholeness according to the analogy of faith, where in Scripture Wesley draws for his material. Wesley does quote or allude to Romans more than any other biblical book,[27] but more important is *where* he gestures to Romans, for it shows how his analogy of faith is indebted to a certain tradition of reading Paul in Western Christianity.[28] Romans 5 appears at the end of the creation and fall narrative, establishing the current crisis precipitated by that narrative as one of humanity being under judgment and condemnation.[29] John 3:16 opens the next section,[30] but the juxtaposition of the first and second Adams has hermeneutical priority over this verse, teasing out the symmetry between death and eternal life as accomplished by parallel representatives of the human race. Significantly, paraphrases of Rom 8:1 and 3:24—"there is no more condemnation for us" (because of the sacrifice of the second Adam); and "justified freely by his grace through the redemption that is in Jesus Christ"—close out the narrative in §9.

Wesley then explains what justification is, arguing, "The plain scriptural notion of justification is pardon, the forgiveness of sins."[31] Again, quotations and paraphrases from Romans are central: due to propitiation made by Christ's blood, God the Father "showeth forth his righteousness (or mercy) by the remission of the sins that are past" (cf. Rom 3:25); "Blessed are they (saith he) whose iniquities are forgiven, and whose sins are covered. Blessed is the man to whom the Lord will not impute sin (4:7, 8)"; and persons are "reconciled to God through his blood" (cf. Rom 5:9, 10). The Pauline themes are all there, in choice places, arranged to reflect the forensic sense of soteriology that was the assumption of the day.[32] Justification is found in Paul, but Paul's voice here is

---

26. "Justification by Faith," §I.8, *Works*, 1:186. The section is summed up well in §9: The first Adam sins, making all "children of wrath" so that "Judgment came upon all men to condemnation." Yet with the sacrificial death of the second Adam, God reconciles himself with the world and "hath given them a new covenant" (§I.9, *Works*, 1:187).

27. Direct quotations of or allusions to Genesis, Wisdom, Isaiah, all four Gospels, and several New Testament epistles besides Romans are all discernible in this section.

28. This can be termed *Augustinian*, for it has its roots in Augustine's reading of Romans, although David Curtis Steinmetz shows how that interpretation was itself an interpretation of Augustine by Luther (*Luther in Context* [Bloomington: Indiana University Press, 1986], ch. 2). It was Luther's preface to Romans that was being read when Wesley's heart was "strangely warmed" at Aldersgate, and of course his own Anglican tradition taught the primacy of justification as found in the Articles of Religion and the Edwardian *Homilies*.

29. "Justification by Faith," §I.6, *Works*, 1:185.

30. "Justification by Faith," §I.7, *Works*, 1:185.

31. "Justification by Faith," §II.5, *Works*, 1:189.

32. See Outler's comment on the forensic sense of justification (§II.1, n. 38, *Works* 1:187).

the voice of Scripture, and other passages Wesley recruits for his sermon gain their meaning by aligning with justification by faith as found in Romans. Yet what Wesley takes for granted as the Bible's message is, from a postcritical standpoint, a reading; that is, it is one possible way of construing the text due to certain assumptions and certain questions.

Toward a Wesleyan Hermeneutical Context

The Changing Assumptions and Questions
Wesley's reading of Scripture and the core place he gives to justification has found a normative place in the Wesleyan tradition.[33] Scott J. Jones has recently asserted that "no…compelling arguments have been advanced in the last two hundred years" that can undermine the basic doctrinal scheme of the analogy of faith, including the privileged status of justification by faith.[34] This categorical dismissal of contemporary biblical scholarship on Romans and justification perhaps pays too high a price, but for the moment a specifically hermeneutical matter demands attention.

Hans-Georg Gadamer has shown that the projection of the fore-meanings that constitute our fore-understandings onto a text we are interpreting often creates a sense of dissatisfaction when the text does not deliver a meaning expected—or even a meaning at all.[35] To combat this, Gadamer counsels the hermeneutical practice of openness, whereby one constantly questions one's assumptions and expectations, of the prejudices that define our subjectivity.[36] For Gadamer, "The important thing is to be aware of one's own bias, so that the text can present itself in all its otherness and thus assert its own truth against one's own fore-meanings."[37] Coupled with Gadamer's attention to historical context and the text's alterity, this means two things: first, readers need questions to ask of the text for meaning to be generated; second, the questions change through history, because the historical, tradition-constituted context in which we interpret texts changes.

Wesley's reading of Scripture, and the place of justification in his doctrinal scheme, may be understandable in light of the assumptions and questions of his day. However, to assert as Jones does that nothing in the last two hundred years challenges Wesley's reading, risks dehistoricizing Wesley's interpretation of Scripture by divorcing it from the particular hermeneutical aims of his time, and threatens the same dehistoricization of the Wesleyan tradition today, if the

---

33. The *Book of Discipline of The United Methodist Church*, for example, names justification as part of its "doctrinal heritage," and includes it in the Standards and General Rules (§§101 and 103).

34. Scott J. Jones, "The Rule of Scripture," in *Wesley and the Quadrilateral*, 58.

35. Gadamer, *Truth and Method*, 270.

36. Gadamer, *Truth and Method*, 271.

37. Gadamer, *Truth and Method*, 271-72.

historical difference is not acknowledged. This would make it impossible to maintain the Wesleyan tradition of interpretation on MacIntyre's criteria for a tradition's extension, for it fails to take seriously how the context of interpretation has evolved, and thereby ignores potential problems that, if left unaddressed, could effectively terminate the tradition.

If it is true that the questions now are different, and justification can no longer be employed hermeneutically as Wesley does, it is incumbent upon those in the Wesleyan tradition to accept the new challenges of interpretation, to confront and be confronted by the biblical text anew, if they wish to perpetuate their ecclesial identity. Not only is this important for a MacIntyrean philosophy of tradition, it is important for the Wesleyan tradition specifically. Jones' comment is made after acknowledging that the analogy of faith for Wesley is *the* depiction of the general tenor of Scripture, and that Wesley would not change his reading without convincing biblical argumentation.[38] If we read Wesley with an eye to learning practices of holiness (e.g., theological interpretation as a craft) as I am doing here, then the practice of biblical interpretation is essential to the Wesleyan identity. The altering hermeneutical landscape dictates that how we understand that interpretive practice must shift from some of Wesley's assumptions, even as it reopens the way to taking other of his assumptions seriously again. If that interpretive ethos was as important to Wesley as Jones suggests, then an interpretation of Scripture that has integrity as faithful to the gospel would surely be more Wesleyan than distilling doctrine from Scripture and maintaining its primacy without serious biblical engagement. Two considerations suggest that Wesleyans can no longer assume Wesley's reading of justification.

First, there is the problem of unity and diversity in Scripture. Different perspectives in Scripture, especially the differences between the four Gospels, have long been acknowledged. Occasionally, as with Tatian's *Diatesseron* or Augustine's *Harmony of the Gospels*, a consonance has been sought, although the church has on the whole seen fit to allow the tensions generated by differing Gospel accounts to stand. In modernist biblical criticism, however, directed by its own type of historical consciousness, the New Testament was recognized as a conglomeration of different traditions or schools of Christianity in antiquity, whether Petrine, Pauline, Johannine, or some other. The Bible was now a hodgepodge of competing "pre-orthodox" versions of the faith.[39]

---

38. Jones, "The Rule of Scripture," 58.
39. See, e.g., James D. G. Dunn, *Unity and Diversity in the New Testament: An Inquiry into the Character of Earliest Christianity* (3rd ed.; London: SCM, 2006). On the question of how early anything like "orthodoxy" can be detected in Christianity and its relation to the early church's diverse portrayals of Jesus, see Rowan Williams, "Does it Make Sense to Speak of Pre-Nicene Orthodoxy?" in *The Making of Orthodoxy: Essays in Honour of Henry Chadwick* (ed. Rowan Williams; Cambridge: Cambridge University Press, 1989), 1-23.

As late- or postmodern biblical scholarship has changed its ideas about history and applied more recent literary studies to Scripture, the particularity of the final form of the text has made gains on (though by no means supplanted) "behind the text" studies. With this has come appreciation for the distinctiveness of different biblical writers, including how each depicts salvation.[40] This does nothing to how the concept of justification itself is understood, but it does relegate it to the Pauline texts in which it is prominent (viz., Romans and Galatians). Whatever the meaning of justification in Paul, one should not presume Romans speaks for other New Testament books on what salvation is.

Second, if modern and postmodern ways of handling canonical diversity have challenged the hermeneutical priority of justification by faith, what justification means within Paul's writings has also come under reexamination in recent decades. Thus the second factor that indicates a change in hermeneutical context from Wesley's is the "New Perspective," as it is known. Adherents to this position have variously asserted that justification by faith is not based on a dichotomous paradigm of faith versus works.[41] Rather, Jews observed the Law in response to God's gracious initiative, and Christ's mission was the covenantal restoration of God's people. Far from being the private gospel of Protestantism, the gospel is a social reality ultimately cosmic in scope. As for justification, as Wesleyan scholar Michael Gorman puts it,

---

40. For a helpful probing of the positive implications of this diversity in a postmodern milieu, see Luke Timothy Johnson, "Fragments of an Untidy Conversation: Theology and the Literary Diversity of the New Testament," in *Biblical Theology: Problems and Perspectives* (ed. Steven J. Kraftchick, et al.; Nashville, TN: Abingdon, 1995), 276-89. A similar essay focusing on the "fourfold Gospel" is Francis Watson, "Are There Still Four Gospels? A Study in Theological Hermeneutics," in *Reading Scripture with the Church*, 95-118. For a look at a New Testament book, the Gospel of Luke, that conscientiously distinguishes that book's view of soteriology from other canonical voices, see Joel B. Green, *The Theology of the Gospel of Luke* (New Testament Theology; Cambridge: Cambridge University Press, 1995), 124-29.

41. The seminal text in the argument is E. P. Sanders, *Paul and Palestinian Judaism: A Comparison of Patterns of Religion* (Philadelphia: Fortress, 1977). See the several writings of James D. G. Dunn, including his commentary, *Romans* (2 vols.; Word Biblical Commentary 38A-B; Dallas: Word, 1988); and idem, *The New Perspective on Paul: Collected Essays* (Wissenschaftliche Untersuchungen zum Neuen Testament 185; Tübingen: Mohr Siebeck, 2005). Other recent and accessible discussions of the issues surrounding this reading of Paul are Michael J. Gorman, *Apostle of the Crucified Lord: A Theological Introduction to Paul and His Letters* (Grand Rapids, MI: Eerdmans, 2004); also N. T. Wright, *What Saint Paul Really Said: Was Paul of Tarsus the Real Founder of Christianity* (Grand Rapids, MI: Eerdmans, 1997). For a sympathetic and sophisticated critique of the New Perspective from a major contributor to theological hermeneutics, see Francis Watson, *Paul and the Hermeneutics of Faith* (London: T & T Clark, 2004). Watson's position in *Paul* puts him close to the New Perspective, though not without qualification. See also Francis Watson, "Paul the Reader: An Authorial Apologia," *Journal for the Study of the New Testament* 28 (2006): 363-73.

Justification, then, is about reconciliation with God and membership in God's covenant community. For Paul, this takes place by God's initiative to grace, to which humans respond in faith—trust, obedience, and public confession. Faith is not merely a onetime act of response to the gospel but an ongoing covenantal relationship with God that is itself a kind of crucifixion and resurrection, so that the covenantal obligations can now be fulfilled.[42]

In general, New Perspective scholarship, thanks to sociohistorical insights not available to Wesley, has redefined justification by faith significantly enough to create a real difference between itself and Wesley's doctrine. The faith versus works polemic has been disarmed, and the communal dimension of justification has emerged. Any soteriological reading that wishes to stand in the Wesleyan tradition will therefore have to account for this difference. However, given my argument about an altered hermeneutical landscape in which to read Scripture, it should be clear I am not claiming Wesley erroneously diverged from the "true" or "original meaning" of justification in Romans.[43] What Francis Watson says about Paul's interpretation of the Pentateuch could be said about Wesley's interpretation of Romans: "It is not enough to attend to what Paul says about the scriptural text; it is also important to attend to what the scriptural text might have to say about its Pauline appropriation. Granted that such an appropriation will never be a simple repetition of a given semantic content, how far can the text be said to lend itself to this appropriation?"[44]

How far does Scripture lend itself to Wesley's appropriation of it in his soteriology? Wesley believed it to be plainly in Scripture.[45] How we answer that (and here Scott J. Jones would seem to agree) depends in large part on the questions we ask the text, questions that have changed (and here Jones would seem not to agree) as the context in which we read Romans has changed. This includes socio-historical research, but not so that it could be recruited to establish an original meaning independent of hermeneutical appropriation. Instead, this research enters into what Watson calls the "intertextual field" of the Wesleyan tradition, problematizing Wesleyans' reading of some of their authoritative texts, namely Scripture and Wesley, but also putting pressure on Wesleyans to reinterpret their formative texts.[46]

---

42. Gorman, *Apostle*, 138.

43. In fact, Wesley's covenantal reading of Rom 9 otherwise seems quite friendly to this development.

44. Watson, *Hermeneutics of Faith*, 5.

45. Although Wesley was not a postcritical interpreter, it is at least interesting to note his willingness to give up his understanding of salvation if a better understanding could be shown to him from Scripture ("Preface," *Sermons*, §§ 8-9, *Works*, 1:107).

46. In discussing intertextual fields, Watson refers to how new writings (such as Paul's once were) enter into a matrix of already communally agreed upon scriptural

Of course, modern work on the unity and diversity of Scripture would seem to marginalize justification, precluding it from "speaking" for the entire Bible. Yet as Jones argues, justification continues to hold its place within Wesleyan soteriology.[47] In chapter eight I will entertain a Wesleyan grammar that differs from Wesley's analogy of faith, but may be more appropriate for a Wesleyan theological hermeneutic of Scripture. For the moment I will accept justification's place but look at it in light of the New Perspective. This rereading of justification will introduce ecclesiology into the concept, tying it in with both the work of the Holy Spirit in the economy of salvation, and the need for a communal context for Wesleyan interpretation.

Rereading Justification
What of Romans and how we understand justification in it? Whereas Wesley's reading of Romans emphasized justification as the removal of guilt in an individual within a faith-versus-works matrix, Richard Hays, a Wesleyan biblical scholar, has argued that Paul's reading of Israel's Scripture (in Romans as elsewhere) is *ecclesiocentric*;[48] it is focused on the corporate reality of the church. According to Hays, "Paul uses Scripture primarily to shape his understanding of the community of faith; conversely, Paul's experience of the Christian community—composed of Jews and Gentiles together—shapes his reading of Scripture."[49] Francis Watson, however, prefers to subsume issues of ecclesiology to soteriology, arguing other themes in Paul are covered by this

---

writings, reinterpreting some of those writings and creating expectations for future interpretations (Watson, *Hermeneutics of Faith*, 3).

47. See, e.g., Ted A. Campbell, *Methodist Doctrine: The Essentials* (Nashville, TN: Abingdon, 1999), 56; also Oden, *Scriptural Christianity*, 197-203. On 23 July 2006 The World Methodist Council gave its official endorsement, in tandem with Lutherans and Catholics, of *The Joint Declaration on the Doctrine of Justification*, which in part affirmed the importance of the doctrine in soteriology.

48. Richard B. Hays, *Echoes of Scripture in the Letters of Paul* (New Haven, CT: Yale University Press, 1989), 86.

49. Hays, *Echoes of Scripture*, 86. Hays does later qualify his "ecclesiocentric" designation in appreciative response to a critique by James A. Sanders, who offered instead a "theocentric" hermeneutic in Paul. Hays admits any thematic centricity is artificial, but claims, "The distinctive character of the hermeneutic can be displayed only in its capacity to incorporate all of the community's experience into the *story* of God's redemptive righteousness." With Paul, says Hays, theocentricism and ecclesiocentrism must complement one another, which I take to mean neither can truly be central. See Richard B. Hays, *The Conversion of the Imagination: Paul as Interpreter of Israel's Scripture* (Grand Rapids, MI: Eerdmans, 2005), 171. Nevertheless, my drawing from Hays (who incidentally does not finally surrender his stress on the place of the church in Paul's hermeneutics) is meant to help establish the reorientation of approach to Romans from that of Wesley.

one.[50] Whatever the case, a contemporary reading of Romans suggests that, indeed, Paul's argument in Romans is concerned not with justification as the central theological theme of the gospel, but with God's work of constituting a people from both Jews and Gentiles.[51] The mystery God has made known in these last days is that these people are one, the body of Christ, the ones who dwell in the Spirit since the Spirit of God and Christ dwells in them. This is set out from the beginning in Paul's greeting to the Roman church:

> Paul, a servant of Jesus Christ, called to be an apostle, set apart for the gospel of God, which he promised beforehand through his prophets in the holy scriptures, the gospel concerning his Son, who was descended from David according to the flesh and was declared to be Son of God with power according to the Spirit of holiness by resurrection from the dead, Jesus Christ our Lord, through whom we have received grace and apostleship to bring about the obedience of faith among all the Gentiles for the sake of his name, including yourselves who are called to belong to Jesus Christ. (Rom 1:1-6)

As we can see, Paul is dealing with the makeup of the church as the people of God's gracious election (cf. 9:25, 26).[52] Persons enter into the new life of the Holy Spirit through baptism, whereby we die with Christ in expectation of the resurrection (6:3, 4). Gorman explains the process this way:

---

50. "[W]hat is at issue is not the church or God *per se*, but the people of God as constituted by the divine electing decision" (Watson, *Hermeneutics of Faith*, 20). It does not appear that the difference in thematic emphases in Hays and Watson cancel each other out, and here one may note how systematic categories can be artificial when made to characterize a biblical text. Watson concedes Hays' point that God's activity as told in Scripture and its work in forming a people must be held together, with the proviso that, essentially, Hays should share Watson's views on divine agency and intertextuality.

51. For Gorman, this means the gospel in Paul is personal, just not private. "It is the announcement of God's good news for all humanity, for all creation," so that "realities like 'justification' and 'salvation' are social or corporate realities; we experience them with other people" (*Apostle*, 110). The disagreement between Hays and Watson may result from their use of systematic categories to describe Romans' message. Certainly in Romans the creation of a people—the church—is part of God's salvific mission in the world, and this holds whether we term Romans "ecclesiocentric" or subsume ecclesiology under soteriology.

52. As Dunn says, "a Jewish gospel for Gentiles" (*Romans*, 5). Hays' construal is more comprehensive: "The fundamental problem with which Paul is wrestling in Romans is *not* how a person may find acceptance with God; the problem is to work out an understanding of the relationship in Christ between Jews and Gentiles...Is God the God of Jews only (as he would be if justification were contingent upon keeping the Law)? Is he not the God of Gentiles also?" (*Conversion*, 69).

It is important to see how closely connected baptism and faith are for Paul. People are baptized "into" Christ ([Romans] 6:3; Galatians 3:27; Gk. *eis*) and they believe *into* (Gk. *eis*) Christ (Galatians 2:16). They are two inseparable sides of one coin; the combination of conviction and confession (cf. Romans 10:5-13) brings about justification (with the promise of future salvation) and entry into the community. What Paul says of baptism can also therefore be predicated of faith: it is a kind of death experience, a cocrucifixion with Christ, as Paul specifically says in Galatians 2:15-20.[53]

Therefore, when Paul introduces the concept of adoption in Romans 8, it should be understood as the incorporation through baptism of all who have responded to the message of salvation, that is, those who have demonstrated the faith of Abraham. In fact, Abraham as the paragon of saving faith indicates the scope of the economy of salvation, for to Abraham it was promised that he would be the father of many nations (4:16, 17; Gen 15:5; 17:5). The fulfillment of God's plan of salvation has implications that extend even to all creation (8:19-23), so that as those who have the first fruits of the Spirit, the church participates in the divine life as the foretaste of the redemption of all things.

On this reading, justification in Romans points away from the dichotomous framing of faith and works in Wesley. Paul portrays Israel as having always understood its election to be based on grace, so that keeping the Law is the condition for remaining in the covenant, not gaining entrance to it.[54] The personal experience of salvation by grace is not fundamental for Paul, but the consistency and fulfillment of God's purposes in bringing Jews and Gentiles into the salvation of Jesus Christ through the Spirit. The children of Abraham are not all his true descendants according to the flesh, but instead children of the promise to Abraham (Rom 9:7-8).[55] These children are the ones who demonstrate saving faith in Christ, who possess the Spirit of adoption which cries out "Abba, Father," this same Spirit being a seal upon them of their redemption, "For all who are led by the Spirit of God are children of God" (8:14). Through this work of the Spirit, believers are conformed to the image of God's Son, "in order that he might be the firstborn within a large family" (8:29). Therefore justification "is reconciliation with God in the present, together with certain hope of salvation (acquittal and glory) in the future, based on the death

---

53. Gorman *Apostle*, 369.

54. Also known as "covenantal nomism," this is a basic contention of a New Perspective reading of Paul. Judaism was not a religion of works in contrast to Christianity as a religion of grace (cf. Sanders, *Paul and Palestinian Judaism*, 422-23).

55. Cf. Rom 4:1-5 and Wesley's commentary in his *Notes upon the New Testament* on these verses, which cast God's interaction with Abraham forensically with Abraham having righteousness imputed to him due to his faith, not by works. For an analysis of how Abraham's place in the economy of salvation should be understood in Romans 4, see Hays, *Conversion*, 61-84.

of Christ in the past, and all known through the gift of the Spirit."[56] It is a covenantal relationship between God and his people, a reality toward which the Law has always pointed. The integrity of this covenantal relationship is upheld by God's righteousness, that is, by his faithfulness to Israel.

What does this summary rereading do for a Wesleyan soteriology? For one, it makes the covenantal formation of a people integral to the gospel. In doing so, the individually focused forensic nature found in Wesley's soteriology is diminished. At the future judgment those with the faith of Abraham, the children of God adopted by the Spirit and conformed to the image of Christ, will be justified, and the Spirit presently witnesses to this future. Within the covenantal motif, baptism as entry into this people is important, and as already indicated, the Holy Spirit is indispensable in this work of grace. The Spirit's adoption is an act of new birth, enacted in baptism, whereby persons are incorporated into the body of Christ. The Spirit therefore institutes and constitutes the church; the church is integral to the Spirit's mission in the economy of salvation.

In this chapter I am concerned with developing the soteriological context of a Wesleyan theological hermeneutic of Scripture, the Spirit-formed church, which I am weaving together from strands taken from the previous two chapters on Frei and Wesley. So far I have worked to articulate the soteriological context on the level of the divine mission, taking Wesley's sensitivity to the place of the Spirit in the economy of salvation, and broadening it beyond Wesley's more individualistic doctrine of justification by faith to a more corporate and communal version of that doctrine. I will now turn to context on the semiotic level with the intention of bringing the means of grace—including theological interpretation—into contact with what I have done so far.

Wesley on the Means of Grace
A second look at Wesley's sermon "The Means of Grace" will serve to expose the point of weakness in Wesley's ecclesiology, as well as show where revision can occur. There, Wesley sets out to answer his quietist critics who believe any outward showing of religion is superfluous, in deference to the grace God works inwardly in all who believe. Wesley begins by affirming outward religion is powerless without a "religion of the heart"; "God is a Spirit," writes Wesley, quoting John 4:24, "and they who worship him must worship him in spirit and truth…" He goes on:

> …therefore, external worship is lost labour without a heart devoted to God; that the outward ordinances of God then profit much when they advance inward holiness, but when they advance it not are unprofitable and void, are lighter than vanity; yea, that when they are

---

56. Gorman, *Apostle*, 379.

used, as it were, *in the place* of this, they are an utter abomination to the Lord.[57]

The means are to be adhered to because the church has recognized them as the ordinary channels by which grace is mediated. And they are not only useless, but an abomination to God if separated from the end of religion, namely, knowledge and love of God; they are further without profit if separated from the Spirit of God.[58] Wesley accepts the *Book of Common Prayer*'s definition of a sacrament in its *Catechism*, that a sacrament is "an outward and visible sign of an inward and spiritual grace."[59] Wesley's use of this to describe the means of grace, the chief of which are prayer, searching the Scriptures, and the Lord's Supper, evinces the basic orientation of his soteriology. It is the conversion of the person in the heart that is the real foundation of the faith -- something inward and invisible.

Ola Tjørhom has claimed that both pietism and liberalism anthropologize theology by appointing the heart and/or soul as the ground of religion, making both inherently anti-sacramental and anti-ecclesiological. The result is the church "as a purely practical framework"[60] However, as William R. Crockett and others have argued, Wesley was hardly anti-sacramental.[61] Neither was Wesley anti-ecclesiological, as I have already argued, in the sense that he acknowledged the Church of England as the home in which he learned the faith and, ostensibly, remained committed to throughout his life. However, Wesley's soteriology does make the heart the "site" of salvation, and the church does function pragmatically for him as the place where one's salvation is subsequently worked out.

I have already noted Wesley's point that the means are to be used because the church has recognized them as the ordinary channels of grace. Combined with the definition of the means he took from the Thirty-nine Articles, it is fair to say that although Wesley had a problematic ecclesiology, it was in part because he largely assumed an ecclesiology. Or at least, he assumed a church, the Church of England.[62] Wesley connects the need for the means with Christ's atoning work. Taking up a phrase used by some, that "Christ is the only means

---

57. "The Means of Grace," §I.4, *Works*, 1:379.

58. "The Means of Grace," §II.3, *Works*, 1:382.

59. "The Means of Grace," §II.1, *Works*, 1:381.

60. Ola Tjørhom, *Visible Church, Visible Unity: Ecumenical Ecclesiology and "the Great Tradition of the Church"* (Collegeville, MN: Liturgical, 2004), 7.

61. William R. Crockett, *Eucharist: Symbol of Transformation* (New York: Pueblo, 1989), 197-215.

62. As with most of Wesley's theology, Outler thinks Wesley's ecclesiology "an interesting amalgam" of sources and influences ("Do Methodists Have a Doctrine of the Church?" in *The Wesleyan Theological Heritage*, 214-15). Wesley and early Methodism were not exercised by ecclesiology proper because there was no intention of becoming a church apart from the Church of England.

of grace," Wesley concurs insofar as this means Christ is the only *meritorious cause* of grace.[63] It is only through the blood of Christ that propitiation for sin is secured. The atonement that is effected through Christ and must be embraced on faith by the sinner in need of salvation is in focus, a focus reinforced by Wesley's claim that God uses the means for conveying grace "to the souls of men."[64] Wesley's evangelical ministry aimed to save souls, and so it was soteriology, not ecclesiology, that marks his terms for entry into his bands and societies, for instance.[65]

Moreover, the *signum/res* distinction undergirding the Church of England's definition of sacraments, combined with Wesley's bias toward interiority in opposition to formalism, is problematic.[66] In part, Wesley wishes to affirm that the signs themselves are not the power; the power comes from the Spirit who works through them. He tries to keep the outward sign and invisible grace tied together (since he also had to distinguish himself from enthusiasts),[67] but ecclesiology is simply not constitutive for either Wesley's view of salvation or his view of the means of grace. By correlating what is invisible with what is interior, Wesley seems to allow a dualism that could be taken to make what is outward and visible secondary and inessential. This certainly poses a threat to a view such as Rowan Williams', which tries to hold together Spirit and *humanum*; or Frei's view, which tries to hold together intention and action so as to make belief an embodied reality or nothing at all.[68]

Insofar as these views are a point of departure in this chapter, I want to move away from the interior and invisible content of Wesley's *signum/res* definition. Wesley combines interiority and the invisibility of God in a way that,

---

63. "The Means of Grace," §II.4, *Works*, 1:382-83.
64. "The Means of Grace," §II.1, *Works*, 1:381.
65. Prospective members must desire only "to be saved from their sins and to flee from the wrath to come." See Outler, "Do Methodists Have a Doctrine of the Church?" 212-13.
66. I refer to the distinction between a sign (*signum*) and the thing it signifies (*res*). For the paradigmatic treatment of this distinction in Western Christianity, see Augustine, *On Christian Teaching* (Oxford: Oxford University Press, 1997), Book III.
67. Knight, *Presence*, 188.
68. Williams has very similar ideas on interiority as Frei, due to the common influence of Wittgenstein: "Religious interiority...means the learning of patterns of behaviour that reinforce the awareness of my finite and provisional status, my being in time. It is neither a flight from relation, not the quest for an impossible transparency or immediacy in relation but that which equips us for knowing and being known *humanly*..." ("The Suspicion of Suspicion: Wittgenstein and Bonhoeffer," in *Wrestling with Angels: Conversations in Modern Theology* [ed. Mike Higton; Grand Rapids, MI: Eerdmans, 2007], 199).

if not revised, could remain permanently unstable as a ground for the ecclesiological advances I am attempting.[69]

Baptism as Paradigmatic Means of Grace

In revising the means of grace to make it a focal concept for joining Spirit, church, and interpretation, I turn to a particular means of grace, baptism.[70] I have already shown how baptism, on the rereading of justification in Romans given above, is the covenantal gateway to the people God has formed through Christ in the Spirit. As the rite of initiation into the church, baptism has a special function in the economy of salvation, for the nature of baptism sets the pattern for the whole of Christian life.[71] And it is with baptism that a decisive shift in Wesley's theology is detectable. Despite the soteriological and ecclesiological problems of his later view, which is contemporaneous with the soteriology I have been examining, I will show that his earlier position on baptism possesses the resources to assist in my agenda here.

Wesley does have two views on baptism. According to Albert Outler, Wesley's "evangelical concern was to separate 'the new birth' from all 'external acts' in order to support his new emphasis on 'conversion.'"[72] In actuality,

---

69. The potential problems extend beyond ecclesiology. Such a stress on interiority and invisibility may be heard as having a gnostic ring to it that could threaten the materiality of creation, limiting the cosmic scope of the gospel to the individualized, and possibly de-historicized, soul. This risks not only the eschatological dimension of salvation, but the materiality and permanence of the incarnation as well, since it is Christ's human righteousness that is imputed to persons in Wesley's theology, as will be discussed in chapter seven. For a thoughtful treatment of these issues, see Douglas Farrow, *Ascension and Ecclesia: On the Significance of the Doctrine of the Ascension for Ecclesiology and Christian Cosmology* (Grand Rapids, MI: Eerdmans, 1999).

70. Debate actually exists as to the status of baptism as a means of grace in Wesley, particularly since it does not show up on Wesley's list as an ongoing means. The debate revolves around whether baptism as initiatory event has a continuous significance in the Christian life. Knight argues it does, but has to go beyond Wesley's words—and rely on circumstantial evidence—to make his case (*Presence*, 188-91). Some of the difficulty stems from the definition Wesley uses for the means, which is the same as that of the Church of England's sacraments, and though all sacraments are means, not all means are sacraments. As should be clear, I am assuming the ongoing significance of baptism, and am using the common definition between sacraments and means in Wesley as the inroad for my argument.

71. Aidan Kavanagh, *The Shape of Baptism: The Rite of Christian Initiation* (New York: Pueblo, 1978), 162. See also the remarks by John H. Erickson in "Baptism and the Church's Faith," in *Marks of the Body of Christ* (ed. Carl E. Braaten and Robert W. Jenson; Grand Rapids, MI: Eerdmans, 1999), 44-58. Similarly, Knight says that baptism "provides descriptive and enacted access to the identity of God, and thus gives distinctive shape to our understanding of who God is, and what God has done and is doing through the sacrament" (*Presence*, 188).

72. See "The New Birth," § IV.1, *Works*, 2:197, n. 66.

according to the "later Wesley," justification and the new birth are simultaneous. In justification God does something for us, namely, forgives our sins. In the new birth God does something in us; he renews our fallen nature. But "in order of thinking, as it is termed, justification precedes the new birth. We first conceive his wrath to be turned away, and then his Spirit to work in our hearts."[73] The new birth, for Wesley, is the birth by the Spirit, whereas baptism is birth by water. The two are not the same, however. Using the Church of England's definition of a sacrament, Wesley argues that the new birth—the birth by the Spirit—is the inward grace, while baptism—the birth by water—is the outward sign. He goes on to reason that a person can be baptized yet still sin, therefore one can be "born of water," but not of the Spirit, reiterating what is truly essential. Wesley's fear of formalism, of having the appearance of godliness while denying the power of it (cf. 2 Tim 3:5) drives his evangelical message for true inner transformation. Sacraments and ecclesiology are ordered by this priority.

This was not always Wesley's position, however. According to Outler, Wesley originally held, as did many in the Church of England before him, that the new birth and baptism did in fact belong together. In the 1758 *A Treatise on Baptism*, Wesley—via his father Samuel—demonstrates a view with a higher ecclesiology than later, as baptism is seen as "the initiatory sacrament, which enters us into covenant with God."[74] What this then includes is washing away of sins by the applied merits of Christ's death,[75] and baptism as "the stipulation, contract, or covenant of a good conscience with God" whereby we are admitted into the church.[76]

In fact, here the true resource in Wesley's thought for a more comprehensive ecclesiology is present, for he writes,

> By baptism, we who were 'by nature children of wrath' are made the children of God. And this regeneration which our Church in so many

---

73. "The New Birth," §1, *Works*, I:45.

74. *A Treatise on Baptism*, §I.1, n. p., *Works on CD-ROM*. Three years before John Wesley's birth Samuel Wesley authored the manual that his son would later publish, in abridged form, as *A Treatise on Baptism*. Though his father's words, Wesley took them for his own, and in the secondary literature the ideas of *A Treatise* are regarded as John's (I am grateful to Randy L. Maddox for bringing this to my attention). Says Outler, "In judging such a literary 'borrowing,' it is useful to realize that Wesley and his eighteenth-century colleagues generally understood this as a form of *endorsement*" (Outler, *John Wesley*, 86, n. 1; italics original). I will follow suit by regarding the ideas of *A Treatise* as John's.

75. Wesley cites Eph 5:25, 26, "He gave himself for the Church, that he might sanctify and cleanse it with the washing of water by the word," which Wesley takes to mean "in baptism, the ordinary instrument of our justification" (*A Treatise on Baptism*, §II.1 n. p., *Works on CD-ROM*).

76. *A Treatise on Baptism*, §§II.2-3, n. p., *Works on CD-ROM*.

places ascribes to baptism is more than barely being admitted into the Church, though commonly connected therewith; being 'grafted into the body of Christ's Church, we are made the children of God by adoption and grace.' This is grounded on the plain words of our Lord: 'Except a man be born again of water and of the Spirit, he cannot enter into the kingdom of God' (John 3:5).[77]

The Spirit has a marked role here, as it is the Spirit who washes and sanctifies, and by whom all are baptized into the church, the body of Christ.[78] And the role of covenantal entry into the church through baptism is perhaps given greatest prominence when Wesley writes, "Baptism doth now save us, if we live answerable thereto; if we repent, believe, and obey the gospel: Supposing this, as it admits us into the Church here, so into glory hereafter."[79] The later concern with the inward and outward aspects of the means of grace can be found,[80] and the forensic edge to his soteriology is there, but Wesley succeeds in tying Spirit, church, and the means of grace together in a way that his later message loses.

There is a lingering tension, however, that I wish to alleviate, and it stems from Wesley's reliance, even in his earlier view, on the Church of England's definition of the means. To stabilize the ground for ecclesiology that my rereading of justification and the place of baptism together open for Wesleyan theological hermeneutics, I look to William J. Abraham. Abraham offers a definition of the means of grace capable of avoiding the problems of Wesley's definition, yet is likewise thoroughly soteriological:

> Means of grace presuppose a complex theological vision of creation and redemption. They take as given the existence of God, the estrangement of human agents from their true destiny, and a network of divine action in the salvation of the world. Within this vision means of grace refer to various materials, persons, and practices that function to reconnect human agents with their divine source and origin. They are akin to medicine designed to heal and restore human flourishing; they are akin to various exercises appointed to reorient the whole of human existence to its proper goal. Their natural home is the Church. In fact they are brought into existence by the Church, as she is guided in her pilgrimage into the kingdom of God.[81]

---

77. *A Treatise on Baptism*, §II.4, n. p., *Works on CD-ROM*.
78. *A Treatise on Baptism*, §§II.1, 3, n. p., *Works on CD-ROM*. Wesley goes on to argue, "From which spiritual, vital union [effected by the Spirit] with him [Christ] proceeds the influence of his grace on those that are baptized; as from our union with the Church, a share in all its privileges, and in all the promises Christ has made to it" (II.3).
79. *A Treatise on Baptism*, §II.5, n. p., *Works on CD-ROM*.
80. *A Treatise on Baptism*, §III.1, n. p., *Works on CD-ROM*.
81. William J. Abraham, *Canon and Criterion*, 1. I draw on Abraham here without subscribing to the whole of his programme, trading as it does on a sharply drawn

There is no reason to read Abraham here as perpetuating the interiority of his ecclesial forebear. Instead, Abraham's definition invites a fuller recognition of the church in the economy of salvation, while not putting the cosmic reach and future dimension of eschatology at risk. If anything, Abraham could stand to make a trinitarian grammar more explicit in the above statement, but surely there is nothing that precludes my concern for a strong Spirit/church connection.[82]

The fallacy in Wesley's later view is not his insistence that the "real" work of baptism is done by God, but his association of that divine work with what is inward and invisible. However, combining Wesley's earlier view of baptism as the covenantal entering into the church with Abraham's definition of the means of grace preserves the best of Wesley's later insistence, that the grace at work is God's, without placing the church's role in the economy of salvation in jeopardy. The *humanum*—to borrow Williams' term—that is created and sustained by the Spirit ("the Lord, the giver of life," as the Nicene Creed says), is naturally served by those "various exercises" whose "natural home is the Church"—to borrow from Abraham—because the one divine purpose of creation is fulfilled in salvation.

As for baptism's place as the portal into the church, John H. Erickson writes, "Baptism is a gracious gift of God, whereby through created realities we enter into participation in divine life itself. Ultimately God is both the giver and the gift."[83] Erickson continues:

> Baptism is...the sacrament of our unity with Christ, of our participation in his paschal mystery. But to be baptized into Christ means to be baptized into his body, which is the church (1 Corinthians 12:13). Baptism is initiation into the mystery of Christ and initiation into the church. It is the sacrament of our unity *with* Christ and at the same time the sacrament of our unity *in* Christ.[84]

To enter into the divine life is to become an adopted child of God, and the place where this is worked out is in the church.[85] God's priority over the

---

distinction between canon and criterion that may be analytically possible, but does not appear to fare as well historically. For his follow-up to the agenda laid out in *Canon and Criterion*, see his recent *Crossing the Threshold of Divine Revelation* (Grand Rapids, MI: Eerdmans, 2006).

82. Besides the lack of mention of the Spirit, Abraham is noticeably silent about the christological telos of the means: that Christ is the image of God to which the church is being restored.

83. Erickson, "Baptism and the Church's Faith," 50-51.

84. Erickson, "Baptism and the Church's Faith," 51.

85. Wainwright, quoting the Nairobi Conference, wonders whether the witness of the Spirit so prized in the Wesleyan tradition may not be located within the corporate reality of the church (*Methodists in Dialog*, 21).

church's rituals is preserved, but the church has a real and necessary part—necessary because God has graciously renewed it to be the body of Christ. One works out one's salvation as rebirth into the divine life through entry into the corporate fellowship of the church as the people of God, body of Christ, and temple of the Spirit.

If we now press further, and combine this with the analysis of justification in the New Perspective, what is gained by my examination of Wesley and the means of grace? First, Wesley's earlier view on baptism, espoused in *A Treatise on Baptism*, is fairly compatible with recent scholarship. As seen above, Wesley regards baptism as covenantal initiation into the church, and therefore the decisive step in cleansing from sin by the Spirit and the securing of eternal salvation. This fits with Michael Gorman's understanding of baptism and justification as entry into the covenantal community. Justification is not simply the imputation of a status, or even the transformation of a person as a phenomenon contained within the self or heart. It is entry into a new reality. As Paul writes in Romans, believers now "walk in newness of life" (6:4). Through confession of faith and baptism the Spirit now inducts us into the people of God. Sanctification is therefore a journey in which those adopted as children of God are made into the image of God, who is Christ.

As a matter of fact, it is just here that we can theologically and hermeneutically begin to overcome the gap that opens between Christ identified in Scripture and the reading community in Frei. Gorman, in examining the Pauline corpus, makes a series of statements about Christ's "benefits" made available through the gospel. According to Gorman, Christ is believers' righteousness, mediator and peace, sacrifice, liberation and freedom, life, community, indwelling power, demonstration of divine agapé, holiness, security, salvation, hope, and goal or telos.[86] As Watson argues, it is in Paul's reading of Israel's Scripture that his christology emerges; Christ is textually mediated, in other words.[87] In the next chapter I will discuss in detail meaning as something generated out of interpretation, rather than as something found within a constitutive element of interpretation (the text or the reader, for example), but for the moment it can suffice to posit that encountering the identity of Christ through such a generative interaction binds our understanding and identities to Christ in the very act of reading Scripture, which is where Christ is identified. It is through this generation of Christ's identity as the church's act of understanding its Scripture that the Holy Spirit conforms the church to the image of God, that is, Christ.[88]

---

86. Gorman, *Apostle*, 111-12.

87. A point Watson already makes in *Text, Church, and World*, 223-31.

88. Together with Gorman's list of Christ's benefits, spelled out as predicate nominatives, this can serve as a postcritical reworking of Melanchthon's *pro nobis* insight, that to know (the textually mediated) Christ is to know his benefits.

I argued earlier that baptism holds a special place among the means of grace. It does not simply alleviate the effects of original sin, for within it is the entire paschal content and patterning of the Christian faith. Baptism is the covenantal entry into the life of God, which is made available for our sanctification in the church. To be born of water and Spirit is to be adopted as a child of God, so that the Spirit witnesses with our spirit that we are children of God. Thus, the Spirit renews the image of God, Christ, in us as we enter the body of Christ. Put differently, baptism is a sign, but not necessarily or solely of something inward and invisible. Instead, it points to the very visible transformation of a people who are themselves a sign of the presence of the Holy Spirit in the world.

7. Appropriating Wesley II

In chapter two, while surveying earlier efforts at delineating a Wesleyan theological hermeneutic of Scripture, I noted Joel Green's insight that much of what makes a Wesleyan hermeneutic "Wesleyan" is that Wesleyans do it. Similarly, while dialoguing with Hans Frei's hermeneutics, I cited Kathryn Tanner on the integral relation between identity and text: "Questions of faithfulness to one's communal identity become questions of textual interpretation, broadly construed."[1] Tanner is indicating that by returning to certain authoritative texts, a community's identity is sustained over time.

Of course, those same authoritative texts must be reinterpreted across constantly changing times, as MacIntyre's work on traditions showed in chapter two. The pressures of shifting contexts, assumptions, and questions lead traditions into crises that founders and earlier generations could not foresee. Identities are sustained in interpretation, but they are not static. In the act of interpretation, there is both continuity and discontinuity in identity, but this is mirrored in the text as well. Meanings can also change over time—justification by faith being the most prominent example I have looked at so far—even as some continuity is maintained.

Green's observation took its force partially from being contrasted with what might be considered the true goal of developing a Wesleyan hermeneutic—that is, forging a method or technique that ensured a "Wesleyan" outcome. Green's point is therefore two-pronged: it privileges identity as an important theme in a Wesleyan hermeneutic, while also raising issues about how theological interpretation creates that identity consistently when a method or technique cannot be used to guarantee the outcome ahead of time.

In this chapter I will focus on the issue of Wesleyan identity and interpretation in a Wesleyan theological hermeneutic of Scripture, emphasizing the interrelationship between reader and text.

The content of this chapter is divided into two parts, patterned after Green's twofold point above. First, I will examine the dynamic nature of meaning. Turning to the reception theory of Umberto Eco, I will consider interpretation as the production of meaning. The remainder of the chapter will explore the concept of the Wesleyan model reader through hermeneutical engagement with both Wesley's and biblical texts and offer a description of what is "Wesleyan" about a Wesleyan theological hermeneutic.

I tap Eco for a variety of reasons. He was among the first theorists to emphasize the reader in a clearly postmodern way, but unlike more radical reader-response theories, he contends it is the *text* that is interpreted, not the reader's drives. As a result, Eco is able to account for the potential multiple interpretations of a text, and provides a moderate postmodern theory that allows

---

1. Tanner, "Plain Sense," 69.

for textual polysemy without capitulating to the idea that texts can be made to say whatever the reader wants.

Eco has also explored the similarities between post- and premodern interpretation, and the place he gives to the importance of the inner coherence of the text in validating interpretive conjectures is especially commensurable with Wesley's belief in the analogy of faith as describing the general tenor of Scripture. Eco accounts for the social production of a text, involving authors and readers, but is nuanced enough in his distinction between "model" and "empirical" authors and readers that he does not fall into some of the problems now associated with authorial intent. His idea of the reader's being invited to "make the work" contributes a way for combining the dynamic nature of meaning with Wesley's call for holiness, and interpretation as a means of grace. Eco also probes the shared background—the "social treasury"—shared by authors and readers in order for interpretation to be valid. His treatment of the difficulties in this regard is helpful since this study is seeking to construct a theological hermeneutic in the Wesleyan tradition, as opposed to simply repeating Wesley's hermeneutics.

In particular, Eco's concept of the model reader will prove fruitful, and act as the bridge to part two of this chapter, on figural reading and the formation of Wesleyan identity. Figural reading is traditionally the way Christians have read the literal sense of Scripture both to see it as a singular witness to the God Christians worship as Father, Son, and Holy Spirit, as well as to make sense of their own lives. This "style" of interpretation is to a significant extent a result of the aims, dispositions, and practices readers are "schooled" in as members of a community, to recall Charles Wood's point from chapter three.

Frei's work on figural reading was suggestive, but his commitment to the literal ascriptive identity of Jesus—though very important in repairing modernism's fracturing of the Bible—maintained a distance from the identity of the church as the community of interpretation. Following Dawson, I noted this created problems for a hermeneutic concerned with discipleship and holiness, and looked to Dawson to indicate a more soteriological direction.

In this chapter I return to Dawson's work, developing figural reading soteriologically, then combine figural reading with Eco's model reader to what makes a Wesleyan model reader, thus styling model reading as a form of figural interpretation. This move will be predicated on a discussion of the aims, dispositions, and practices of Wesleyans.

Umberto Eco's Reception Theory

Open Texts and Model Readers

Eco does not merely expound upon "texts," "authors," and "readers," but upon *open* and *closed* texts, and *empirical* and *model* authors and readers. For Eco the interpretive process begins not simply when a text is engaged by a reader, but even at the point of a text's production by an author. The communication that occurs through textual generation and interpretation is not a mere matter of code transmitted between Sender, Message, and Addressee:

> The existence of various codes and subcodes, the variety of sociocultural circumstances in which a message is emitted (where the codes of the addressee can be different from those of the sender), and the rate of initiative displayed by the addressee in making presuppositions and abductions—all result in making a message (insofar as it is received and transformed into the *content* of an *expression*) an empty form to which various possible senses can be attributed.[2]

There is variability, in other words, that permeates a text, not only within the actual structure of the document created, but within the contexts of its creation and interpretation, including those persons involved in each pole of the text's existence. All of these factors contribute to the meaning that comes from the act of reading.

When Eco speaks of a *text*, he means "a network of different messages depending on different codes and working at different levels of signification."[3] Authors write texts with what Eco calls a *model reader* in mind. A model reader is a "possible reader...supposedly able to deal interpretively with the expressions in the same way as the author deals generatively with them."[4] For this to happen, a model reader must share with the author certain customs and codes, which can be detected in the work to be interpreted. This includes what Eco calls "a specific encyclopedic competence" that is embodied in an interpretive community.[5]

However, texts are often interpreted against a different background of codes than those of the author; therefore, the ability of the author to account for this (or not) in imagining a model reader results in a text that is either *open* or *closed*. Closed texts "obsessively aim at arousing a precise response on the part of more or less precise empirical readers," and are therefore "open to any possible 'aberrant' decoding."[6] Closed texts are sensitive to variability, which means that too much deviation from the rather narrowly conceived conditions for the model reader the author envisioned will in fact fail to result in that model reader. Open texts can handle variability, and successfully result in the model reader they are designed to create.[7]

---

2. Umberto Eco, *The Role of the Reader: Explorations in the Semiotics of Texts* (Advances in Semiotics; Bloomington: Indiana University Press, 1979), 5.
3. Eco, *Role*, 5
4. Eco, *Role*, 7.
5. Eco, *Role*, 7.
6. Eco, *Role*, 8.
7. "What I call open texts are...reducing [aberrant presuppositions and deviating circumstances] as indeterminacy, whereas closed texts, even though aiming at eliciting a

Although the concept of openness may suggest hermeneutical free rein over the text by the interpreter, Eco assures us that texts cannot be used however we want.[8] There is, in other words, "text intent" (*intentio operanis*); a text has "certain structural devices that encourage and elicit interpretive choices."[9] Of course an author provides the codes, but it is the text that is the device from which are generated model readers; the author does not herself generate them.[10]

What an open text does is to invite the reader to "make the work" with the model author.[11] For this to occur, it is not the reader alone who is "modeled" in interpretation. Empirical authors, that is, the persons who actually generate the text, imagine model readers. However, the empirical reader—the person who actually interprets that same text—executes her interpretation in part by imagining a model author. According to Eco, an author "is nothing but a textual strategy establishing semantic correlations and activating the model reader."[12] The empirical reader, in turn, tries to be a model reader as per the text being interpreted by offering a conjecture about the text's intent, imagining in the process a model author.[13]

According to Wolfgang Iser, the work of art is paradigmatic for how semiotics frames textual interpretation.[14] In this vein Eco writes,

---

sort of 'obedient' cooperation, are in the last analysis randomly open to every pragmatic accident" (Eco, *Role*, 7).

8. Eco, *Role*, 9.

9. Umberto Eco, *The Limits of Interpretation* (Bloomington: Indiana University Press, 1990), 50. Eco lists examples of how a text can be read badly—for instance, reading Kafka's *The Trial* as "a trivial criminal novel"—and this makes for an interesting observation about so much modernist biblical studies. If, broadly speaking, a model reader of the Bible is one who reads it as Christian Scripture, many modernist interpreters who have abided by the canons of modern historicism have been "negative model readers" (cf. *Role*, 9-10).

10. At a time in interpretation theory where the reader has received so much attention, the absence of the author and its effect on hermeneutics and meaning has been a regular concern. But Eco's theory shows there is also the problem of the absent reader when an author writes a text. Can the author anticipate her reader in such a way as to provide the textual prompts and markers that will succeed in generating a model reader? "Text intent" is Eco's way of keeping the text situated within a deliberate communicative action between author and reader without either declaring the author "dead," or turning to authorial intent to the exclusion of the reader's participation in the production of meaning.

11. Eco, *Limits*, 63.

12. Eco, *Role*, 11.

13. Cf. Umberto Eco, *Interpretation and Overinterpretation* (Cambridge: Cambridge University Press, 1992), 64.

14. Wolfgang Iser, *How to Do Theory* (How to Study Literature; Malden, MA: Blackwell, 2006), 71. Gadamer likewise turns to art as a way of discussing hermeneutics (*Truth and Method*, 102-61).

> A work of art is a complete and *closed* form in its uniqueness as a balanced organic whole, while at the same time constituting an *open* product on account of its susceptibility to countless different interpretations which do not impinge on its unadulterable specificity. Hence every reception of a work of art is both an *interpretation* and a *performance* of it, because in every reception the work takes a fresh perspective for itself.[15]

In other words, the work *qua* work remains; its integrity, or "unadulterable specificity," is not violated by the inevitable interpretation of it. In fact, this interpretation is mandated by the work. This idea stems from Eco's contention that the purpose of a text is to generate a model reader. An open literary work's purpose is to be "performed" by an interpreter; otherwise, it becomes something other than what its author created it to be. Yet because the work is open, interpretive possibilities can abound without compromising the intent of the text. As already established, the intent of an open work is for this very abundance to be present for the model reader to be activated:

> Every performance *explains* the composition, but does not *exhaust* it. Every performance makes the work an actuality, but is itself only complementary to all possible other performances of the work. In short, we can say that every performance offers us a complete and satisfying version of the work, but at the same time makes it incomplete for us, because it cannot simultaneously give all the other artistic solutions the work may admit.[16]

Other performances are possible, and for a given performance to be successful, for it to actually provide a version of the work, one must interpret the text instead of use it. By *using* a text Eco means "to start from it in order to get something else, even accepting the risk of misinterpreting it from the semantic point of view."[17] Here the intent of the text is ignored, and the model reader never materializes.[18]

Put concisely, texts create model readers who attempt a conjecture of the text's intent by conceiving a model author. Out of this process, the structure of codes within the text and the context in which the encyclopedic knowledge is shared between author and reader—both come into play. Interpretation is therefore dynamic and social. One does not look through a text to find the meaning beneath the words; neither does one "discover" meaning in the words of the text, as if the text were a container. And, finally, one does not interpret in

---

15. Eco, *Limits*, 49.
16. Eco, *Limits*, 58-59.
17. Eco, *Limits*, 57.
18. Eco concedes, however, that every empirical reading is a mixture of both (*Limits*, 62).

a vacuum, but is socialized into that encyclopedic, social treasury from which one draws to read.

Since the empirical author is absent from the interaction of text and reader, and since a text must be read for a model reader to be activated, Eco's theory puts the emphasis on the reader. Eco's is not a radical reader-response vision, however.[19] On the one hand, the text places limits on what readings can arise between itself and the empirical reader. On the other hand, Eco also believes agreement is possible, if not about what makes a superior interpretation, at least about what makes an inferior one.[20]

There has to this point in my study been a lingering question about how to account for the variance between contemporary Wesleyan readings of Scripture, and Wesley's readings of Scripture, a question made somewhat pressing by Frei's conception of the literal sense as something formal, which can differ in different communities. In chapter four I drew on Charles Wood's argument that the meaning of the literal sense was obvious to readers, but that its obviousness was due to the habits of perception one was "schooled" into. The real question has to do with meaning—what it is, where it comes from, and how it can be both continuous and discontinuous with the past. Eco presents a way of answering this by how he understands reader, text, and context. Therefore I will briefly elaborate upon his contribution under three interrelated headings, *the production of meaning, the directions of meaning,* and *the spaces of meaning.*

The Production of Meaning

Eco shows how the numerous variables that go into creating and interpreting a text *produce* meaning. In other words, meaning is not found as an object with its own integrity independent of the reader, but emerges from the entire textual process at the point where the model reader is generated. The message that comes through the text's intent is "an empty form to which various possible senses can be attributed."[21] Already the kinship to Frei's formal account of the literal sense should be apparent.

Texts are not inert objects acted upon methodologically by a reader who discovers the one correct meaning. Rather, texts have numerous (though not

---

19. See Eco's analysis of "unlimited semiosis" and "hermetic drift" associated with deconstruction (*Limits*, 27-32). "To privilege the initiative of the reader does not necessarily mean to guarantee the infinity of readings. If one privileges the initiative of the reader, one must also consider the possibility of an active reader who decides to read a text univocally: it is a privilege of fundamentalists to read the Bible according to a single literal sense" (*Limits*, 51). In light of Eco's theory as a whole, it should be obvious he is not using "literal sense" in the same way as Frei.

20. Eco argues that "a theory of interpretation—even when it assumes that texts are open to multiple readings—must also assume that it is possible to reach an agreement, if not about the meanings that a text encourages, at least about those it discourages" (*Limits*, 45).

21. Eco, *Role*, 5.

infinite) meanings, what is sometimes referred to as a *surplus of meaning*.[22] A reader comes to the text from a particular point, with questions, and this stimulates the interpretive process that births meaning. The inexhaustible nature of a text, its polysemy, permits continued rereadings, the occasion for which is created by the context of the reader. After all, as Eco notes, the background of the reader is typically different than the author's, but this can be the fertile ground that raises new questions that drive rereadings.[23]

The Directions of Meaning
On the one hand, texts open "to the fore," a phenomenon engendered by the text's polysemy.[24] The textual intent is to generate a model reader, and in seeking that generation it invites the empirical reader to "make the work," by deftly navigating the variables of interpretation.[25] On the other hand, there is a circularity to reading, or what is commonly called the *hermeneutical circle*. Essentially, the hermeneutical circle operates at two levels, that of how our preunderstanding affects our reading of a text, which results in understanding that in turn becomes our new preunderstanding at a rereading; and there is the movement between the whole of a text and its parts.[26]

Meaning therefore accrues over time, and a history of interpretation builds up, creating the social treasury that belongs to a community of interpretation. Through it all, the text maintains an otherness, or alterity, that keeps it from being overrun by this accrued history of meaning.[27] Another way to put this is that the openness of the text is always in tension with interpretive closure, decisions within a tradition of interpretation to take a text a certain way. This situation is partially a result of the text's polysemy, and partially the result of the interpreter making judgments about a text. In the Wesleyan tradition, a certain reading of justification by faith is a closure on the text, and it remains closed when this reading becomes assumed and developed systematically apart from Scripture. But as I showed last chapter, numerous factors have reopened how

---

22. Paul Ricoeur, *Interpretation Theory: Discourse and the Surplus of Meaning* (Fort Worth, TX: Texas Christian University Press, 1976).

23. Eco, *Limits*, 58. As J. Severino Croatto writes, "the reservoir of meaning residing in a text...depends on the *text*, and on the *life* that gives orientation to the question addressed to that text" (*Biblical Hermeneutics: Toward a Theory of Reading as the Production of Meaning* [Maryknoll, NY: Orbis, 1987], 50).

24. Croatto, *Biblical Hermeneutics*, 30.

25. Eco, *Limits*, 63.

26. The former level came to prominence in the twentieth century, first proposed by Heidegger and then developed for contemporary hermeneutics by Gadamer. For the account of this development, see Gadamer, *Truth and Method*, 268-69. Obviously this newer sense beginning with Gadamer reflects twentieth-century hermeneutics' unique preoccupation with the reader-subject. The latter level, of course, has already been encountered in Wesley and the prior history of interpretation.

27. For more on alterity, see Gadamer, *Truth and Method*, 271-72.

justification is read, and at the point of that reopening the Wesleyan tradition is faced with the kind of interpretative conflict that can potentially extend it through a context different from Wesley's.

Again following Eco, it is the text that is interpreted, not the reader's drives (or even the mere reiteration of a tradition of interpretation[28]), so in opening to the fore the text presents itself to the reader as something to be dealt with on its own terms, which are in part presented through the structured code of the language on the page. The model of circularity makes sense of the elements of reader and text within a context, and both the polysemy of the text and the occasion for interpretation brought on by questions within a context gives the rationale for how the literal sense can be something formal.

The Spaces of Meaning
The language on the page contributes to the otherness of a text, but that is not the only resource a text has available to it. There is also the socio-historical context in which the text was created by the empirical author. A text comes to a reader from a different point in time, and these three, the past context, the text itself, and the present interaction of the reader with that text, comprise the spaces of meaning.

It is here that a redefined role for historical criticism is legitimate. To once again look to the example of the previous chapter, gaining an understanding of Paul's first-century context helps open up a reading of justification by faith different from Wesley's. Historical criticism contributes a consciousness to the difference in contexts that creates questions. The key is not to allow that socio-historically derived knowledge of difference to become absolute, a possibility foiled to a degree by the text itself. Working on the assumption of an absolute difference in context between present and past, and further assuming the "real," singular meaning of a text was located in that past, historical criticism often tried to bypass the text as it is received in the church through reconstructions of the text's development. But by respecting the literal sense of the text, the language on the page is taken seriously in its own right, and the theological context of interpretation is preserved, since it is the church that hands down its Scripture through history. For this reason, the canonical, final form of Scripture is taken at face value. From a theological perspective this is actually the approach that best respects its otherness, for it is in this mode that the Bible is read as Christian Scripture.

As a text, Scripture is analyzable as a structural whole, containing all the various elements that make it a communicative entity. Werner Jeanrond[29] observes that a text exists at three levels, meaning, grammar, and printing, and

---

28. To simply reiterate a tradition of interpretation would be to use, rather than interpret, the text, and turn a tradition into an ideology. More will be said about this for a Wesleyan theological hermeneutic in chapter seven.

29. For what follows, see Jeanrond, *Theological Hermeneutics*, 84-91.

that these are linguistically studied through semantics, syntactics, and pragmatics. Semantics is concerned with the meaning of words and texts; syntactics with how words and sentences connect; and pragmatics with the conditions external to linguistic communication. Furthermore, texts fit within genres, and how they so fit—in what ways they do or do not observe the conventions of a genre—is the style evinced in a text. This stylistic negotiation of a genre that produces a text is called a textual strategy, of which there are four: narration, argument, description, and instruction. The use of these strategies in multiple combinations in the production of the text leads to multiple possibilities for analysis in reading. And this analysis is part of the answering of questions that lead a reader to a text to begin with, but the structural elements themselves cannot account for this. The text as a linguistically constituted, structural whole is therefore itself a "space" for meaning, but it is not the sole locus of meaning's production.

The final space to consider, and the one that has commanded the most attention in recent decades, is the space "in front of" the text. The text comes to the present from its past creation and interpretation, and opens to the fore where it meets the reader in the production of meaning. This meeting is an invitation to "make the work," to generate the model reader as per the text's intent. Even in the circularity of hermeneutics, that circularity remains essentially in front of the text as the production of meaning between the text and reader. Likewise, the incorporation of the past through historical criticism is brought to bear on the production of meaning. Here is the space of the reader, and exploration of this space has led to questions about the aims, dispositions, and reading conventions that inform the reader's interpretive encounter with a text. All three of these spaces come into play in the production of meaning, but they converge in front of the text where reader and text meet in a particular context.

Evaluating Eco's Contribution
This elaboration on Eco's reception theory contributes to my discussion by giving an account of how meaning is produced that compliments Frei's work on the literal sense and the grammar of the faith, but presses forward where Frei was apprehensive. It is an "alternative logic" which Frei said we need to even be able to read, but the soteriological ends of reading in Wesleyan hermeneutics discipline it. It does not so much tell us what is "really" happening when we read as it helps us see how a Wesleyan reading of Scripture today might differ from Wesley's reading of that same Scripture in the eighteenth century. In other words, it allows the literal sense to be the result of a communal consensus that may change over time with changing contexts.

Yet it also shows how the production of meaning can involve and change readers, opening the door to talk about figural reading today. To that end, my discussion will now move to the formation of the Wesleyan identity, the Wesleyan model reader, which emerges from the reader, text, and context relationship. The concept of the model reader helpfully reinforces the following.

First, it reinforces the integrity of the text as something not acted upon, but that itself acts upon the reader. A text has an intent to activate a model reader, and this asks of the reader a conformance to that intent insofar as a reader is interested in interpreting that text, not merely using it. But Gadamer has shown how all readers come to texts with preunderstandings, with assumptions, that must be brought to the fore through questioning. Similarly, Charles Wood has argued that the literal sense of a text is plain to those schooled into a certain set of "conventions of reading, with the capacities and dispositions, linguistic and personal, which the reader brings to the text, by virtue of having been formed in a community."[30] Becoming a model reader, then, demands that an empirical reader be willing to alter her assumptions and dispositions when necessary. Accordingly, when reading Scripture as Wesleyans, the question of what makes a Wesleyan model reader must begin with the "interpretive aims, interests, and practices"[31] into which Wesleyans are "schooled" (to again use Wood's term) by participation in Wesleyan communities.

Second, the model reader is an identity concept, and in the history of Christian interpretation, figural reading has been an important strategy in Christians' surrendering one identity to allow Scripture to reshape them into another. The nature of being a Wesleyan model reader, therefore, is a matter of figural reading. Below, I will develop model reading as a figural activity, whereby the process of producing meaning results in the transformation of the Wesleyan reader. The attributes a reader brings to the text (aims, dispositions, etc.) are through the figural refashioning of the reader changed (though they may also be reinforced), leading to the performance of Scripture in a certain way of life. As Nicholas Lash argues, "[T]he fundamental form of the Christian interpretation of scripture is the life, activity and organization of the believing community. The performance of scripture *is* the life of the church."[32] Far from this being a merely human endeavor, however, this is part of the Spirit's reinterpretation of the reader of Scripture, resulting in holy living. A Wesleyan model reader is someone who reads as a response to grace within the economy of salvation.

Finally, the model reader concept is helpful in appropriating from Wesley, who was concerned with being a real, or "altogether Christian";[33] who ruminated on what it meant to be a Methodist;[34] and of course who preached a new birth whereby we died as slaves to sin to be reborn as children of God.[35] These themes from Wesley's writings, transmogrified into a contemporary

---

30. Wood, *Christian Understanding*, 40.
31. As put by Fowl, *Engaging Scripture*, 55-56.
32. Nicholas Lash, *Theology on the Way to Emmaus* (Eugene, OR: Wipf and Stock, 2005), 43.
33. E.g., "The Almost Christian," *Works*, 1:131-141.
34. E.g., *The Character of a Methodist*, *Works*, 9:31-46.
35. E.g., "Justification by Faith," *Works*, 1:181-199.

hermeneutic, can help Wesleyans make sense of their interpretive engagement with Scripture in a context that in significant ways differs from Wesley's. Let me first begin, however, to treat the Wesleyan model reader through discussing the aims, dispositions, and practices that form readers in a Wesleyan community of interpretation.

Forming the Wesleyan Model Reader

The Aims, Dispositions, and Practices of the Wesleyan Model Reader
To uncover the aims, dispositions, and practices of Wesleyan reading, I will follow Frei and observe how the Wesleyan grammar of faith governs the reading of the literal sense. Due to the communal nature of theological interpretation, and Wesley's soteriological concerns, how does the analogy of faith shape the life of Wesleyans, particularly as that life includes theological interpretation? And with the privileged place Wesley's writings have in this study, the more specific question may be, what do we learn from Wesley?

In his tract *The Character of a Methodist*, Wesley sets out "the *principles* and *practice* whereby those who are called 'Methodists' are distinguished by other men."[36] After setting aside misconceptions of Methodism as being defined by "*opinions* of any sort," "*words* or *phrases* of any sort," "*actions, customs,* or *usages* of an *indifferent* nature," or "by laying the *whole* stress of religion on any *single part* of it,"[37] Wesley argues that "a Methodist is one who has 'the love of God shed abroad in his heart by the Holy Ghost given unto him'; one who 'loves the Lord his God with all his heart, and with all his soul, and with all his mind, and with all his strength.'"[38] What follows is an elaboration on the love of God that reads like a scriptural collage of nearly forty biblical quotes and allusions, encompassing rejoicing, thanksgiving, hope, praise, and ceaseless prayer.[39] Wesley then similarly spells out love of neighbor. At the core of this love for others is purity of heart, achieved because God's love has purged the Methodist of sinful behaviors and attitudes in exchange for "bowels of mercies, kindness, humbleness of mind, meekness, long-suffering," and the ability to forgive.[40]

Wesley then points out that a Methodist not only aims at, "but actually *attains*" living a life "all to the glory of God."[41] These are not merely ideas, in

---

36. *The Character of a Methodist*, §2, *Works*, 9:32 (italics original).
37. *The Character of a Methodist*, §§1-4, *Works*, 9:33-35 (italics original).
38. *The Character of a Methodist*, §5, *Works*, 9:35.
39. *The Character of a Methodist*, §§6-8, *Works*, 9:35-37. By saturating his depiction of Methodist character in the biblical idiom, Wesley demonstrates his own principle stated earlier in the tract that Methodists "express Scripture truths in Scripture words" (§2, *Works*, 9:34).
40. *The Character of a Methodist*, §10, *Works*, 9:38. Wesley quotes here from Col 3:12.
41. *The Character of a Methodist*, §14, *Works*, 9:39 (italics original).

other words, but descriptions of actual beliefs and practices of Methodism, which in the end Wesley indicates is simply "real Christianity."[42]

The impressive collection of quotations and allusions here and in *The Character of a Methodist* is hardly haphazard, but again reflect the internal logic of the analogy of faith governing Wesley's language about God and Christian life. This can be coupled with the rule for life Wesley drafted for the bands and societies, which I discussed in chapter four. There, Wesley related how his first society came to be: he was approached by eight to ten persons "deeply convinced of sin, and earnestly groaning for redemption," wishing "to flee from the wrath to come."[43] This disposition of repentance gave way to groups created to provide an environment for those "having the form, and seeking the power of godliness"; people seeking prayer and "exhortation, and to watch over one another in love, that they may help each other to work out their salvation."[44] Considering that Wesley believed the Methodists not only attempted, but actually attained what they set out for, it follows that the aim of a Wesleyan hermeneutic is no less than the attainment of the perfect love of God and neighbor in the heart and life—Wesley's doctrine of Christian perfection.[45]

Broadly, and obviously, Wesley teaches Wesleyans to approach the Bible soteriologically. The ultimate goal or aim of theological interpretation is that "happy shore" Wesley writes about in the preface to his *Sermons*.[46] He obviously endorses humility, the heart of a repentance that earnestly desires to experience the fullness of Christian faith. Hermeneutically, this means coming to Scripture expectantly, looking for the Spirit to work through the text to effect transformation resulting in holiness. In other words, it means reading Scripture as a means of grace.[47]

Set within the analogy of faith and these aims and dispositions, the interpretive practices, or as Wood called them, "reading conventions," of Wesley that I examined in chapters four and five have their purpose, namely, reading according to the general tenor and the primacy of the literal sense. But these practices are of a piece with the practices of holiness Wesley commended, such as works of piety and mercy. How we read Scripture and how we live are fused together; the analogy of faith, as I showed in chapter four, is a description

---

42. Cf. *The Character of a Methodist*, §18, *Works*, 9:42.
43. "General Rules," §1, *Works*, 9:69.
44. "General Rules," §2, *Works*, 9:69.
45. This of course is a doctrine Wesley believed was thoroughly biblical, as I showed in my examination of "On Perfection" in chapter five.
46. "Preface," *Sermons*, §5, *Works*, 1:105.
47. Here the importance of the question—first discussed in chapter four in connection with justification by faith—is again worth asserting, since questioning keeps us from allowing our dispositions and assumptions to harden into ideologies that are above reproach. Instead of simply acting upon the text, our prejudices toward it are exposed and held up for scrutiny. For more on prejudices, see Gadamer, *Truth and Method*, 272-73.

of both Scripture and life. To be schooled in the practices, including the reading conventions, of the Wesleyan tradition is to be schooled in a life of holiness, both within and without.

In sum, what makes a Wesleyan model reader is someone who approaches Scripture soteriologically, with humility and the desire for the Spirit to work through that particular means of grace. Soteriological reading by its nature expects Scripture to change readers from one identity to another, to *convert* and *sanctify* them, leading then to "the end of religion" via "the way to heaven." For Wesleyans in a postcritical milieu, this change can be expedited through a recognition of the assumptions they bring to Scripture. Recognizing these aims, dispositions, and practices is one ingredient of a theological interpretation of Scripture. The transformation of a reader's identity, quite possibly a conversion away from those prior characteristics, comes through a figural engagement with Scripture, to which I will now turn.

Figural Reading and Wesleyan Identity

Hans Frei's work, as shown in chapter three, has done much to bring figural reading back into biblical interpretation. Its loss, which he documents in *Eclipse*, has been detrimental to both the Christian reading of the Bible as a unified witness to the God Christians worship as Father, Son, and Holy Spirit, as well as how the church makes sense of its life and mission in the world. Frances Young, commenting on the traditional place of figural reading in Christian identity, writes, "The way that people understood their own lives was once shaped by patterns and models found in Scripture, and, conversely, people read their own lives into Scripture."[48] This grasp of figural reading's import to Christian identity and hermeneutics has spurred a recovery of the practice. "The loss of figural reading is not the loss of an exegetical technique," writes Christopher Seitz. "It is the loss of location in time under God."[49]

Building on Frei's work in chapter three, I turned to John David Dawson for a more soteriological construal of figural reading, one that brought Jesus' identity and that of Christian readers in the church into closer proximity. Dawson's definition of figural reading is worth repeating:

> Figural reading in the Christian tradition seeks to express the dynamic process of spiritual transformation in ways that respect the practitioners' commitment to both past and future, both old identity

---

48. Frances M. Young, *Brokenness and Blessing: Towards a Biblical Spirituality* (Grand Rapids, MI: Baker Academic, 2007), 20.

49. Seitz, *Figured Out*, viii. With Seitz and Young, see Ephraim Radner, *The End of the Church: A Pneumatology of Christian Division in the West* (Grand Rapids, MI: Eerdmans, 1998); idem, *Hope among the Fragments: The Broken Church and Its Engagement of Scripture* (Grand Rapids, MI: Brazos, 2004); R. R. Reno, *In the Ruins of the Church: Sustaining Faith in an Age of Diminished Christianity* (Grand Rapids, MI: Brazos, 2002); O'Keefe and Reno, *Sanctified Vision*.

and newly refashioned identity. Imbedded in figural practice is all the drama of discerning the point of existence and identifying one's place in it, figured as a journey from a former mode of existence through various states of transformation toward some ultimate end.[50]

For Wesley, this end is happiness ("the end of religion")—that is, the knowledge and love of God, for which we are created. This experience of happiness occurs when the Holy Spirit adopts us as children of God, renewing the image of God, Christ, within us.

Although taking figural reading in this way will infuse a subjective element into the textually mediated Jesus identified in Scripture—a move Frei does not appear ready to concede in his latest writings—I will argue on theological and hermeneutical grounds that this is permissible in the Wesleyan tradition. Being a Wesleyan model reader of Scripture means having one's identity transformed from slave to child, opening up a life of "scriptural holiness." This holiness is modeled on Christ himself whose identity is located within Scripture. Within a postmodern approach to interpretation, one in which the reader participates in generating the meaning of the text, the kind of segregation Frei desires between Jesus and his reading followers is not sustainable. Jesus' identity is not self-contained or even fully exhausted by his relationship to his Father in abstraction from Scripture. But, because Christ's identity is textually mediated, it is also inextricably tied to the community of interpretation known as the Body of Christ, the church.

In comparing figural reading in Hans Frei and Origen, Dawson observes, "If Frei's conception of personal identity is anchored in narrative depictions that lend stability, definition and, above all, continuity of character, Origen's conception stresses the ongoing and (as yet) unfinished fashioning of personhood"; "Radical change does not threaten identity but promises its consummation."[51] Both men have different theological intentions, leading to different depictions of how Jesus is related to believers. Frei stresses ongoing distance between the two; Origen stresses their relation and how that relation "transforms the reader, impelling him or her further along the pathway of personal spiritual regeneration."[52]

---

50. Dawson, *Figural Reading*, 216.
51. Dawson, *Figural Reading*, 194.
52. Dawson, *Figural Reading*, 186. To be specific, Dawson is discussing Origen's *allegorical* reading compared to Frei's *figural* reading. Since the comparison between Frei and Origen is not the object of my attention, I will refrain from discussing the distinction between figuration and allegory here. Dawson's book is in part an argument against conflation of the two. According to him, failure to distinguish between figuration and allegory "simply blocks understanding of what Christian interpretation of Hebrew Scripture (or…maybe…the Old Testament) is all about" (*Figural Reading*, x). For more on the distinction, see O'Keefe and Reno, *Sanctified Vision*, 20-22.

What Dawson writes approvingly of Origen is largely applicable to Wesley. What, after all, is Wesley's typology of the natural, legal, and evangelical person, if not a continuum of "radical change" that "does not threaten identity" but assumes its promised "consummation"? To further unpack the differences between Frei and Origen, Dawson considers each theologian's interpretation of 2 Corinthians 3, where Paul writes about the veil of Moses, a passage significant not only for the issues of identity, but also for reading the Bible as two united testaments in one Scripture.[53] To look at the same passage as Wesley comments on it in his *Notes upon the New Testament* reveals much about the relation of figural reading to the formation of identity for him, and moves us beyond what a Wesleyan reader brings to Scripture to how theological interpretation of Scripture shapes identity.

The Veil of Moses and the Wesleyan Model Reader
In 2 Corinthians 3, Paul claims he and his associates do not need written letters commending them to the Corinthians, because their letters are written on the hearts of those same Corinthians (vv. 1-6). In his *Notes upon the New Testament*, Wesley reads Paul as expounding upon the differences between the Mosaic law ("the letter" of v. 6) and the gospel ("the Spirit" of v. 6).[54] Paul goes on to juxtapose the "ministration of death" with the "ministration of the Spirit" (v. 7), and sets the latter over the former as superior, using as a key image the veil Moses placed over his face to shield himself "so that the children of Israel could not look steadfastly to the end of that which is abolished" (v. 13).

Then comes a pivotal verse that opens sustained reflection on the transformation of identity in Wesley's theological hermeneutics: "But their (Israel's) understandings were blinded; and until this day the same veil remaineth unremoved on the reading of the Old Testament, which is taken away in Christ. But the veil lieth on their heart when Moses is read to this day. Nevertheless, when it shall turn to the Lord, the veil shall be taken away" (vv. 14-16). Wesley's comment on v. 14, at the phrase "reading of the Old Testament," might be striking for the modern-day hermeneut: "The veil is not now on the face of Moses, or of his writings, *but on the reading of them, and on the heart of them that believe not*...."[55] The veil is over the act of reading and

---

53. And in tandem with this Dawson looks at Exodus 34. Although I here look at Wesley's reading of Paul and the veil of Moses, his comments on the Exodus passage are unremarkable and so are irrelevant for my purposes.

54. Scripture verses will be quoted as they appear in Wesley's *Notes upon the New Testament*.

55. *Notes upon the New Testament*, 453. Note how Wesley's Bible refers to the "reading of the *Old Testament*" where modern translations translate παλαιᾶς διαθήκης as "old covenant." Note too how Wesley casually refers to "his (Moses') writings" as synonymous with the "Old Testament." The contrast between the theological climate in which Wesley interpreted and the present one, where many Christian scholars refer no

the heart of the unbeliever, not "on the face of Moses or of his writings"—not on the text itself.

From here Wesley works with an assumption that salvation in Christ is tied to one's ability to read Scripture. The removal of the veil (v. 16) allows one to "see with the utmost clearness, how all the types and prophecies of the law are fully accomplished in [Christ]."[56] This work of liberation is an act of the Spirit (v. 17), and the believing reader is freed not only to see the typological unity of Scripture, but the change in her own identity. Paul writes, "And we all with unveiled face, beholding as in a glass the glory of the Lord, are transformed into the same image, from glory to glory, as by the Spirit of the Lord" (v. 18). For Wesley, the "glass" in which the Lord's glory is beheld is "the mirror of the Gospel," and to be "transformed into the same image" means, "Into the same love, from one degree of glory to another, in a manner worthy of his almighty Spirit." Whereas Moses veiled God's glory from Israel, "We behold his glory in the glass of his word, and our faces shine too. Yet we veil them not, but diffuse the lustre which is continually increasing, as we fix the eye of our mind more and more steadfastly on his glory displayed in the Gospel."[57] To read Scripture is to be transformed, and this by the Spirit; it is a means of grace. Three points need further consideration.

The first is the transformation of our identities and its relation to Jesus' identity. Frei maintains that the uniqueness of Jesus' identity was connected to his being the Son who reveals the Father, and that this keeps him at a remove from others. Yet Wesley takes 2 Corinthians to say that Christ, who is the image of God, transforms us into that same image. This does not do any violence to Jesus' identity, as Wesley's comment on 2 Cor 4:4 shows. For the phrase "hath blinded," Wesley writes, "Illumination is properly the reflection or propagation of light, from those who are already enlightened to others."[58] This illumination comes from Christ, "who is the image of God" (4:4). At this phrase Wesley comments, "Hence we also may understand how great is the glory of Christ. He that sees the Son sees the Father in the face of Christ. The Son exactly exhibits the Father to us."[59] If, in Frei, Jesus as ascriptive subject is distanced from us by virtue of his revealing the Father, does this not distance the Father from us as well? For Wesley, this is not so; the Son as image reveals the Father, and it is

---

longer to the Old Testament but to the "Hebrew Bible," (and, hence, would prefer the less overtly Christian term "Old Testament" in v. 14) could not be clearer.

56. *Notes upon the New Testament*, 453.

57. *Notes upon the New Testament*, 454.

58. *Notes upon the New Testament*, 454. For more on illumination in Wesley, see Long, *Moral Theology*, 82-83, 110-12.

59. *Notes upon the New Testament*, 454.

this revealing through his glory that illuminates, changing us into that same image.[60]

Is this the supercession of Jesus' identity? Not at all, and this brings me to my second point. Wesley takes Paul's phrase "are transformed into the same image" (3:18) to mean, "Into that same love, from one degree of this glory to another, in a manner worthy of his almighty Spirit."[61] God "hath shined into our hearts, to enlighten us with the knowledge of the glory of God in the face of Jesus Christ" (4:6).[62] For Wesley, the knowledge and love of God is the end for which humanity is created, the experience of which is happiness. The renewal of the image is induction into the love of God, and as Dawson says, love is a relation.[63] Jesus' glory *must*, for those who will respond to the gospel, have a salvific effect, but note too that "his almighty Spirit" performs this effect. For Wesley, it is not simply a matter of negotiating the proximity of two identities, Jesus' and ours. There is even a certain crudity about doing so, when instead it is more appropriate to speak of the Holy Spirit.[64] It is the Spirit who relates us to Christ in love; the Spirit is the agent of transformation, who works through Scripture as a means of grace.[65] Another way of putting this is that the Spirit *reinterprets* our identities, so that our reading of Scripture, our interpretation of Jesus' identity, is responsive to grace.

And finally, our ability to read the literal sense is tied to this work of salvation. Paul's claim that when Israel turns to the Lord, "the veil shall be taken away" (3:16), leads Wesley to state, "That very moment, and they see *with the utmost clearness*, how all the types and prophecies of the law are fully accomplished in him."[66] Reading Scripture as a means of grace, as a channel through which the Holy Spirit renews the image of God in us and changes us from slaves to sin into children of God, is a condition for the literal sense to be seen for what it is.

---

60. God the Father "is himself our light," writes Wesley; he is "the fountain of (light)," who gives his light to the Son, who in turn gives it to us. See Wesley's comments on 3:6. This gifting of God's light comes, as we will see directly, by the Holy Spirit.

61. *Notes upon the New Testament*, 454.

62. For Wesley "the glory of God" means, "Of his glorious love, and of his glorious image" (*Notes upon the New Testament*, 454).

63. Dawson, *Figural Reading*, 206.

64. Wesley takes "the ministration of the Spirit" in 3:8 to simply mean "the Christian dispensation" (*Notes upon the New Testament*, 453).

65. See Wesley's comment on 3:6. On the phrase, "but the Spirit," he writes, "The Gospel, conveying the Spirit to those who receive it" (*Notes upon the New Testament*, 453).

66. *Notes upon the New Testament*, 453 (italics added).

Figuration and Imitation
Wesley's commentary shows how the identities of Jesus and readers of Scripture are closely bound to the text, so that it is through the text that the Spirit brings readers into an encounter with Jesus that changes them. Figural reading here is about Wesley's and his readers' location within the whole of Scripture. Scripture is able to truthfully describe the soteriological state of persons before God regardless of historical location, for God is author not only of Scripture, but also of life, faith, and salvation.[67] Scripture reveals not only God to us, but us to ourselves, so that we see our need for God. Due to this soteriological context, Paul is not only addressing the Corinthians in his day, but he is addressing all Christians everywhere. To read figurally here is to hear the address of Scripture as directed to the church reading now.

Wesley's comments help Wesleyans hear Scripture as address and/or description, making the invitation to take up the aims, dispositions, and practices described in 2 Corinthians a real possibility to be embraced or rejected.[68] Wesley makes this figural assumption that Scripture is directed to him and his readers whenever he refers to, for example, an "altogether Christian."[69] To accept that identity as readers is to believe in Christ, and it is to be transformed by the Spirit-inspired interaction with Scripture, a soteriological act that presumes God is speaking to us through the Bible.

This is especially evident in Wesley's thirteen discourses, *Upon Our Lord's Sermon on the Mount*, where he examines Christ's teachings on "true

---

67. "Sermon on the Mount, III," §IV, *Works*, 1:530; "Sermon on the Mount, IV," §II.1, *Works*, 1:540; "Sermon on the Mount, V," §I.4, *Works*, 1:553; "Sermon on the Mount, VI," §III.4, *Works*, 1:578. Cf. "The Circumcision of the Heart," §II.4, *Works*, 1:411; "Spiritual Worship," §II.1, *Works*, 3:95; "The More Excellent Way," §IV.2, *Works*, 3:271; *A Farther Appeal to Men of Reason and Religion*, §I.6, *Works*, 11:107-108.

68. By "description" I mean that for Wesley readers can glean from throughout the Bible a composite portrait of what a Christian should be in terms of attributes, behaviors, and so on. See, e.g., *A Plain Account of Genuine Christianity*, where Wesley concludes a discussion of Christian character by stating, "This is the plain, naked portraiture of a Christian." He then turns to the reader and demands a response to the Scripture-informed character he has described, "Is it your own," before admonishing the reader to become "altogether a Christian" (*John Wesley* [ed. Albert C. Outler; New York: Oxford University Press, 1964], 187, 188). See also, "The Almost Christian," *Works*, 1:131-41.

69. In addition to the previous citations, see Wesley's considerations for what makes a Methodist in *Thoughts upon Methodism*. There he is clear that Methodism is "only plain scriptural religion," and not a recent innovation (§8, *Works*, 9:527-30). Similarly, in *The Character of a Methodist*, Wesley's description of "the mark of a Methodist" is typical and typically scriptural: "a Methodist is one who has 'the love of God shed abroad in his heart by the Holy Ghost given unto him'; one who 'loves the Lord his God with all his heart, and with all his soul, and with all his mind, and with all his strength'" (§5, *Works*, 9:35). "Methodist" is therefore a figurally constituted identity for Wesley.

religion."[70] To be changed into the image of God means we are to live like him, to imitate him; we are to be what we were created to be originally;[71] we are to love and enjoy God forever.[72] To imitate God is to be holy and perfect as God is holy and perfect,[73] and since God is revealed in Christ, so that through him we see "the fountain of beauty and love, the original source of all excellency and perfection,"[74] then the imitation of Christ is the appropriate response to Scripture.

For Wesley this response is striving after righteousness: "Righteousness...is the image of God, the mind which was in Christ Jesus. It is every holy and heavenly temper in one; springing from as well as terminating in the love of God as our Father and Redeemer, and the love of all men for his sake."[75] As Wesley claims elsewhere, Christ's righteousness belongs to divine nature itself, but the righteousness he here means is Christ's *human* righteousness.[76] For Wesley, we aim for righteousness, the image of God renewed in us, which is true happiness. In this sense, we participate in the divine nature.[77] Since for Wesley we are to imitate whom we love,[78] to have "the mind that was in Christ" means we are "to walk as Christ also walked."[79] Saying the same thing differently, Wesley states

---

70. "Sermon on the Mount, I," §I.1, *Works*, 1:475. See Wesley's summary remarks, "Sermon on the Mount, X," §§1-3, *Works*, 1:650-651.

71. "Sermon on the Mount, II," §II.6, *Works*, 1:498.

72. "Sermon on the Mount, XIII," §II.2, *Works*, 1:692; cf. idem, §III.11, *Works*, 1:698; also, "Sermon on the Mount, III," §I.2, *Works*, 1:511; "Sermon on the Mount, VIII," §§6, 21, *Works*, 1:615, 626; "Sermon on the Mount, IX," §§5, 15, *Works*, 1:635, 639; "Sermon on the Mount, X," §7, *Works*, 1:653.

73. "Sermon on the Mount, III," §IV, *Works*, 1:530.

74. See especially, "Sermon on the Mount, IV," §1, *Works*, 1:531-532.

75. "Sermon on the Mount, II," §II.2, *Works*, 1:495. Cf. "Sermon on the Mount, I," §I.11, *Works*, 1:481; "Sermon on the Mount, XIII," §II.1, *Works*, 1:691.

76. For Wesley, this human righteousness has both internal and external aspects. Internally, it is "the image of God...a copy of the divine righteousness, as far as can be imparted to a human spirit," containing "every...holy and heavenly temper" (§I.2, 452-53). The external has negative and positive aspects. Negatively, Christ committed no sin. Positively, he perfectly performed his Father's will ("The Lord Our Righteousness," §§I.1-3, *Works*, 1:452-53).

77. As Long observes, in "The Great Privilege of Those That Are Born of God," Wesley combines 2 Cor 4:6 (cited above) and 2 Pet 1:4 to show how the renewal of the image through Christ's illumination is our entry into divine participation (*Moral Theology*, 132).

78. Cf. "Sermon on the Mount, IV," §III.4, *Works*, 1:544; "Sermon on the Mount, XIII," §II.2, *Works*, 1:692; also, *Genuine Christianity*, §I.4, *John Wesley*, Outler, 184. Cf. "Sermon on the Mount, III," §I.11, *Works*, 1:516; and "Sermon on the Mount, III," §§III.13, IV, *Works*, 1:530.

79. "Scriptural Christianity," §4, *Works*, 1:160-161. In *Thoughts upon Methodism*, Wesley refers to "the mind that was in Christ" as "the essence of religion" (§9), the content of which is "holiness of heart and life" (§§9, 8, respectively, *Works*, 9:529).

that we ought to "follow...after the image of God."[80] To do this is to take on another set of behaviors rooted in who God is; it is to "be merciful as thy Father in heaven is merciful; it is to be "purified from every unholy affection";[81] it is to have our aims, dispositions, and practices transformed as our identities are transformed. Our dispositions are changed from those of scribes and Pharisees,[82] to those of being children of God.[83] And as children of God birthed by the Spirit through belief in Christ, our dispositions are rooted in the very nature of God himself.[84]

Holiness is thus what a Wesleyan model reader calls the performance of Scripture. It is "to love God in the manner Scripture describes, in the manner God himself requires of us, and by requiring engages to work in us."[85] If in coming to Christ in Scripture we believe, holiness must follow from that interpretive encounter.[86] In revealing these things to us in Scripture, God also "engages to work in us." Through Scripture God teaches and graciously enables obedience. Performing Scripture is therefore traversing "the way to heaven," but traversing as a response to grace.[87]

To perform Scripture is to read it as a means of grace, since we use it "with a constant eye to the renewal of your soul in righteousness and true holiness."[88] A Wesleyan is socialized into this approach through learning the analogy of faith, making the analogy a prejudice that informs a Wesleyan's pre-understanding when coming to Scripture. In reading Scripture as a means of grace, Wesley teaches that we should approach prayerfully,[89] and that a

---

Consistent with his priority of the inward, Wesley claims imitation begins in the mind ("Sermon on the Mount, IX," §6, *Works*, 1:636).

80. "Sermon on the Mount, XIII," §III.10, *Works*, 1:697.

81. "Sermon on the Mount, III," §I.2, *Works*, 1:510; "Sermon on the Mount, XIII," §III.11, *Works*, 1:698.

82. "Sermon on the Mount, V," §§IV.1-13, *Works*, 560-71.

83. Or, as in the case of the thirteenth discourse, readers are invited to figurally assume the identity of him who "buildeth his house upon a rock" in Matthew 7 ("Sermon on the Mount, XIII," §§II.1-4, *Works*, 1:691-93). The dispositions Wesley references are taken from the Beatitudes in the thirteen discourses, but also from the fruit of the Spirit list Paul gives in Galatians 5. See, e.g., "Sermon on the Mount, V," §IV.13, *Works*, 1:571; also "Sermon on the Mount, XIII," §III.12, *Works*, 1:698.

84. "[I]t is impossible to hide your lowliness and meekness and those other dispositions whereby ye aspire to be perfect, as your Father which is in heaven is perfect" ("Sermon on the Mount, IV," §II.2, *Works*, 1:539).

85. "Sermon on the Mount, IX," §5, *Works*, 1:635.

86. Cf. "Sermon on the Mount, V," §III.9, *Works*, 1:560.

87. "Sermon on the Mount, XI," §II.2, *Works*, 1:668, and §3, where he also refers to this as "the way of universal holiness"; "Sermon on the Mount, XII," §I.4, *Works*, 1:677.

88. "Sermon on the Mount, IV," §III.6, *Works*, 1:545.

89. See his comments in the preface to his *Notes upon the Old Testament*, §§17-18, where he interweaves prayer, the analogy of faith, and reading the Old Testament (*Notes upon the Old Testament*, n. p., Wesley Center Online; http://wesley.nnu.edu/john_wesley/

threefold usage of Scripture is appropriate: reading, meditating, and preaching. These together Wesley calls "searching the Scriptures."[90] Interpreting Scripture in this way leads to holiness through the Spirit's work of grace. Holiness is therefore both prejudice and performance of Scripture for the Wesleyan model reader, as through sanctification one receives the knowledge and love of God and attains the true end for which humanity is created: happiness.

Holiness and the Production of Meaning
A Wesleyan understands herself to be a model reader of Scripture because she comes to the text expectantly, seeking "the way to heaven." This posture of expectation supposes the Bible to be an open text, for though its history of interpretation stretches back thousands of years, the church continues to witness—and Wesley's writings are part of this witness—to God's address through it. More specifically, to regard the Bible as an open text is to regard it as *Scripture*, a soteriological approach that assumes Scripture to be one means of grace at the church's disposal within the economy of salvation.

Going further, to read the Bible as Scripture is to accept that Scripture is a text with the intent to activate a model reader, an "altogether," or "real" Christian—or as Wesley elsewhere puts it, a Methodist. That intent is nothing less than God's original intent for humanity to live in communion with him, to love and enjoy him forever. To submit ourselves to that intent is therefore to accept Scripture's invitation to "make the work," to participate in the production of meaning.[91] This work-making is also an act of participation in the life of God, for through it the Spirit converts and sanctifies readers. By reading in this way we make use of Scripture as a means of grace, so that the openness of the text corresponds to an openness in us to the Spirit's work. As a result, to read soteriologically, as Wesley teaches, is to have the image of God renewed within us so that we are renewed in the life for which God created us.

Because Scripture both reveals God and instructs us in holiness, God is both author of Scripture and author of life. For the Wesleyan model reader who approaches the Bible soteriologically, the model author she envisions is to be found in Christ himself, who is the image of God. The identities of Christ and reader are textually mediated, which has a double significance. As *textually* mediated, Christ is understood to be part of God's salvific activity that is witnessed to in Old and New Testaments taken together. Christ is therefore understood only in light of the Law, Psalms, and Prophets, as well as how the New Testament church interprets these writings. Likewise, readers are called to perceive themselves by these same writing—to figurally enter and inhabit the "world" of Scripture in order to know God as he is (Father, Son, and Holy

---

notes/otpreface.htm; accessed January 2008).
    90. Wesley actually lists *hearing* alongside reading and meditating, but preaching is essentially what he means ("Means of Grace," §III.7, *Works*, 1:387).
    91. Cf. Long, *Moral Theology*, 132-38.

Spirit; but also the God of Abraham, Isaac, and Jacob; the God who delivered Israel out of Egypt, and so on), and to understand themselves as this same God intended them to be (children of God, the Body of Christ, the temple of the Spirit).

As textually *mediated*, the nature of the economy of salvation as Dawson reminds us is preserved, "the reality and the proper characterization of a divine performance in the material world of space and time, a performance that defines the personal, social, ethical, and political obligations of Christians in the present, as well as their stance toward past and future."[92] God comes to us through Scripture, but God is not contained within Scripture. Christ has "ascended to the right hand of God the Father almighty," but the identity of Christ, which comes to us in Scripture, is only apprehended by us as we interpretively engage it. Thus, to know Christ in Scripture requires us to share in the production of meaning. To "make the work" of Scripture is to help "make" Christ's identity insofar as we perform Scripture according to its soteriological intent. Since we are to imitate the one we love, the imitation of the textually mediated Christ in holy living is the performance of Scripture most appropriate to its intent; the model reader mirrors the model author. Interpretation is not contained within the text, but involves us as our identities are reshaped. Through our imitation of Christ, we "follow a better pattern," so that the Author of life, "by the finger of God," has "transcribed into our own hearts" the "perfect law of liberty": "the genuine religion of Jesus Christ."[93]

This performance calls us to repentance and to be grafted into God's people. We are remade as the Body of Christ through being birthed by the Holy Spirit. Accordingly, a Wesleyan model reader will adopt aims, dispositions, and practices commensurate with the witness of Scripture: the love and knowledge of God; love of neighbor; hungering and thirsting for righteousness; repentance and humility; works of piety and mercy; and much else besides. The identity of Jesus Christ cannot be held at a distance in the way Frei wanted. The identification of Christ in Scripture, the Spirit's continued appropriation of Scripture as a means of grace, and the Wesleyan model reader's performative imitation of Christ make this impossible.

However, Christ's identity is not overwhelmed or lost for three reasons. First, as Eco shows, every performance explains a work, but does not exhaust it. The identity of Jesus within Scripture is never finally interpreted because it is textually mediated. Second, because it is textually mediated, Christ is not contained within Scripture, but is made known to us through it. Although Scripture's depiction of Christ is part of the economy of salvation, Christ is not the text itself. And third, because the righteousness we receive as the image of God is renewed in us is simply the restoration by grace of God's creative intent, we do not overwhelm Christ's identity because we never cease to be creatures.

---

92. Dawson, *Figural Reading*, 216.
93. "Sermon on the Mount, III," §§III.13, IV, *Works*, 1:530.

The righteousness Christ gives us is his human righteousness. That is, we do not receive the divine nature itself by participating in the means of grace. We become only by grace what he is by nature.

Scripture's intent being what it is, a Wesleyan model reader's life of holiness is the appropriate performance of Scripture, allowing Wesleyans to retain Wesley's theme and ethos of "scriptural holiness." This has two hermeneutical implications. First, Wesleyan model readers interpret Scripture according to its literal sense, which is the form of Scripture's reception in the Wesleyan tradition, a ruled reading that takes Scripture to have a narrative unity. It is in this sense the Bible as Scripture is first approached. Second, it means a figural entry into Scripture, insofar as we share in the life of Christ by ourselves becoming children of God through the Spirit, is an extension of the literal sense. This simply means the literal sense has priority, and that it is God in Christ *as he is identified in Scripture* that is interpreted, so that figural reading always takes its point of departure from there.[94] Both of these are practices Wesleyans are socialized into by their communities. God addresses us through Scripture, and the biblical text can also accurately describe the aims, dispositions, and practices a Wesleyan model reader should assume.

---

94. To echo Eco, it is the *text* that is interpreted, not the reader's drives.

8. A Wesleyan Theological Hermeneutic of Scripture

In this study I have attempted to develop a Wesleyan theological hermeneutic of Scripture. My approach to the task was initially set up by Alasdair MacIntyre's work on how traditions are extended through time in the face of new challenges. Confronted with the limitations of what have become the conventional methods of Wesleyan theology, I determined to take a tradition-constituted tack, and reinterpret Wesley's writings with a view to learning theological interpretation as a craft. I then turned to Hans Frei's hermeneutics in chapter three for direction on how to appropriate Wesley's hermeneutics. After surveying Wesley's hermeneutics in chapters four and five, I focused on the soteriological context of a Wesleyan hermeneutic in chapter six, then the interrelationship between reader and text as the figural fashioning of the Wesleyan model reader in chapter seven.

This chapter will complete my proposal of a Wesleyan theological hermeneutic, then offer a demonstration of that hermeneutic. To begin with, I will take up a discussion of some final matters relating to the Wesleyan hermeneutic I have been developing. Essentially, I will probe issues of continuity and discontinuity between a Wesleyan hermeneutic, as this proposal has developed one, and Wesley's hermeneutics. First I will take up the issue of ruled reading, discussing the place of the analogy of faith in a Wesleyan hermeneutic. Considering the way Wesley's doctrine of justification has been recast here as a reading of Scripture, and how Pauline influence in Wesley's hermeneutics has been exposed, can the analogy of faith continue as the rule for reading Scripture for Wesleyans? I will argue that it cannot, and give an alternative. I will further argue, however, that it is not the analogy of faith per se that makes a Wesleyan hermeneutic Wesleyan, and bring together many of the themes already discussed to describe the robust nature of a Wesleyan theological hermeneutic. I will then demonstrate the Wesleyan theological hermeneutic I am proposing through a sermon. At the sermon's close I will offer some analysis of certain aspects of it, then draw my conclusion.

From Wesley to Wesleyan

One thread running throughout the preceding chapters has been that of identity. As I showed in chapter one, there is no shortage of proposals today in theological interpretation of the Bible. By and large, these proposals are set within general problems that have developed in modernity, potentially affecting all who work within the guilds of biblical studies and systematic theology, regardless of confessional background. Some, such as Stephen Fowl, have contended that doctrinal traditions play more of a role in these proposals than is sometimes acknowledged, but significant work in theological interpretation within a particular tradition has been less forthcoming than more generalized approaches.[1]

After taking stock of the contemporary landscape of theological interpretation, I noted the need for a Wesleyan voice beyond what has so far been offered. Interacting with Wesleyan scholars such as Robert Wall and Joel Green raised many issues pertinent to my aims. Both discuss Wesleyan hermeneutics primarily in terms of continuity from within the Wesleyan tradition. Wall remarked that at the very least Wesleyans would interpret within the tradition traceable back to John Wesley. Green observes that much of what makes a Wesleyan hermeneutic Wesleyan is that it is Wesleyans who do the interpreting. Both discussed the formation of the Wesleyan identity within Wesleyan communities, and the need to adopt certain themes and dispositions as signature components of being Wesleyan.

In agreement with Green, I argued that there is no technique or method for determining a Wesleyan hermeneutic ahead of time. It is at this point that the issue of continuity and discontinuity appears, opening the door both for creative reflection on identity in the Wesleyan tradition, as well as variability. Forfeiting the (illusory) quest for a Wesleyan method is also the forfeiting of the (equally illusory) ability to control the outcome of the endeavor. MacIntyre shows how practitioners could only extend a tradition through the creative, skillful reinterpretation of authoritative materials. But this skill is made up of judgments based on experience, not predetermined steps that will automatically give a guaranteed result. The skillful reinterpretation is needed for a Wesleyan theological hermeneutic, not only because of the problems with the well-worn approaches of modern Wesleyan theology, but also because the present milieu and the milieu of Wesley are separated by over two hundred years that have rendered a very different situation than Wesley's. We cannot simply repeat Wesley's hermeneutics; we must appropriate them. But how, then, can we tell that a Wesleyan theological hermeneutic is *Wesleyan*?

Given the ground already covered in these pages, I will not entertain that question as a theoretical one. Instead, I will turn to what it is that makes up the grammar that rules the Wesleyan theological hermeneutic I have been crafting. Additionally, I will deal with how it differs from the analogy of faith, the grammar that ruled interpretation for Wesley. This will give me solid ground for wrestling with issues of continuity and discontinuity between Wesley's hermeneutics and a Wesleyan hermeneutic.

Wesleyan Ruled Reading and the Analogy of Faith
A subtle tension in this study has endured since chapter four. There, while developing the soteriological context for my proposal, I took up the privileged role of justification by faith in Wesley's hermeneutics. Justification is one of the defining articles of Wesley's soteriology, appearing in virtually every construal

---

1. Fowl, *Theological Interpretation*, Part Four.

of his analogy of faith.² However, in chapter six I demonstrated how the privileging of justification by faith was challenged by modern criticism on the unity and diversity of the Bible, then looked at a redefinition of justification in light of New Perspective scholarship. Though I made positive use of that scholarship, moving from an individualistic soteriology to a communal-covenantal one, the problem of unity and diversity has lurked close at hand. In other words, whether one agrees with the general orientation of New Perspective scholarship, justification is a Pauline doctrine, found in Romans and Galatians, and can only continue in the privileged position Wesley grants it at the expense of other voices in Scripture. Moreover, as I showed in chapter five, although Wesley takes his concept of new birth from John 3, the content comes from primarily Pauline sources. Additionally, Wesley's understanding of original sin is deeply indebted to his reading of Paul, as per his Augustinian-Protestant heritage.

If a doctrine like justification by faith can no longer speak for all of Scripture as *"the* biblical view" of salvation, its ability to function hermeneutically within the analogy of faith is diminished, since the analogy serves to articulate the general tenor of Scripture. To loosen those doctrinal threads in Wesley's theological hermeneutics is to begin to loosen the connection between Wesley's analogy of faith, which is composed primarily of the doctrines above, from Scripture. It also throws into doubt Scott J. Jones' statement that "no compelling arguments have been advanced in the last two hundred years" that could displace the analogy of faith for Wesleyans.³ In fact, here one of the major gaps between Wesley in the eighteenth century and Wesleyans in the twenty-first presents itself. Wesley's hermeneutics, rooted as they were in the late-medieval/early modern world of the Reformation, could assume that the analogy of faith just was the message of Scripture. In today's postcritical age, ruled readings such as the analogy of faith are just that: *readings*. Scholars realize other readings of the biblical texts are possible, but that does not mean all are equal or appropriate in every situation. In light of modern and postmodern criticism of the Bible's unity and diversity, a ruled reading has to be argued for. As Richard Hays has said,

> The understanding of Scripture as a coherent dramatic narrative is rightly done *"in light of the church's rule of faith."* In other words, the Bible's coherence cannot simply be read off the surface of the text as though it were self-evident to any impartial reader.... On the contrary, the skilled exegete must come to the text with the hermeneutical guidance of the distilled wisdom of a historically

---

2. E.g., see Wesley's comments on Rom 12:6, *Notes upon the New Testament*, 397, n. 6; "Preface," *Notes upon the Old Testament*, §18, n. p., *Works on CD-ROM*; "The Causes of the Inefficacy of Christianity," §6, *Works*, 4:89. Cf. "Justification by Faith," *Works*, 1:181-99; also, *The Principles of a Methodist*, *Works* 9:47-66.

3. Jones, "The Rule of Scripture," 58.

grounded interpretive community, the church. Why is this so? Because the Christian Bible is already narratively shaped, in the very act of its collection and preservation, by the church in order to remember and proclaim the gospel.[4]

Hays realizes a Christian ruled reading is not the only option for theological interpretation, but it is the most appropriate one within the context of the church, and the church can claim a privileged seat at the table of biblical interpretation because the Bible is the church's book, its Scripture. In a postcritical milieu, a gap between readings and texts has opened up that Wesley, living under different assumptions, did not have to contend with. Wesley did not see the analogy of faith as a rule for reading in the sense contemporary scholars do; it simply was for him the message of Scripture.

Nevertheless, intrinsic to my argument in chapter six was that Wesley's doctrine of justification is a *reading* of the biblical text, ruled by the analogy of faith that featured it as a basic article of Christianity. To unpack the hermeneutical significance of this point, it will be helpful to recall a portion of Eco's reception theory. Eco argued that an empirical author who could account for a model reader in a different semiotic background would produce an open text.[5] An open text invites an empirical reader to "make the work," by becoming the model reader compatible with the text's intent. The model reader becomes such by conjecturing about the inner coherence of the text's intent as encoded by the model author. This conjecture takes the form of a performance of the text by the interpreter, which explains, but does not exhaust, the text.[6] Meaning is generated out of this interaction, and this meaning brings closure to certain interpretive possibilities, but it does not drain the text of its surplus of meaning.

Thus, Wesley's doctrine of justification is a reading based on the analogy of faith as a conjecture of the Bible's inner coherence.[7] As a reading, justification is a closure of the biblical text, and that closure becomes permanent when justification is then abstracted from the text and developed systematically. Two things happen at that point: if justification continues to be regarded as the biblical message of salvation, then as new understandings of the biblical text come to light—whether literary, or having to do with its socio-historical background—persisting in that closure becomes an instance of using the Bible,

---

4. Richard B. Hays, "Can Narrative Criticism Recover the Theological Unity of Scripture?" *Journal of Theological Interpretation* 2 (2008): 203 (italics original). Hays' views expressed here are not uncommon in the literature. See, e.g., Fowl, *Theological Interpretation*, 24-31; also, Wall, "Reading the Bible," 96-99.

5. Eco, *Role*, 7.

6. Eco, *Limits*, 58-59.

7. I single out justification here because I have already given it extensive treatment in the thesis, which is a result of its being Wesley's "core belief," to use Robert Wall's term again. But what is said here about justification as a reading applies to any of the concepts in Wesley's analogy of faith.

rather than interpreting it. A second consequence is that the analogy of faith no longer functions hermeneutically, becoming instead the template for a Wesleyan systematic theology. However, insofar as Wesleyans are interested in returning again and again to the Bible as Scripture (which entails regarding the Bible as an open text), and insofar as the background against which Wesleyans have continued reading the Bible has changed, both the closure (e.g., justification as an abstracted doctrine) and the conjecture (the analogy of faith in its hermeneutical role) may no longer be adequate.

The depiction of the analogy of faith as hermeneutical conjecture actually fits quite well with the understanding of rules for reading in antiquity, when Christian "rules of faith," or "rules of truth," first came to prominence. In the ancient world a Christian ruled reading was in fact a "hypothesis" (ὑπόθεσις) of Scripture. As John Behr observes, a hypothesis in antiquity could be a plot or outline that guides the creation of a literary work. Or it could be a goal that orients someone toward a certain end. Whatever the case, "if the goal proves unattainable or if the conclusions derived from the supposition turn out to be manifestly false, then the hypothesis in question must be rejected."[8] As the term came to be used by early Christians, a hypothesis was the first principle that made knowledge of God possible. It was eventually used by Irenaeus to show why the Valentinians read the Bible the way they did as a departure from the gospel.[9]

The analogy of faith is Wesley's hypothesis for the right ordering of the overarching narrative, or the general tenor, of Scripture. But as a hypothesis, the analogy of faith is tentative, despite Wesley's belief in the equivalence of the analogy with the message of Scripture. As the context for theological interpretation in the Wesleyan tradition has changed—and with it many of the questions and assumptions Wesley may have taken for granted—a more appropriate hypothesis needs to be posited. This of course will lead to new readings of particular concepts like justification that may differ from both Wesleyans of the past and Wesley himself, but if we are able to adopt Wesley's ethos of openness to "plain scriptural proof"—in contemporary idiom, if we are open to rereadings of Scripture—we should not fear that a rereading of justification might lend itself to altering Wesleyan identity, since this is, in part, what reading a text scripturally does.[10]

Although justification by faith and other doctrines in Wesley's soteriology have remained important for Wesleyans, it is unclear whether the analogy of

---

8. Behr, *The Way to Nicaea*, 32-33.
9. Behr, *The Way to Nicaea*, 31-32.
10. See Wesley A. Kort, *"Take, Read": Scripture, Textuality, and Cultural Practice* (University Park: Pennsylvania State University Press, 1996). Kort's theory of scriptural reading, however, presses the liminal aspect too far, as if reading a text scripturally only serves to upset and alter identity.

faith per se has enjoyed the same prestige.[11] Whatever the case, I have been building up to the suggestion that a Wesleyan theological hermeneutic of Scripture need not subscribe to John Wesley's rule for reading, the analogy of faith. Before asking what kind of ruled reading might replace it, two additional points about the displacement of Wesley's ruled reading from a Wesleyan hermeneutic can be made.

First, in a tradition-constituted framework such as what I have taken from MacIntyre, the re-opening of a hermeneutical engagement with the analogy of faith is precisely what we should expect. Where MacIntyre is most helpful in discussing traditions is in showing how various stages tend to play out, replete with crises that challenge the integrity of a tradition. Resourcefulness is required if the tradition will survive. Relativizing the analogy of faith as one possible hypothesis of Scripture's message may represent a crisis for some, but Wesleyan theologians today have the resources to move beyond it.

Second, even if this displacement of the analogy of faith is viewed as a crisis for Wesleyan identity, the scope of the crisis should be circumscribed. In other words, although the extension of a tradition through time involves the passing down of themes, practices, and beliefs, it would be reductionistic to tie a tradition's identity to just one theme, even one as historically important as justification, or just one practice, such as reading by the analogy of faith.[12] None of this means that original sin, or justification by faith, or other doctrines cannot continue to be explored as concepts of theological plenitude, but the status they enjoyed for Wesley in his time may be a casualty of the present age in which Wesleyans continue reading the Bible as their Scripture.

One might protest, wondering where this revision of Wesley's doctrine and hermeneutics should end. If, for example, justification by faith can no longer be employed hermeneutically as Wesley employed it, does that not sever a crucial tie with Wesley that makes the identity "Wesleyan" empty? Yet undoubtedly some beliefs and practices that were once considered indelibly Wesleyan have been jettisoned, and it is not unreasonable that some Wesleyan themes and practices that have fallen into disuse could eventually be recovered.[13] The difficulty of the tradition-constituted framework is that, because it forsakes

---

11. After all, justification, new birth, and the rest are usually discussed in Wesleyan theology as systematic doctrines, apart from hermeneutics, marginalizing questions about the analogy of faith. Cf. Ted A. Campbell, *Methodist Doctrine*, 56; and Oden, *Scriptural Christianity*, 197-203.

12. For an interesting look at how the Lutheran theologian Dietrich Bonhoeffer moved away from Luther's two-kingdoms theme as a critical engagement with his own tradition, see Klemens von Klemperer, "Beyond Luther? Dietrich Bonhoeffer and Resistance against National Socialism," *Pro Ecclesia* 6 (1997): 184-98.

13. For a lamentation of the Wesleyan tradition's losses, see Abraham, "The End," 17-18. Lester Ruth's *Early Methodist Life and Spirituality: A Reader* (Nashville, TN: Kingswood, 2005) places on display many attitudes, themes, beliefs, and practices that seem to have remained in the distant past.

methods for skilled judgments, there can be no clearly defined criteria for what is expendable and what is essential. Nevertheless, the examination of issues in chapter five, and their reiteration and further development here, provide ample theological and hermeneutical reasons for continuing on.

Certainly numerous elements in theological interpretation today are examples of the recovery of Christian beliefs and practices from earlier eras. Of these elements in recovery, ruled reading has established itself as a major theme in theological interpretation, as Hays' quotation above evinces. It is therefore somewhat ironic that the analogy of faith would decrease as advocacy of ruled readings is on the increase. What, then, is a viable option for a ruled reading of Scripture for a Wesleyan hermeneutic?

In "The 'Literal Reading' of Biblical Narrative," Hans Frei introduces ruled reading in this way: "The creed, 'rule of faith' or 'rule of truth' which governed the Gospels' use in the church asserted the primacy of their literal sense."[14] Frei combines creed and rule of faith, insinuating they are essentially the same.[15] Scholars today have continued in that vein, exploring particularly how the Nicene Creed can rule Scripture and life.[16] Although there may be some differences historically speaking between the rule of faith and the creed, the creed today is useful due to its fixed nature and historical endurance; it provides a relatively stable point of departure at a time when the unity of neither church nor Bible can be assumed.

The creed, then, does possess a hermeneutical function today, communicating a sensibility, a pattern for perceiving the Bible as Scripture. But using the creed hermeneutically does not mean trying to correlate propositions with biblical texts. It is perhaps for this reason R. R. Reno has referred instead to the Nicene *tradition*, saying,

> [T]he rule of faith cannot be limited to a specific set of words, sentences, and creeds. It is instead a pervasive habit of thought, the animating culture of the church in its intellectual aspect.... This is why Irenaeus is able to appeal to the rule of faith more than a century before the first ecumenical council, and this is why we need not

---

14. Frei, "Literal Reading," 122.

15. As a historical matter, Wolfram Kinzig and Markus Vinzent debate this, though not in direct conversation with Frei. According to them, creeds are fixed declarations of allegiance, whereas rules of faith (which possibly hailed from earlier times; Kinzig and Vinzent argue for evidence of the Roman Creed as early as the second century), were ad hoc doctrinal summaries recruited for theological argumentation, and were more fluid in structure and wording ("Recent Research on the Origin of the Creed," *Journal of Theological Studies* 50 [1999]: 540-41).

16. E.g., Radner and Sumner, eds., *The Rule of Faith: Scripture*; Reno, "Series Preface," 14; Wall, "Reading the Bible," 88-107; cf. David S. Yeago, "The New Testament and the Nicene Dogma: A Contribution to the Recovery of Theological Exegesis," in *The Theological Interpretation of Scripture*, ed. Fowl, 87-100.

itemize the contents of the Nicene tradition in order to appeal to its potency and role in the work of interpretation.[17]

As a result the rule cannot be reduced to the creed, but it does take its point of departure from it. That sensibility or habituated perception is the shape of the creed itself, outlined as it is into the three *hypostases* of the Godhead—God the Father, God the Son, and God the Holy Spirit. The threefold Name gives structure to the creed, and of course hearkens back to the font of the liturgical use of the threefold Name in the church, baptism.[18]

But why is this rule of faith exempt from the problems of the analogy of faith? Why is it not the case that, just as the analogy of faith was set aside as an inadequate hypothesis after a rereading of doctrines like justification, that a rule of faith in the Nicene tradition cannot also suffer the same fate? One answer is that it already has, as so much biblical scholarship in the past two hundred years attests. But more importantly, these questions point back to the same problem of unity and diversity in the Bible that led to my rereading of justification by faith. How does this rule of faith, as a recovery of the Nicene tradition, deal with the problem of unity and diversity?

Although I cannot offer a full-scale treatment of the problem, some important points can be made. Richard Hays, in an article I have already looked to, offers some important reflections on this very topic. Hays argues that one reason we struggle to find unity in Scripture may be that our ideas of unity are too simplistic. The criteria by which we try to discern unity may be "too flat and literalistic." We tend to look for unity "at the level of the conceptual articulations of the individual authors," which Hays considers "too narrow a textual field." In his opinion, "the unity we seek must be discerned through the texture of the whole divinely scripted performance. It is this totality that bears witness to the identity of God rendered in the dramatic narrative."[19]

In working toward what he means by dramatic narrative, Hays begins by demonstrating the shortcomings in historical and literary methods for securing biblical unity. After going on to dismiss methods in general, Hays makes a theological assertion: "Christian Scripture is unified only insofar as it reaffirms Israel's *Shema* by witness to one God: the God of Abraham, Isaac, and Jacob, and the God and Father of Jesus Christ."[20] Hays declares, however, that this

---

17. Reno, "Series Preface," 14.

18. Kinzig and Vinzent show how the Roman Creed (precursor to the Apostles' Creed) and the various rules of faith had a common origin in baptismal practice, though apparently the rules and creed did not directly influence each other ("Recent Research," 540-50).

19. Hays "Theological Unity," 202.

20. Hays, "Theological Unity," 200. For an example of exhaustive treatment of the biblical narrative that proceeds on just this assertion, see Christopher J. H. Wright, *The Mission of God: Unlocking the Bible's Grand Narrative* (Downers Grove, IL: InterVarsity, 2006).

theological claim is not enough, given the complexity of the biblical canon. Looking for a more satisfactory answer, he takes as his point of departure a thesis from the Scripture project that "Scripture is rightly understood in light of the church's rule of faith as a coherent dramatic narrative." Hays then explains what exactly is meant by "coherent dramatic narrative": "It will contain numerous voices, diverse characters, and many discrete scenes. It will unfold across time, and its words and images will gather dense significations as the plot develops. Consequently, its meaning can be grasped only when the totality of the action is considered from its endpoint."[21]

Hays unpacks the Scripture Project's thesis, arguing that to read Scripture as a coherent dramatic narrative in light of the rule of faith is to recognize God as author and chief actor, and as working through the dramatic narrative "to transform the audience."[22] He then offers this summation:

> [T]he unity of the Bible is grounded in the ongoing action of the one God who is both its central character and its ultimate author. Because God is one, Scripture turns out to be coherent. That is what is meant by the claim that "God is the author of Scripture's unity: the Bible's many human characters, and even the human authors of the individual biblical writings, are taken up into the complex dramatic design of the One from whom are all things and for whom we exist.[23]

Hays' argument echoes much of what has already been said here about a soteriological approach to theological interpretation, especially from within the Wesleyan tradition. God is author of both Scripture and life, and works through Scripture's interpretation as a means of grace to draw persons along the way to heaven toward the end of religion, which is knowledge and love of God.

Combined with the insights I gleaned from him earlier on the rule of faith and the church as the privileged interpreter of its Scripture, Hays' article is valuable in both reaffirming the truly theological core of the Bible, and exposing how methods that operate on merely the historical and literary levels are too myopic and wrongheaded, on their own, to take the Bible on its own terms (that is, the terms of the community of faith who read it as Scripture) as an instrument both used by, and pointing to, God. This does not rule out other critical approaches, but it does domesticate them to the theological purpose of Scripture. Hays accomplishes this from a postcritical perspective, recognizing the reality of the problem of Scripture's unity and diversity. "The more complex the drama," he writes, "the more is required of the audience by way of patient, mature, reflective reception."[24]

---

21. Hays, "Theological Unity," 201.
22. Hays, "Theological Unity," 201.
23. Hays, "Theological Unity," 202.
24. Hays, "Theological Unity," 201.

What, however, does this approach say about where the unity of Scripture is located? Certainly that unity cannot be reduced to the text itself, as Hays indicates. As my constant emphasis on theological interpretation as a means of grace suggests, Scripture is not an end in itself. Scripture and its interpretation are part of a larger divine economy; Scripture is a witness to God's action in the world, and faithful interpretation of Scripture by the church is testimony to the continued action of the Father, Son, and Holy Spirit. Unity cannot be found merely on the level of the text, but within the totality of the church's life. It is reflected partially in Scripture, in creed, and in faithfulness. But this "unity" is not the same thing as conceptual neatness; it does not sidestep the partial, human act of interpretation.

For a Wesleyan theological hermeneutic in this postcritical era, this means traversing the way to heaven may not be as clear-cut and simple as a three-step typology of natural-to-legal-to-evangelical, but it may be truer to the realities of the present, preserving Rowan Williams' admonition from chapter six that we open ourselves to the hermeneutical work of the Spirit in redefining our identities, but not at the expense of the *humanum*—in this case both the fact that it is humans who do the hard work of interpretation within the constraints of our time, and that the Bible is a cultural product, encompassing an array of genres and voices from across centuries that nevertheless testify to the one God. This interpretation is not limited at the textual level, but is also reflected in the everyday lives of believers.

A final couple of thoughts on ruled reading are in order. What, it may be asked, makes this rule of faith I am arguing for particularly *Wesleyan*? This rule of faith remains "Wesleyan" in the sense that, first, Wesley's soteriological hermeneutics assumed the work of the triune God in the economy of salvation, allowing him to focus on the individual's experience of grace. For different reasons—many of which I have examined—the emphasis has shifted back to the triune God who authors Scripture and life, away from the experience of the reader. Yet this is no less soteriological, since it is God who is creator and redeemer; as numerous psalms attest, God is our salvation.

Second, this rule of faith is Wesleyan in the sense that, rooted as it is in the church's primitive baptismal practice and Nicene orthodoxy, it truly is part of "the old religion," that Wesley always claimed his Methodist movement really was in the first place. In other words, adopting this rule of faith within a Wesleyan theological hermeneutic of Scripture retrofits a basic belief of Wesley's about the Wesleyan identity for a postcritical time. It is part of the catholic tradition Wesley always believed Methodism was a recovery of in the first place.

In this section I have dealt with the nature of a ruled reading for a Wesleyan hermeneutic that takes seriously the consequences of living in a different context from Wesley. Considering how "Wesleyan theology" is often presented systematically as a series of doctrinal themes reflected in the analogy of faith, a Wesleyan theological hermeneutic may appear a drastic departure from what some may consider vital to Wesleyan identity. I have tried to address that issue, but a Wesleyan theological hermeneutic cannot be limited to doctrine and ruled reading. After all, as Wesley said in *The Character of a Methodist*, Methodism is not limited to opinions of any sort, but to a life fully lived to the glory of God. In the following section I will try to give a sense of this by weaving together several elements presented so far for a Wesleyan theological hermeneutic of Scripture.

A Wesleyan Theological Hermeneutic of Scripture
My intention here is to take three points established earlier—searching Scripture as a means of grace, baptism as the paradigmatic means of grace, and God as author of Scripture and life—and combine them with the concept of the model reader and a rule of faith in the Nicene tradition to offer a Wesleyan theological hermeneutic that is soteriological.

The means of grace comprise the life of the church. As William Abraham says, "Means of grace presuppose a complex theological vision of creation and redemption. They take as given the existence of God, the estrangement of human agents from their true destiny, and a network of divine action in the salvation of the world." The various means of grace "reconnect human agents with their divine source and origin."[25] The means of grace are the ordinary channels by which the Holy Spirit restores in us the image of God, who is Jesus Christ the Son, refashioning our fallen identities into children of our heavenly Father. They give us "a complex theological vision of creation and redemption," that is, they teach us that we are creatures who were made for communion with the divine source of all life, which the church worships as Father, Son, and Holy Spirit. One of these means of grace is theological interpretation, which is not a dispassionate, "scientific" analysis of the Bible, but a way of reading the Bible as Scripture; it is a way of opening ourselves to this particular channel of grace, so that by the Spirit's presence we can work out our salvation.

Persons enter into the life of church, and therefore the network of means of grace, through the sacrament of baptism. I argued in chapter five that baptism, as the rite of initiation into the church, is the paradigmatic means of grace. It is the pattern of life for the paschal mystery of faith in the church, and that pattern is the triune Name itself into which persons are baptized. Baptism "is a gracious gift of God, whereby through created realities we enter into participation in divine life itself. Ultimately God is both the giver and the gift."[26] In other words, "Father, Son, and Holy Spirit" both identifies God, and gifts to us a new identity: "Baptism is initiation into the mystery of Christ and initiation into the church. It is the sacrament of our unity *with* Christ and at the same time the

---

25. Abraham, *Canon and Criterion*, 1.
26. Erickson, "Baptism and the Church's Faith," 50-51. "Giver" and "gift," as Erickson uses them here, certainly resemble how Hays uses "author" and "chief actor" above.

sacrament of our unity *in* Christ."[27] By joining ourselves to Christ, we receive by grace the filial identity that he possesses by nature.

But as Hans Frei showed, Christ is identified in the biblical narrative. Reading the Bible as Scripture—as a means of grace—is to acknowledge the literal ascriptive identity of Jesus. The identity of Jesus in Scripture, of course, is unintelligible apart from the Father and Spirit, but we learn to recognize this because our habits of perceiving have been fundamentally shaped by the triune Name into which we were baptized, and reinforced by ongoing participation in the divine life through the means of grace. But literal ascriptive identity of Jesus is also an identity that, as we open ourselves to it in theological interpretation, transforms our own identities by the work of the Spirit.

This is where the concept of model reader proved helpful in chapter seven. The concept frames interpretation as an act where the reader attempts to read a text in accord with the text's intent, as the empirical author encodes it. The empirical reader, by imagining the model author through the act of interpretation, becomes the model reader of the text. Given the intertwining of divine authorship of Scripture and life, I argued that the divine identity is disclosed through the text in the person of Jesus Christ who is the divine image of God. Therefore, Wesley's hermeneutical example encourages us to approach Scripture expectant of transformation from slaves of sin to children of God, where the filial identity of Christ mediated by Scripture is granted to us through adoption by the Holy Spirit. Holiness, becoming like Christ, bearing the fruit of the Spirit—these essentially synonymous concepts show that the Wesleyan reader is approaching Scripture as a model reader. To know God as he is revealed in Scripture is to love God, since knowledge of God requires our openness to him in response to his gracious initiative. "Father, Son, and Holy Spirit" is the internal logic or grammar of the faith, ruling all of Christian life within the church, including theological interpretation of Scripture.

By tying together a ruled reading from the Nicene tradition with baptism and theological interpretation, this discussion reinforces a key point in a Wesleyan theological hermeneutic as a soteriological approach to the Bible: God is the author of both Scripture and life. Scripture was written as a means for God to bring his creative purposes to fulfillment through the economy of salvation. As this occurs, our identities are transformed through adoption into children of God. This is the case for a Wesleyan theological hermeneutic, not because we privilege a Pauline doctrine or book, and not because we subscribe to Wesley's analogy of faith, but because the Son has made it possible for us to participate in his identity as the image of God through being adopted by the Spirit, who refashions us into children of our heavenly Father.

Both life and Scripture are to be read in light of the rule of faith, as God has authored both. The rule truly is the internal logic of the community of faith, as Frei taught, giving coherence to the semiotic system of the church's sacramental

---

27. Erickson, "Baptism and the Church's Faith," 51.

life, and allowing theological interpretation to produce a soteriological meaning out of its engagement with Scripture. Thus, the literal sense of a Wesleyan theological hermeneutic is the soteriogical sense. Through grace the literal sense is a reading of Scripture that perceives the triune pattern of biblical unity, and opens the reader to have her own identity shaped by the encounter with God. It is not limited to the words and grammar on the page of the text, but looks through the Bible to both the living God attested to therein, and the living community of faith that continues to regard the Bible as its Scripture.

Demonstration of a Wesleyan Theological Hermeneutic of Scripture

To this point I have addressed some final matters in my constructive proposal of a Wesleyan theological hermeneutic of Scripture. However, as I stated at the outset of this study, my intention has been to develop and demonstrate a Wesleyan hermeneutic. In this section I will make good on that intention, offering a sermon. As I mentioned in chapter five, the sermon was essential to Wesley as a minister, and was his preferred genre of theological interpretation. Along with the concern of much theological hermeneutics to bring academy and church closer together, it therefore seems fitting to offer a sermon as an example of Wesleyan interpretation. Following the sermon I will offer some reflections on its hermeneutical inner workings, before concluding.

Sermon for the Fourth Sunday of Lent[28]
(Num 21:4-9; Ps 107:1-3, 17-22; Eph 2:1-10; John 3:14-21)
Lent has been wearing on for some time now; this is the fourth Sunday of Lent. Whatever zeal we had in making our sacrifices a few weeks ago has probably passed. The journey to the cross, and eventually on to Easter morning, is long and arduous, and we may ask ourselves whether this is all worth it. If we allow one of our readings this morning, from Numbers 21, to guide our thinking about Lent, then we know that we are not merely wandering around, but are being led. Not only that, but when combined with another reading, from John 3, we learn our destination. God is leading us to himself. He is both guide and destination, and he has freed us up to make this trip. Like the Israelites, we are traveling, but whereas they traversed a space—the wilderness—we are traversing a time. *Lent* is the name of that time we cross, and the "distance" is between God and us. It takes time to arrive at God, and in the meantime, our personal topographies are re-landscaped in an act of new creation we call *sanctification*. If the reading from Numbers does anything else, it teaches us to be good traveling companions, because Israel did not know how to behave itself on its trip through the wilderness.

---

28. This is a revised version of a sermon preached by Steven Joe Koskie Jr., 22 March 2009, at Antioch United Methodist Church in Simsboro, Louisiana. Biblical quotations are from the NRSV.

What I want to do this morning is begin with the reading from Numbers and try to get a sense of what is going on there. Then we will turn to the Gospel reading, from John 3, because there Jesus references something from Numbers 21 while having his famous conversation with Nicodemus, who as much as anything is trying to figure out from Jesus where "this" (Jesus' ministry) is all going, we might say.

Here is the passage:

> From Mount Hor they set out by the way to the Red Sea, to go around the land of Edom; but the people became impatient on the way. The people spoke against God and against Moses, "Why have you brought us up out of Egypt to die in the wilderness? For there is no food and no water, and we detest this miserable food." Then the LORD sent poisonous serpents among the people, and they bit the people, so that many Israelites died. The people came to Moses and said, "We have sinned by speaking against the LORD and against you; pray to the LORD to take away the serpents from us." So Moses prayed for the people. And the LORD said to Moses, "Make a poisonous serpent, and set it on a pole; and everyone who is bitten shall look at it and live." So Moses made a serpent of bronze, and put it upon a pole; and whenever a serpent bit someone, that person would look at the serpent of bronze and live. (Numbers 21:4-9)

Had we begun reading a little before, we would know that Mount Hor is where the priest Aaron died, and that the Israelites had just defeated the Canaanites in battle. Now Israel is moving on, and we know where, to the promised land. But it says they became impatient and began to complain against God and Moses. At this point we get some interesting coordinates about where Israel is.

"Why," Israel asks in verse 5, "have you brought us up out of Egypt to die in the wilderness?" Taking this with the information from verse 4, Israel is now in the wilderness, between Egypt and the promised land. The wilderness through which Israel is moving has been seen variously as the site both of God's presence and absence, of testing, as well as a state of separation from God resulting from sin. It is the perfect setting for the Lenten journey we find ourselves undertaking. Israel is here in the wilderness trying to go around Edom "by the way of the Red Sea," the Red Sea of course being the site of God's dramatic act of deliverance, crushing Pharaoh's army after Israel had crossed on dry land.

As a quick aside: If we allow that *space* and *place* are rarely accidental in Scripture (that is, movement through space such as "ascending" and "descending" often means more than simply up or down, but may indicate proximity to God; and a location is typically about more than a point of mere geography), then what emerges here at the beginning of our reading is a layout, a topography, of where Israel is.[29] *Where* in a geographical sense, yes, but *where* in a theological sense as well: where in relation to God.

For this reason the proximity to Edom is interesting here. Edom is also Esau, Israel's (or Jacob's) brother, who sold his birthright to the patriarch for some kind of red lentil soup. The text in Genesis says, "Thus Esau despised his birthright" (Gen. 25:34). Jacob inherits the promise originally made to Abraham and passed down to Isaac, making the Israelites descendants of the promise. True to the covenant, God delivers Israel from Egypt and brings them into the wilderness to make them into a people at Sinai.

Despite this, Israel's trust of God and Moses has been tenuous from the beginning of the Exodus, and it is obvious here that Israel does not yet understand who this God is, and why the path his servant Moses is taking them on is any better than the life of slavery they lived in Egypt. The way from Egypt, along the Red Sea, ought to be a way of life, as those who were not a people are being made into a people. Seemingly a death trap for Israel as it fled Egypt, God cut through the chaos of the sea to open new earth leading to freedom. This fails to occur to the Israelites, who lament their eminent doom at the hands of God and Moses. Instead, Israel implies it would be willing to switch course, preferring the life-less realm of slavery under Pharaoh. So we find Israel here in Numbers 21 complaining against God and Moses about their plight and specifically about their food. The children of the promise do not seem to comprehend what it is they are heirs to. They are very close to Edom indeed.

God's response is to send poisonous serpents among the Israelites. The bites of these snakes were fatal, and the text says many Israelites died. The people appeal to Moses to pray to God on their behalf, which he does, and God instructs Moses to make a serpent and set it on a pole. Moses obeys, fashioning a serpent of bronze. From then on anyone who was bitten could look at the bronze serpent and live.

The whole incident is more than a little puzzling. Perhaps we can make sense of God sending the serpents as a punishment, but why the bronze snake in response? Are we to assume the poisonous snakes remained? Why did God not get rid of them?

We can linger over these questions, but I want to first press ahead to the Gospel of John. In this reading, Jesus references the incident we have just looked at. The scene is Jesus' clandestine meeting, under darkness, with Nicodemus. The reading throws us into the middle of their conversation, but in brief, Jesus is trying to get Nicodemus (who has come to him) to understand "heavenly things" (3:12). John, as effectively as any scriptural writer, uses spatial metaphors to make his points, though not only spatial metaphors. He arrays a series of contrasts to create a world in which the Word has come into

---

29. A general discussion on space and place in Scripture is John Inge, *A Christian Theology of Place* (Explorations in Practical, Pastoral, and Empirical Theology; Aldershot: Ashgate, 2003), esp. ch. 2.

creation to tabernacle with humanity. Here, "heavenly" and "from above" are contrasted with "worldly" and "from below." Similarly, darkness and nighttime are contrasted with light and daytime. Hate is opposed to love; sight is distinguished from blindness; and so on. If Jesus' use of these things in John 3 is any indication, the purpose of this imagery is to teach us the ways of God (or "the way," as in "the way, the truth, and the life," John 14:6). For Nicodemus to arrive at nighttime is not a good sign regarding him, and his lack of understanding is congruent with the setting. "Are you a teacher of Israel," Jesus asks just prior to our reading, "and yet you do not understand these things?" (3:10).

We pick up with verse 14:

> And just as Moses lifted up the serpent in the wilderness, so must the Son of Man be lifted up, that whoever believes in him may have eternal life. For God so loved the world that he gave his only Son, so that everyone who believes in him may not perish but may have eternal life. Indeed, God did not send the Son into the world to condemn the world, but in order that the world might be saved through him. Those who believe in him are not condemned; but those who do not believe are condemned already, because they have not believed in the name of the only Son of God. And this is the judgment, that the light has come into the world, and people loved darkness rather than light because their deeds were evil. For all who do evil hate the light and do not come to the light, so that their deeds may not be exposed. But those who do what is true come to the light, so that it may be clearly seen that their deeds have been done in God. (John 3:14-21)

Note first how the reference to Moses and the serpent in the wilderness is somehow the key to what Jesus is saying about himself: "And just as Moses lifted up the serpent in the wilderness, so must the Son of man be lifted up." Why? "That whoever believes in him may have eternal life." To be "lifted up" here means to be crucified, as we learn elsewhere in John (cf. John 8:28; 12:32-34).

Then comes a verse we all know well—maybe too well to allow it to do its work of shaping us in the ways of God, as Nicodemus apparently needed that shaping. The verse is John 3:16: "For God so loved the world that he gave his only Son, so that everyone who believes in him may not perish but may have eternal life." What I want to draw attention to is the phrase "so loved." As Methodists, we have been taught to read this as a statement of the degree of God's love for us. John Wesley, after all, said that we should make our religion a religion of the heart, and his Aldersgate experience centered on his realization of God's love for him. John 3:16 seems to fit this perfectly, and there is no doubt most people read it this way.

Another possibility, however, is to read the phrase as referencing something else. The Greek word οὕτως can certainly be translated "so," but that does not have to have the sense of *degree*. It could also mean "thus" or "in this way." Jesus has just mentioned Moses raising up the serpent in the wilderness and drawing a parallel to his own experience as Son of Man. Apparently what happened in Numbers 21 sets the pattern for what will happen to him. Jesus has primed both Nicodemus and us to look at an action of God in the past to be able to identify an action of God in the present. Then comes verse 16 where Jesus appears to elaborate on this patterned action. We might, therefore, read John 3:16 like this: "For God loved the world in this way"; or maybe better, "For this is how God loved the world: that he gave his only Son, so that everyone who believes in him may not perish but may have eternal life." Now the phrase "so loved" is not referring to the degree of God's love, but to what it looks like—not *how much*, but *how*. The "so loved" points to what comes next, but it does so in light of what came before. The shape of what God is doing now is patterned after the earlier action of Numbers 21.

This way of reading John 3:16 is supported by a truism or principle of Christian faith, that we know who God is by what God does. We do not have access to the inner workings of God's "psychology," as if God were simply a more powerful version of ourselves, who as a result loves us "*so* much"—far more than we can love him. Instead of looking for God's motivations for having Jesus "lifted up," or sending poisonous serpents whose venom is nullified by a bronze serpentine image, we begin with God's act, and the decisive act is the life, death, and new life of Jesus of Nazareth. Jesus, by pointing to the act of God's love—what it looks like—points us to himself, and now the interplay between our two readings begins to open up.

"Indeed," Jesus says, "God did not send the Son into the world to condemn the world, but in order that the world might be saved through him. Those who believe in him are not condemned; but those who do not believe are condemned already, because they have not believed in the name of the Son of God" (3:17-18). Jesus is not concerned with the serpent per se, but with what its being lifted up effects, how that makes sense of his own lifting up to come. The lifting up of the bronze serpent was not an act of condemnation, but an act designed to bring life. Israel, unable to grasp God's purposes in bringing them through the wilderness, learn who this God is who brought them out of Egypt, and in the process are molded into God's people. The lifting up of the bronze serpent is not a signal of condemnation, but a sign of life, pointing to the God who is using the wilderness plight to make Israel into his chosen people. In the same way, the Son has not come into the world to condemn it, but to bring eternal life. It is an act of judgment meant to goad Israel into repentance. Those who refuse the light of the Son are already condemned because they love darkness (John 3:19-20). "But those who do what is true come to the light, so that it may be clearly seen that their deeds have been done in God" (John 3:21).

Refusing to look at the bronze serpent would not condemn a poisoned Israelite; that person was already "condemned" by being bitten. God may have sent the poisonous serpents, but their purpose was not to end the unfolding drama of redemption. This seems to be the psalmist's take, at least. In Psalm 107, which thanks God for deliverance, the psalmist, referring to "the redeemed of the Lord," says,

> Some were sick through their sinful ways, and because of their iniquities endured affliction; they loathed any kind of food, and they drew near to the gates of death. Then they cried to the LORD in their trouble, and he saved them from their distress; he sent out his word and healed them, and delivered them from destruction. Let them thank the LORD for his steadfast love, for his wonderful works to humankind. (Psalm 107:17-21)

The episode with the serpents is a microcosm of the way of the wilderness, and combined with Jesus' words in John 3, we begin to grasp better the way of repentance and preparation we call Lent. Yet Jesus' words, and the story of Numbers 21:4-9, come to us after the first Easter. As Paul says in our last reading, from Ephesians, we were once dead in our trespasses, but God "made us alive together with Christ" (Eph 2:5). Israel had to be remade into God's people through the discipline of the wilderness; so too, we experience the discipline of Lent as a means of grace, so the Holy Spirit can remake us. It takes time to arrive at God, but it is the time it takes for each of us to be renewed in the divine image. As Paul goes on to say: "For we are what he has made us, created in Christ Jesus for good works, which God prepared beforehand to be our way of life" (Eph 2:10).

Lent is the church's Exodus, but we are traveling across time, not wilderness. We will not be crossing a river at the journey's end, but the cross of Good Friday. And our promised land is not fertile soil, but an Easter morning that dawns "in Christ," as Paul says.

We began this morning mapping out the landscape of Israel's location in Numbers 21. Like Israel, we need to learn whom this God is who has brought us into this land called Jesus Christ where we travel the journey of sanctification. We are heading toward the cross, and as the cross comes into view we are further defined, but so too is God defined for us—unless we stay in the dark like Nicodemus. In the same way Jesus teaches that his coming was not a signal of condemnation, what God is doing now through Lent is shaping us through the "way of life" he has prepared for us in Christ. This is the God who awaits us at the end of the Lenten journey, but who is also accompanying us along the way.

Analysis of the Theological Hermeneutics of the Sermon
The sermon is a lectionary-based elucidation of the church's experience of Lent. Involving as it traditionally does various levels of self-mortification, and

extending forty days from Ash Wednesday to Easter, Lent is intended to bring Christians to the point of repentance as preparation for Good Friday and, finally, Easter. The sermon remains on the level of Scripture's literal sense, but as a sermon, reading the literal sense is easily extended figurally to invite the congregation into the vision for the Lenten journey that is being created.

Seizing on the forty days and the lectionary reading from Numbers, I try to give a figural depiction of Lent as the church's Exodus, but as a temporal and theological journey rather than a geographical one. To move in that direction, I try to show how even the geographical journey of Numbers is theological, as Israel is being transformed through its hardship into a people God has set aside for himself. The intention is to encourage the congregation, as it hears the text read and explored, to picture itself in a similar situation; to begin to make connections with the Israelites on their journey, and themselves as they journey through Lent. The congregation is invited, in other words, to begin assuming the role of model reader.

I then tie the Numbers text figurally with the Johannine reading. Of course, John insists upon this move, as Jesus himself references the episode of Moses lifting up the serpent in the wilderness. The sermon is therefore figural on two levels: it invites the church to see itself within a scripturally inspired divine drama (Lent as Exodus), and it connects Jesus and his mission as an act of God in the New Testament with an act of God in the Old Testament.

The readings from Numbers and John comprise the primary texts for the sermon, with the psalm and reading from Ephesians playing a supporting role. In a sense, the occasion of Lent rules my arrangement and exposition of the lectionary materials. On another level, the texts themselves rule the sermon's narratival logic. This latter ruled reading emerges not simply from settling for the parameters of each lectionary passage, but by "reading around" the passages to give them context. By reading just prior to Jesus' words in John 3:14-21, I can better set the scene for his speech. Likewise, I allude to John 1, 8, and 12, all to give a better sense of that particular Gospel's theological narrative. I do the same thing to a lesser extent with Numbers, to give context to the Israelites' setting when the reading begins at Num 21:4.

Psalm 107 does not deal specifically with the events of Numbers; it discusses God's redeeming work for various groups in a general way. However, the passage quoted in the sermon (107:17-21) works well with the general tenor of the readings. It is used in a supplementary way to expand on the redemptive action of God as it is paralleled in the raising up of the serpent and the raising up of Jesus. Similarly, I bring in Ephesians after returning from the figural reading within the text to the figural context "in front of" the text that I have been inviting the congregation to enter into. Paul's words on moving from death to life further reinforce the logic of the Lent-as-Exodus narrative, and the final verse quoted, Eph 2:10, gives the narrative an eschatological orientation, reminding us that the church's Exodus occurs after Easter and is part of the church's experience of sanctification.

As a final point, the sermon is Wesleyan. I emphasize Lent as a means of grace by which the Holy Spirit sanctifies believers, and offer a different reading of John 3:16 than what is traditional in a Wesleyan perspective. The rereading of John 3:16 has the effect of calling into question a familiar assumption, and reopens a text that had likely been closed for many in the congregation due to a long-held, popular interpretation. My intention with the rereading is that by opening the text, the congregation may likewise open anew to God's address through the reading as a means of grace. The reading therefore exhibits continuity and discontinuity with the Wesleyan identity as that has been connected with a certain reading of John 3:16, but it is thoroughly soteriological.

Moreover, the journey motif, with its promise of a destination, is subtle reference to what Wesley teaches in *The Character of a Methodist*, that a Methodist is someone who not only desires transformation, but will also attain it. By assuming the identity of pilgrims on an Exodus of their own, the congregation is invited to prepare itself for transformation through Good Friday and Easter Sunday.

It is also the case, recalling my emphasis on context, that part of what makes the sermon Wesleyan is not merely the sermon's content, but its delivery within the life of a United Methodist Church that conscientiously sets itself within the Wesleyan tradition. So not only the sermon, but the entire web of beliefs and practices that constitute the congregation contribute to the Wesleyan nature of the sermon.

Conclusion

This study has developed and demonstrated a Wesleyan theological hermeneutic of Scripture. Beginning in the first two chapters, with a survey of both theological hermeneutics in general, and Wesleyan theological hermeneutics in particular, I considered issues and problems for my agenda. Given the distance between John Wesley's hermeneutical context and that of the present day, I turned to Alasdair MacIntyre's work on traditions and crafts for a conceptual orientation, determining to learn theological interpretation as a craft through a skillful reinterpretation of Wesley's texts.

My dialogue with Hans Frei's hermeneutics in chapter three gave me an approach for appropriating Wesley's hermeneutics by focusing attention on context, grammar, ruled reading, and the literal sense. Together, these topics pointed to the question of identity. Frei's work—developed in some instances by others—oriented my appropriation around discerning the semiotic system of Wesley's hermeneutics as the environment in which a ruled reading of the literal sense could flourish after modernist criticism.

I brought this approach to chapters four and five, and examined Wesley's hermeneutics accordingly. Wesley reads Scripture as a means of grace within the economy of salvation, and according to the analogy of faith. For him the literal sense is the soteriological sense of Scripture, through which the Holy

Spirit works to bring persons from sin to salvation and on to the end for which they were originally created, the knowledge and love of God. But it is also the literal-moral and verbal sense, because his reading is concerned with the life of holiness in the life of the reader while refusing to depart from the text's final form.

Chapters six and seven began in earnest my appropriation of Wesley's hermeneutics for a Wesleyan theological hermeneutic of Scripture. Chapter six explored the church as Spirit-formed context, a soteriological setting wherein theological interpretation is practiced as a means of grace. This was developed addressing the ecclesiological deficit in Wesley's thought first through a rereading of justification by faith—moving from an individualistic to a covenantal-communal reading—and showing how the institution of the church is intrinsic to the Spirit's mission in the economy of salvation. I likewise recovered Wesley's earlier view of baptism, which was more ecclesiologically satisfying, to present it as the paradigmatic means of grace that gives shape to the whole of Christian life, including "searching the Scriptures."

Chapter seven took up the dynamic of reader and text in the formation of the Wesleyan identity. Umberto Eco's reception theory assisted conceptually, showing how meaning is produced through the interaction between a text and its model reader. I then fused the model reader with figural reading as that was first introduced by Frei, and then developed by John David Dawson, to ask what it is that makes a Wesleyan model reader. The Wesleyan model reader is a figurally composed identity that is generated out of a reading of Scripture expectant of finding "the way to heaven." Theological interpretation for the Wesleyan model reader is an exercise in sanctification, as holiness is both presupposed and the result of "searching the Scriptures." As a result, holiness is the performance the Bible consonant with reading it as Scripture within the Wesleyan community.

Over the course of my appropriation, beginning with my rereading of justification by faith, the question began to impress itself as to whether a Wesleyan theological hermeneutic would employ Wesley's analogy of faith. In the present chapter, therefore, I confronted this problem, arguing that, as a hypothesis of the Bible's narratival unity, Wesley's analogy of faith must be set aside. In its place, I looked to recent scholarship on ruled readings that take as their touchstone the Nicene Creed. The basic form of the creed, the triune God, was, I argued, a superior hypothesis for Scripture, and no less soteriological than Wesley's analogy of faith. I then offered a description of a ruled reading of the literal sense within a Wesleyan theological hermeneutic as I have developed it here. I then demonstrated this hermeneutic with a sermon that I subsequently analyzed.

Because I have chosen to proceed in this study within a MacIntyrean understanding of tradition-constituted knowledge, the theological hermeneutic offered here is not intended to be definitive. Other interpreters within the Wesleyan tradition might, for instance, broaden their investigation beyond Wesley's writings, or even read Wesley's writings differently. By way of conclusion I offer six characteristics of a Wesleyan theological hermeneutic, as first presented in chapter one:

1) Wesleyan interpretation is theological in that its aim is the knowledge and love of God.
2) Wesleyan interpretation regards the literal sense of Scripture as the soteriological sense, which leads to the knowledge and love of God. The literal sense thus has a salvific effect on the interpreter, incorporating her into the economy of salvation.
3) By recognizing the Bible as Scripture, Wesleyan interpretation is sacramental, regarding the Bible as a means of grace through which the Holy Spirit works to bring us from death to life.
4) As sacramental, Wesleyan interpretation is ecclesially located (that is, it exists within communities known as "Wesleyan").
5) As ecclesially located, Wesleyan interpretation occurs within the ongoing tradition of Wesleyan theology, as a particular expression of the church catholic.
6) Being within the Wesleyan tradition, Wesleyan interpretation will tend to pattern its reading of Scripture according to its concerns with holiness. It grammatically structures the life of sanctification Scripture facilitates through figural reading. Wesleyan readers enter the world of Scripture and embark on the Christian way of life as children of God, a way of life whose end is the Father, Son, and Holy Spirit—an end also known as *entire sanctification*, or *Christian perfection*.

Bibliography

Abraham, William J. *Canon and Criterion in Christian Theology: From the Fathers to Feminism*. Oxford: Oxford University Press, 1998.

_____. "Christian Perfection." In *The Oxford Handbook of Methodist Studies*, ed. William J. Abraham and James E. Kirby, 587-601. New York: Oxford University Press, 2009.

_____. *Crossing the Threshold of Divine Revelation*. Grand Rapids, MI: Eerdmans, 2006.

_____. "The End of Wesleyan Theology." *Wesleyan Theological Journal* 40 (2005): 7-25.

_____. *Waking from Doctrinal Amnesia: The Healing of Doctrine in the United Methodist Church*. Nashville, TN: Abingdon, 1995.

_____. "Wesley as Preacher." In *The Cambridge Companion to John Wesley*. Cambridge Companions to Religion, ed. Randy L. Maddox and Jason E. Vickers, 98-112. Cambridge: Cambridge University Press, 2009.

Abraham, William J. and James E. Kirby, eds. *Oxford Handbook of Methodist Studies*. New York: Oxford University Press, 2009.

Adam, A. K. M., et al. *Reading Scripture with the Church: Toward a Hermeneutic for Theological Interpretation*. Grand Rapids, MI: Baker Academic, 2006.

Alexander, T. Desmond and Brian S. Rosner, eds. *New Dictionary of Biblical Theology*. Downers Grove, IL: InterVarsity, 2000.

Archer, Kenneth J. *A Pentecostal Hermeneutic for the Twenty-first Century: Spirit, Scripture and Community*. Journal of Pentecostal Theology Supplement Series 28. London: T & T Clark, 2004.

Arnett, William M. "A Study in John Wesley's *Explanatory Notes upon the Old Testament*." *Wesleyan Theological Journal* 8 (1973): 14-32.

Augustine. *On Christian Teaching*. Translated and edited by R. P. H. Green. Oxford: Oxford University Press, 1997.

Ayres, Lewis. *Nicaea and Its Legacy: An Approach to Fourth-Century Trinitarian Theology*. Oxford: Oxford University Press, 2006.

Baird, William. *History of New Testament Research*. Minneapolis: Fortress, 1992.

Barr, James. *The Concept of Biblical Theology: An Old Testament Perspective*. Minneapolis: Augsburg Fortress, 1999.

_____. *Holy Scripture: Canon, Authority, Criticism*. Philadelphia: Westminster, 1983.

_____. *Old and New in Interpretation: A Study of the Two Testaments*. London: SCM, 1966.

Barth, Karl. *Church Dogmatics*. Edited by G.W. Bromiley and T.F. Torrance. Edinburgh: T & T Clark, 1958.

_____. *The Epistle to the Romans*. London: Oxford University Press, 1977.

_____. "The Strange New World within the Bible." In *The Word of God and the Word of Man*, 28-50. New York: Harper Torchbooks, 1957.

Bartholomew, Craig G. "Biblical Theology." In *Dictionary for Theological Interpretation of the Bible*, ed. Kevin Vanhoozer, 85-90. Grand Rapids, MI: Baker Academic, 2005.

Bartholomew, Craig G., et al., eds. *After Pentecost: Language and Biblical Interpretation*. Scripture and Hermeneutics Series 2. Grand Rapids, MI: Zondervan, 2001.

Bartholomew, Craig G., et al., eds. *"Behind" the Text: History and Biblical Interpretation*. Scripture and Hermeneutics Series 4. Grand Rapids, MI: Zondervan, 2003.

Bartholomew, Craig G., et al., eds. *Out of Egypt: Biblical Theology and Biblical Interpretation*. Scripture and Hermeneutics Series 5. Grand Rapids, MI: Zondervan, 2004.

Bartholomew, Craig G., et al., eds. *Renewing Biblical Interpretation*. Scripture and Hermeneutics Series 1. Grand Rapids, MI: Zondervan, 2000.

Bass, Dorothy C., ed. *Practicing Our Faith: A Way of Life for a Searching People*. San Francisco: Jossey-Bass, 1997.

Behr, John. *The Way to Nicaea*. Formation of Christian Theology 1. Crestwood, NY: St. Vladimir's Seminary Press, 2001.

Berger, Teresa. *Theology in Hymns? A Study of the Relationship of Doxology and Theology According to* A Collection of Hymns for the Use of the People Called Methodists (1780). Nashville, TN: Kingswood, 1995.

Blocher, Henry. "The Analogy of Faith in the Study of Scripture." *Scottish Bulletin of Evangelical Theology* 5 (1987): 17-38.

Blowers, Paul M. "The *Regula Fidei* and the Narrative Character of Early Christian Faith." *Pro Ecclesia* 6 (1997): 199-228.

Bonhoeffer, Dietrich. *Christology*. London: Collins, 1966.

Borgen, Ole E. *John Wesley on the Sacraments: A Theological Study*. Nashville, TN: Abingdon, 1972.

Braaten, Carl E. and Robert W. Jenson, eds. *In One Body through the Cross: The Princeton Proposal for Christian Unity*. Grand Rapids, MI: Eerdmans, 2003.

Braaten, Carl E. and Robert W. Jenson. "Introduction: Gospel, Church, and Scripture." In *Reclaiming the Bible for the Church*, ed. Carl E. Braaten and Robert W. Jenson, ix-xii. Grand Rapids, MI: Eerdmans, 1995.

Braaten, Carl E. and Robert W. Jenson, eds. *Reclaiming the Bible for the Church*. Grand Rapids, MI: Eerdmans, 1995.

Brown, Delwin. *Boundaries of Our Habitations Tradition and Theological Construction*. SUNY Series in Religious Studies. Albany: State University of New York Press, 1994.

Brown, William P., ed. *Character and Scripture: Moral Formation, Community, and Biblical Interpretation*. Grand Rapids, MI: Eerdmans, 2002.

Bryant, David J. *Faith and the Play of Imagination on the Role of Imagination in Religion: On the Role of Imagination in Religion*. Studies in American Biblical Hermeneutics 5. Macon, GA: Mercer University Press, 1989.

Buckley, James J. "Beyond the Hermeneutical Deadlock." In *Theology after Liberalism: A Reader*, ed. John Webster and George P. Schner, 187-203. Blackwell Readings in Modern Theology. Oxford: Blackwell, 2000.

Buckley, James J. and David S. Yeago, eds. *Knowing the Triune God: The Work of the Spirit in the Practices of the Church*. Grand Rapids, MI: Eerdmans, 2001.

Burnett, Richard E. *Karl Barth's Theological Exegesis: The Hermeneutical Principals of the Römerbrief Period*. Wissenschaftliche Untersuchungen zum Neuen Testament 145. Tübingen: Mohr Siebeck, 2001.

Buttrick, G. A., ed. *Interpreter's Dictionary of the Bible*. Vol. 1. New York: Abingdon, 1962.

Callen, Barry L. and Richard P. Thompson, eds. *Reading the Bible in Wesleyan Ways: Some Constructive Proposals*. Kansas City, MO: Beacon Hill, 2004.

Campbell, Ted A. *John Wesley and Christian Antiquity: Religious Vision and Cultural Change*. Nashville, TN: Kingswood, 1991.

_____. "Means of Grace and Forms of Piety." In *Oxford Handbook of Methodist Studies*, ed. William J. Abraham and James E. Kirby, 280-91. New York: Oxford University Press, 2009.

_____. *Methodist Doctrine: The Essentials*. Nashville, TN: Abingdon, 1999.

Charry, Ellen T. *By the Renewing of Your Minds: The Pastoral Function of Christian Doctrine*. New York: Oxford University Press, 1997.

Chilcote, Paul Wesley. *The Wesleyan Tradition: A Paradigm for Renewal*. Nashville, TN: Abingdon, 2002.

Childs, Brevard S. *Biblical Theology in Crisis*. Philadelphia: Westminster, 1970.

_____. *Biblical Theology of the Old and New Testaments: Theological Reflection on the Christian Bible*. Minneapolis: Fortress, 1993.

_____. "The Sensus Literalis of Scripture: An Ancient and Modern Problem," In *Beiträge zur Alttetamentlichen Theologie*, ed. Herbert Donner, et al., 80-93. Göttingen: Vandenhoeck & Ruprecht, 1977.

_____. "Speech-Act Theory and Biblical Interpretation." *Scottish Journal of Theology* 58 (2005): 375-92.

_____. "Toward Recovering Theological Exegesis." *Pro Ecclesia* 6 (1997): 16-26.

Clapper, Gregory S. "Wesley's 'Main Doctrines' and Spiritual Formation and Teaching in the Wesleyan Tradition." *Wesleyan Theological Journal* 39 (2004): 97-121.

Clines, David J. A., et al. *The Bible in Three Dimensions: Essays in Celebration of Forty Years of Biblical Studies in the University of Sheffield*. Journal for the Study of the Old Testament Supplement Series 87. Sheffield: JSOT, 1990.

Collins, Kenneth J. *John Wesley: A Theological Journey*. Nashville, TN: Abingdon, 2003.

_____. *The Theology of John Wesley: Holy Love and the Shape of Grace*. Nashville, TN: Abingdon, 2007.

Croatto, J. Severino. *Biblical Hermeneutics: Toward a Theory of Reading as the Production of Meaning*. Maryknoll, NY: Orbis, 1987.

Crockett, William R. *Eucharist: Symbol of Transformation*. New York: Pueblo, 1989.

Cummins, S. A. "The Theological Interpretation of Scripture: Recent Contributions by Stephen E. Fowl, Christopher R. Seitz and Francis Watson." *Currents in Biblical Research* 2 (2004): 179-96.

Cunningham, Mary Kathleen. *What Is Theological Exegesis? Karl Barth's Interpretation and Use of Scripture in His Doctrine of Election.* Valley Forge, PA: Trinity Press International, 1995.

Davaney, Sheila Greeve. *Historicism: The Once and Future Challenge for Theology.* Guides to Theological Inquiry. Minneapolis: Fortress, 2006.

Davis, Ellen F. and Richard B. Hays, eds. *The Art of Reading Scripture.* Grand Rapids, MI: Eerdmans, 2003.

_____ and Richard B. Hays. "Nine Theses on the Interpretation of Scripture." In *The Art of Reading Scripture*, ed. Ellen F. Davis and Richard B. Hays, 1-5. Grand Rapids, MI: Eerdmans, 2003.

Dawson, John David. *Christian Figural Reading and the Fashioning of Identity.* Berkeley: University of California Press, 2002.
_____. *Literary Theory.* Guides to Theological Inquiry. Minneapolis: Fortress, 1995.

Donner, Herbert, et al., eds. *Beiträge zur Alttestamentlichen Theologie: Festschrift für Walther Zimmerli zum 70. Geburtstag.* Göttingen: Vandenhoeck und Ruprecht, 1977.

Dunn, James D. G. *The New Perspective on Paul: Collected Essays.* Wissenschaftliche Untersuchungen zum Neuen Testament 185. Tübingen: Mohr Siebeck, 2005.

_____. *Romans.* 2 vols. WBC 38A-B. Dallas: Word, 1988.

_____. *Unity and Diversity in the New Testament: An Inquiry into the Character of Earliest Christianity.* 3rd ed. London: SCM, 2006.

Eberhard, Philippe. *The Middle Voice in Gadamer's Hermeneutics: A Basic Interpretation with Some Theological Implications.* Hermeneutische Untersuchungen zur Theologie 45. Tübingen: Mohr Siebeck, 2004.

Eco, Umberto. *Interpretation and Overinterpretation.* Cambridge: Cambridge University Press, 1992.

_____. *The Limits of Interpretation.* Bloomington: Indiana University Press, 1990.

_____. *The Role of the Reader: Explorations in the Semiotics of Texts.* Advances in Semiotics. Bloomington: Indiana University Press, 1979.

Erickson, John H. "Baptism and the Church's Faith." In *Marks of the Body of Christ*, ed. Carl E. Braaten and Robert W. Jenson, 44-58. Grand Rapids, MI: Eerdmans, 1999.

Fairclough, Norman. *Analysing Discourse: Textual Analysis for Social Research.* London: Routledge, 2003.

Farley, Edward. *Theologia: The Fragmentation and Unity of Theology Education*. Minneapolis: Fortress, 1983.

Farrow, Douglas. *Ascension and Ecclesia: On the Significance of the Doctrine of the Ascension for Ecclesiology and Christian Cosmology*. Grand Rapids, MI: Eerdmans, 1999.

Fish, Stanley. *Is There a Text in This Class? The Authority of Interpretive Communities*. Cambridge, MA: Harvard University Press, 1982.

Florovsky, Georges. *Collected Works of Georges Florovsky*. Belmont, MA: Nordland, 1972.

Ford, David. *Barth and God's Story: Biblical Narrative and the Theological Method of Karl Barth in the "Church Dogmatics"*. Frankfurt am Main: Peter Lang, 1981.

Fowl, Stephen E. *Engaging Scripture: A Model for Theological Interpretation*. Challenges in Contemporary Theology. Oxford: Blackwell, 1998.

_____. "The Importance of Multivoiced Literal Sense of Scripture." In *Reading Scripture with the Church: Toward a Hermeneutic for Theological Interpretation*, by A. K. M. Adam, et al., 35-50. Grand Rapids, MI: Baker Academic, 2006.

_____. "Introduction," In *The Theological Interpretation of Scripture: Classic and Contemporary Readings*, ed. Stephen E. Fowl, xii-xxx. Blackwell Readings in Modern Theology. Cambridge: Blackwell, 1997.

_____. *Theological Interpretation of Scripture*. Eugene, OR: Cascade Companions, 2009.

_____, ed. *The Theological Interpretation of Scripture: Classic and Contemporary Readings*. Blackwell Readings in Modern Theology. Cambridge: Blackwell, 1997.

Fowl, Stephen E. and L. Gregory Jones. *Reading in Communion: Scripture and Ethics in Christian Life*. Eugene, OR: Wipf and Stock, 1998.

Frei, Hans W. *The Eclipse of Biblical Narrative: A Study in Eighteenth and Nineteenth Century Hermeneutics*. New Haven, CT: Yale University Press, 1974.

_____. *The Identity of Jesus Christ: The Hermeneutical Bases of Dogmatic Theology*. Eugene, OR: Wipf and Stock, 1997.

_____. "The 'Literal Reading' of Biblical Narrative in the Christian Tradition: Does It Stretch or Will It Break?" In *Theology and Narrative: Selected Essays*, ed. George Hunsinger and William C. Placher, 117-52. New York: Oxford University Press, 1993.

Bibliography

———. "'Narrative' in Christian and Modern Reading." In *Theology and Dialogue: Essays in Conversation with George Lindbeck*, ed. Bruce D. Marshall, 149-63. Notre Dame, IN: University of Notre Dame Press, 1990.

———. "Response to 'Narrative Theology: An Evangelical Appraisal.'" In *Theology and Narrative: Selected Essays*, ed. George Hunsinger and William C. Placher, 207-12. New York: Oxford University Press, 1993.

———. "Theological Reflections on the Accounts of Jesus' Death and Resurrection." In *The Identity of Jesus Christ: The Hermeneutical Bases of Dogmatic Theology*, 1-49. Eugene, OR: Wipf and Stock, 1997.

———. *Theology and Narrative: Selected Essays*. Edited by George Hunsinger and William C. Placher. New York: Oxford University Press, 1993.

———. "Theology and the Interpretation of Narrative: Some Hermeneutical Considerations." In *Theology and Narrative: Selected Essays*, ed. George Hunsinger and William C. Placher, 94-116. New York: Oxford University Press, 1993.

———. *Types of Christian Theology*. Edited by George Hunsinger and William C. Placher. New Haven, CT: Yale University Press, 1992.

Gadamer, Hans-Georg. *Philosophical Hermeneutics*. Berkeley: University of California Press, 1976.

———. *Truth and Method*. Translated and edited by Joel Weinsheimer and Donald G. Marshall. 2nd ed. London: Continuum, 2004.

Goldingay, John. *Models for Scripture*. Grand Rapids, MI: Eerdmans, 1994.

Gorman, Michael J. *Apostle of the Crucified Lord: A Theological Introduction to Paul and His Letters*. Grand Rapids, MI: Eerdmans, 2004.

Grafton, Anthony. *Defenders of the Text: The Traditions of Scholarship in an Age of Science, 1450-1800*. Cambridge, MA: Harvard University Press, 1991.

Grant, Robert M. and David Tracy. *A Short History of the Interpretation of the Bible*. 2nd ed. Philadelphia: Fortress, 1984.

Green, Garrett. *Imagining God: Theology and the Religious Imagination*. San Francisco: Harper & Row, 1989.

———, ed. *Scriptural Authority and Narrative Interpretation*. Eugene, OR: Wipf and Stock, 2000.

———. *Theology, Hermeneutics, and Imagination: The Crisis of Interpretation at the End of Modernity*. Cambridge: Cambridge University Press, 2000.

Green, Joel B. "Context." In *Dictionary for Theological Interpretation of the Bible*, ed. Kevin J. Vanhoozer, 130-33. Grand Rapids, MI: Baker Academic, 2005.

_____. "Contribute or Capitulate? Wesleyans, Pentecostals and Reading the Bible in a Post-Colonial Mode." *Wesleyan Theological Journal* 39 (2004): 74-90.

_____, ed. *Hearing the New Testament: Strategies for Interpretation*. Grand Rapids, MI: Eerdmans, 1995.

_____. "Is There a Contemporary Wesleyan Hermeneutic?" In *Reading the Bible in Wesleyan Ways: Some Constructive Proposals*, ed. Barry L. Callen and Richard P. Thompson, 123-34. Kansas City, MO: Beacon Hill, 2004.

_____. "Scripture and Theology: Uniting the Two So Long Divided." In *Between Two Horizons: Spanning New Testament Studies and Systematic Theology*, ed. Joel B. Green and Max Turner, 23-43. Grand Rapids, MI: Eerdmans, 2000.

_____. "Scripture in the Church: Reconstructing the Authority of Scripture for Christian Formation and Mission." In *The Wesleyan Tradition: A Paradigm for Renewal*, ed. Paul W. Chilcote, 38-51. Nashville, TN: Abingdon, 2002.

_____. *Seized by Truth: Reading the Bible as Scripture*. Nashville, TN: Abingdon, 2007.

_____. *The Theology of the Gospel of Luke*. New Testament Theology. Cambridge: Cambridge University Press, 1995.

Green, Joel B., and Scot McKnight, eds. *Dictionary of Jesus and the Gospels*. Downers Grove, IL: InterVarsity, 1992.

Green, Joel B., and Michael Pasquarello III, eds. *Narrative Reading, Narrative Preaching: Reuniting New Testament Interpretation and Proclamation*. Grand Rapids, MI: Baker, 2003.

Green, Joel B., and Max Turner, eds. *Between Two Horizons: Spanning New Testament Studies and Systematic Theology*. Grand Rapids, MI: Eerdmans, 2000.

Green, Joel B., and David F. Watson, eds. *Wesley, Wesleyans, and Reading Bible as Scripture*. Waco, TX: Baylor University Press, 2012.

Greene-McCreight, Kathryn. *Ad Litteram: How Augustine, Calvin, and Barth Read the "Plain Sense" of Genesis 1-3*. Issues in Systematic Theology 5. New York: Peter Lang, 1999.

_____. "Literal Sense." In *Dictionary for Theological Interpretation of the Bible*, ed. Kevin J. Vanhoozer, 455-56. Grand Rapids, MI: Baker Academic, 2005.

──────. "Rule of Faith." In *Dictionary for Theological Interpretation of the Bible*, ed. Kevin J. Vanhoozer, 703-04. Grand Rapids, MI: Baker Academic, 2005.

Grider, Kenneth J. "Wesleyanism and the Inerrancy Issue." *Wesleyan Theological Journal* 19 (1984): 51-61.

Grondin, Jean. *Introduction to Philosophical Hermeneutics*. Yale Studies in Hermeneutics. New Haven, CT: Yale University Press, 1994.

Gunton, Colin E. *The Cambridge Companion to Christian Doctrine*. Cambridge Companions to Religion. Cambridge: Cambridge University Press, 1997.

Gunter, Stephen W., et al. *Wesley and the Quadrilateral: Renewing the Conversation*. Nashville, TN: Abingdon, 1997.

Hafemann, Scott J. *Biblical Theology: Retrospect and Prospect*. Downers Grove, IL: InterVarsity, 2002.

Harrison, Peter. *The Bible, Protestantism, and the Rise of Natural Science*. Cambridge: Cambridge University Press, 1998.

Hart, Trevor. "Tradition, Authority, and a Christian Approach." In *Between Two Horizons: Spanning New Testament Studies and Systematic Theology*, ed. Joel B. Green and Max Turner, 183-204. Grand Rapids, MI: Eerdmans, 2000.

Hauerwas, Stanley and L. Gregory Jones, eds. *Why Narrative? Readings in Narrative Theology*. Eugene, OR: Wipf and Stock, 1997.

Hawthorne, Gerald F., et al, eds. *Dictionary of Paul and His Letters*. Downers Grove, IL: InterVarsity, 1993.

Hays, Richard B. "Can Narrative Criticism Recover the Theological Unity of Scripture?" *Journal of Theological Interpretation* 2 (2008): 193-211.

──────. *The Conversion of the Imagination: Paul as Interpreter of Israel's Scripture*. Grand Rapids, MI: Eerdmans, 2005.

──────. *Echoes of Scripture in the Letters of Paul*. New Haven, CT: Yale University Press, 1989.

──────. *The Moral Vision of the New Testament: Community, Cross, New Creation: A Contemporary Introduction to New Testament Ethics*. San Francisco: HarperSanFrancisco, 1996.

Healy, Nicholas. "Hermeneutics and the Apostolic Form of the Church: David Demson's Question." *Toronto Journal of Theology* 17 (2001): 17-32.

Heitzenrater, Richard P. *The Elusive Mr. Wesley: John Wesley His Own Biographer*. Vol. 1. Nashville, TN: Abingdon, 1984.

_____. *The Elusive Mr. Wesley: John Wesley as Seen by Contemporaries and Biographers*. Vol. 2. Nashville, TN: Abingdon, 1984.

Hempton, David. *Methodism: Empire of the Spirit*. New Haven, CT: Yale University Press, 2005.

Higton, Mike. *Christ, Providence and History: Hans W. Frei's Public Theology*. London: T & T Clark, 2004.

_____. "Frei's Christology and Lindbeck's Cultural-Linguistic Theory." *Scottish Journal of Theology* 50 (1997): 92-94.

Holmer, Paul L. *The Grammar of Faith*. San Francisco: Harper & Row, 1978.

Howell, Kenneth J. *God's Two Books: Copernican Cosmology and Biblical Interpretation in Early Modern Science*. Notre Dame, IN: University of Notre Dame Press, 2002.

Hunsinger, George. "Afterword: Hans Frei as Theologian." In Hans W. Frei, *Theology and Narrative: Selected Essays,* ed. George Hunsinger and William C. Placher, 233-70. New York: Oxford University Press, 1993.

_____. *Disruptive Grace: Studies in the Theology of Karl Barth*. Grand Rapids, MI: Eerdmans, 2000.

_____. *How to Read Karl Barth: The Shape of His Theology*. New York: Oxford University Press, 1991.

_____. "Postliberal Theology." In *The Cambridge Companion to Postmodern Theology*, ed. Kevin Vanhoozer, 42-57. Cambridge Companions to Religion. Cambridge: Cambridge University Press, 2003.

Hütter, Reinhard. *Suffering Divine Things: Theology as Church Practice*. Grand Rapids, MI: Eerdmans, 2000.

Inge, John. *A Christian Theology of Place*. Explorations in Practical, Pastoral, and Empirical Theology. Aldershot: Ashgate, 2003.

Iser, Wolfgang. *How to Do Theory*. How to Study Literature. Malden, MA: Blackwell, 2006.

Jeanrond, Werner G. "Karl Barth's Hermeneutics." In *Reckoning with Barth*, ed. Nigel Biggar, 80-97. Oxford: Mowbray, 1988.

_____. *Text and Interpretation as Categories of Theological Thinking.* New York: Crossroad, 1988.

_____. *Theological Hermeneutics: Development and Significance.* New York: Crossroad, 1991.

Jenson, Robert W. *Systematic Theology.* 2 vols. New York: Oxford University Press, 1997.

Johnson, Luke Timothy. "Fragments of an Untidy Conversation: Theology and the Literary Diversity of the New Testament." In *Biblical Theology: Problems and Perspectives*, ed. Steven J. Kraftchick Jr., et al., 276-89. Nashville, TN: Abingdon, 1995.

_____. "Imagining the World Scripture Imagines." In *Theology and Scriptural Imagination: Directions in Modern Theology*, ed. L. Gregory Jones and James J. Buckley, 3-18. Oxford: Blackwell, 1998.

Jones, L. Gregory. "Formed and Transformed by Scripture: Character, Community, and Authority in Biblical Interpretation." In *Character and Scripture: Moral Formation, Community, and Biblical Interpretation*, ed. William P. Brown, 18-33. Grand Rapids, MI: Eerdmans, 2002.

Jones, L. Gregory and James J. Buckley, eds., *Theology and Scriptural Imagination.* Directions in Modern Theology. Oxford: Blackwell, 1998.

Jones, Scott J. *John Wesley's Conception and Use of Scripture.* Nashville, TN: Kingswood, 1995.

_____. "The Rule of Scripture." In *Wesley and the Quadrilateral: Renewing the Conversation.* Gunter, Stephen W., et al. Nashville, TN: Abingdon, 1997.

Kavanagh, Aidan. *The Shape of Baptism: The Rite of Christian Initiation.* New York: Pueblo, 1978.

Kelsey, David H. *Proving Doctrine: The Uses of Scripture in Modern Theology.* Harrisburg, PA: Trinity Press International, 1999.

Kimbrough, S. T., Jr., ed. *Orthodox and Wesleyan Scriptural Understanding and Practice.* Crestwood, NY: St. Vladimir's Seminary Press, 2005.

Kinzig, Wolfram and Markus Vinzent. "Recent Research on the Origin of the Creed." *Journal of Theological Studies* 50 (1999): 535-59.

Klemperer, Klemens von. "Beyond Luther? Dietrich Bonhoeffer and Resistance against National Socialism." *Pro Ecclesia* 6 (1997): 184-98.

Knight, Henry H. III. *The Presence of God in the Christian Life: John Wesley and the Means of Grace*. Pietist and Wesleyan Studies 3. Metuchen, NJ: Scarecrow, 1992.

Kort, Wesley A. *"Take, Read": Scripture, Textuality, and Cultural Practice*. University Park: Pennsylvania State University Press, 1996.

Koskie, Steven J. "Can We Speak of a Wesleyan Theological Hermeneutic of Scripture Today?" In *Wesley, Wesleyans, and Reading Bible as Scripture*, ed. Joel B. Green and David F. Watson, 195-209. Waco, TX: Baylor University Press, 2012.

Kraftchick, Steven John, et al., eds. *Biblical Theology: Problems and Perspectives*. Nashville, TN: Abingdon, 1995.

Kugel, James L. and Rowan A. Greer. *Early Biblical Interpretation*. Philadelphia: Westminster, 1986.

Langford, Thomas A. *Practical Divinity: Theology in the Wesleyan Tradition*. Nashville, TN: Abingdon, 1983.

Lash, Nicholas. "Ideology, Metaphor, and Analogy." In *Why Narrative? Readings in Narrative Theology*, ed. Stanley Hauerwas and L. Gregory Jones, 113-37. Eugene, OR: Wipf and Stock, 1997.

_____. *Theology on the Way to Emmaus*. Eugene, OR: Wipf and Stock, 2005.

Lee, David. *Luke's Stories of Jesus: Theological Reading of Gospel Narrative and the Legacy of Hans Frei*. Journal for the Study of the New Testament Supplement Series 185. Sheffield: Sheffield Academic Press, 1999.

Lessing, Gotthold. *Lessing's Theological Writings*. Edited by Henry Chadwick. London: Adam & Charles Black, 1956.

Levering, Matthew. *Participatory Biblical Exegesis: A Theology of Biblical Interpretation*. Notre Dame, IN: University of Notre Dame Press, 2008.

Lindbeck, George A. "Barth and Textuality." *Theology Today* 43 (1986): 361-76.

_____. *The Nature of Doctrine: Religion and Theology in a Postliberal Age*. Philadelphia: Westminster, 1984.

_____. "The Story-Shaped Church: Critical Exegesis and Theological Interpretation." In Scriptural *Authority and Narrative Interpretation*, ed. Garrett Green, 161-78. Eugene, OR: Wipf and Stock, 1987.

Long, D. Stephen. *John Wesley's Moral Theology: The Quest for God and Goodness*. Nashville, TN: Kingswood, 2005.

Lossky, Vladimir. *The Mystical Theology of the Eastern Church.* Crestwood, NY: St. Vladimir's Seminary Press, 1976.

Loughlin, Gerard. *Telling God's Story: Bible, Church and Narrative Theology.* Cambridge: Cambridge University Press, 1999.

Lowenthal, David. *The Past Is a Foreign Country.* Cambridge: Cambridge University Press, 1985.

Lubac, Henri de. *Medieval Exegesis: The Four Senses of Scripture.* Vol. 1. Grand Rapids, MI: Eerdmans, 1998.

MacIntyre, Alasdair C. *Whose Justice? Which Rationality?* Notre Dame, IN: University of Notre Dame Press, 1988.

_____. *Three Rival Versions of Moral Enquiry: Encyclopaedia, Genealogy, and Tradition.* Notre Dame, IN: University of Notre Dame Press, 1989.

Maddox, Randy L. "The Recovery of Theology as a Practical Discipline." *Theological Studies* 51 (1990): 650-72.

_____. "Respected Founder / Neglected Guide: The Role of Wesley in American Methodist Theology." *Methodist History* 37 (1999): 71-88.

_____. *Responsible Grace: John Wesley's Practical Theology.* Nashville, TN: Kingswood, 1994.

_____, ed. *Rethinking Wesley's Theology for Contemporary Methodism.* Nashville, TN: Kingswood, 1998.

Maddox, Randy L. and Jason E. Vickers, eds. *The Cambridge Companion to John Wesley.* Cambridge Companions to Religion. Cambridge: Cambridge University Press, 2009.

Marshall, Bruce D. "Aquinas as Postliberal Theologian." *The Thomist* 53 (1989): 353-406.

_____. ed. *Theology and Dialogue: Essays in Conversation with George Lindbeck.* Notre Dame, IN: University of Notre Dame Press, 1990.

Martin, Troy W. "John Wesley's Exegetical Orientation: East or West." *Wesleyan Theological Journal* 26 (1991): 104-38.

Matthews, R. D. "Religion and Reason Joined: A Study in the Theology of John Wesley." Th.D. Thesis, Harvard University, 1986.

McCormack, Bruce. "Historical-Criticism and Dogmatic Interest in Karl Barth's Theological Exegesis of the New Testament." *Lutheran Quarterly* 5 (1991): 211-25.

_____. *Karl Barth's Critically Realistic Dialectical Theology: Its Genesis and Development, 1909-1936*. Oxford: Clarendon, 1995.

McGrath, Alister E. *The Genesis of Doctrine: A Study in the Foundation of Doctrinal Criticism*. Grand Rapids, MI: Eerdmans, 1990.

McKnight, Edgar V. and Elizabeth Struthers Malbon, eds. *The New Literary Criticism and the New Testament*. Valley Forge, PA: Trinity Press International, 1994.

Mead, James K. *Biblical Theology: Issues, Methods, and Themes*. Louisville, KY: Westminster John Knox, 2007.

Meadows, Philip R. "The 'Discipline' of Theology: Making Methodism Less Methodological." *Wesleyan Theological Journal* 36 (2001): 50-87.

Moberly, R. W. L. *The Bible, Theology, and Faith: A Study of Abraham and Jesus*. Cambridge Companions in Christian Doctrine. Cambridge: Cambridge University Press, 2000.

Moore, Stephen D. *Literary Criticism and the Gospels: The Theoretical Challenge*. New Haven, CT: Yale University Press, 1989.

Morgan, Robert and John Barton. *Biblical Interpretation*. New York: Oxford University Press, 1988.

Morton, Russell. "Studying Text in a Wesleyan 'Context': A Response to Robert Wall and Joel Green." *Wesleyan Theological Journal* 34 (1999): 243-57.

Mullen, Wilbur H. "John Wesley's Method of Biblical Interpretation." *Religion in Life* (1978): 99-108.

Muller, Richard A. *Prolegomena to Theology*. Post-Reformation Reformed Dogmatics: The Rise and Development of Reformed Orthodoxy, ca. 1520 to ca. 1725. Vol. 1. Grand Rapids, MI: Baker Academic, 2003.

Muller, Richard A. *Holy Scripture: The Cognitive Foundation of Theology*. Post-Reformation Reformed Dogmatics: The Rise and Development of Reformed Orthodoxy, ca. 1520 to ca. 1725. Vol. 2. Grand Rapids, MI: Baker Academic, 2003.

Nassif, Braley, ed. *New Perspectives on Historical Theology: Essays in Memory of John Meyendorff*. Grand Rapids, MI: Eerdmans, 1996.

Noble, Paul R. "The *Sensus Literalis*: Jowett, Childs, and Barr." *Journal of Theological Studies* 44 (1993): 1-23.

O'Collins, Gerald and Daniel Kendall. *The Bible for Theology: Ten Principles for the Theological Use of Scripture*. New York: Paulist, 1997.

O'Keefe, John J. and R. R. Reno. *Sanctified Vision: An Introduction to Early Christian Interpretation of the Bible*. Baltimore, MD: Johns Hopkins University Press, 2005.

Ochs, Peter, ed. *The Return of Scripture in Judaism and Christianity: Essays in Postcritical Scriptural Interpretation*. New York: Paulist, 1993.

Oden, Thomas C. *John Wesley's Scriptural Christianity: A Plain Exposition of His Teaching on Christian Doctrine*. Grand Rapids, MI: Zondervan, 1994.

Osborn, Eric. "Reason and the Rule of Faith in the Second Century A.D." In *The Making of Orthodoxy: Essays in Honour of Henry Chadwick*, ed. Rowan Williams, 40-61. Cambridge: Cambridge University Press, 1989.

Outler, Albert Cook. *Theology in the Wesleyan Spirit*. Nashville, TN: Discipleship Resources, 1975.

_____. "The Wesleyan Quadrilateral—in John Wesley." In *The Wesleyan Theological Heritage: Essays of Albert C. Outler*, 21-37. Grand Rapids, MI: Zondervan, 1991.

Outler, Albert Cook, ed. *John Wesley*. New York: Oxford University Press, 1964.

Outler, Albert Cook, et al. *The Wesleyan Theological Heritage: Essays of Albert C. Outler*. Grand Rapids, MI: Zondervan, 1991.

Palmer, Richard E. *Hermeneutics: Interpretation Theory in Schleiermacher, Dilthey, Heidegger, and Gadamer*. Northwestern University Studies in Phenomenology and Existential Philosophy. Evanston, IL: Northwestern University Press, 1969.

Pasquarello, Michael, III. *Christian Preaching: A Trinitarian Theology of Proclamation*. Grand Rapids, MI: Baker Academic, 2006.

Phelan, James. *Narrative as Rhetoric: Technique, Audiences, Ethics, Ideology*. The Theory and Interpretation of Narrative Series. Columbus: Ohio State University Press, 1996.

Phillips, Thomas E. "Reading Theory and Biblical Interpretation." *Wesleyan Theological Journal* 35 (2000): 32-48.

Powell, Samuel M. and Michael E. Lodahl. *Embodied Holiness: Toward a Corporate Theology of Spiritual Growth*. Downers Grove, IL: InterVarsity, 1999.

Preuss, James Samuel. *From Shadow to Promise: Old Testament Interpretation from Augustine to the Young Luther*. Cambridge: Belknap, 1969.

Radner, Ephraim. *The End of the Church: A Pneumatology of Christian Division in the West*. Grand Rapids, MI: Eerdmans, 1998.

———. *Hope among the Fragments: The Broken Church and Its Engagement of Scripture*. Grand Rapids, MI: Brazos, 2004.

Radner, Ephraim and George R. Sumner. *The Rule of Faith: Scripture, Canon, and Creed in a Critical Age*. Harrisburg, PA: Morehouse, 1998.

Räisänen, Heikki. *Beyond New Testament Theology: A Story and a Programme*. 2nd ed. London: SCM, 2001.

Reno, R. R. "Biblical Theology and Theological Exegesis." In *Out of Egypt: Biblical Theology and Biblical Interpretation*, ed. Craig G., Bartholomew, et al., 385-408. Scripture and Hermeneutics Series 5. Grand Rapids, MI: Zondervan, 2004.

———. *In the Ruins of the Church: Sustaining Faith in an Age of Diminished Christianity*. Grand Rapids, MI: Brazos, 2002.

———. "Origen and Spiritual Interpretation." *Pro Ecclesia* 15 (2006): 108-26.

———. "Series Preface." In *Acts*, by Jaroslav Pelikan. Brazos Theological Commentary on the Bible. Grand Rapids, MI: Brazos, 2005.

Reventlow, Henning Graf. *The Authority of the Bible and the Rise of the Modern World*. Philadelphia: Fortress, 1985.

Richey, Russell E, et al. *Marks of Methodism: Theology in Ecclesial Practice*. United Methodism and American Culture 5. Nashville, TN: Abingdon, 2005.

Ricoeur, Paul. *The Conflict of Interpretation: Essays in Hermeneutics*. Evanston, IL: Northwestern University Press, 1974.

———. *Interpretation Theory: Discourse and the Surplus of Meaning*. Fort Worth, TX: Texas Christian University Press, 1976.

Ricoeur, Paul and John B. Thompson. *Hermeneutics and the Human Sciences: Essays on Language, Action, and Interpretation*. Cambridge: Cambridge University Press, 1981.

Roberts, Alexander, et al. *Ante-Nicene Fathers: The Writings of the Fathers Down to A.D. 325*. Peabody, MA: Hendrickson Publishers, 2004.

Rogers, Eugene, F. Jr. "How the Virtues of an Interpreter Presuppose and Perfect Hermeneutics: The Case of Thomas Aquinas." *The Journal of Religion* 76 (1996): 64-81.

———. "The Mystery of the Spirit in Three Traditions: Calvin, Rahner, Florensky or, You Keep Wondering Where the Spirit Went." *Modern Theology* 19 (2003): 243-60.

Rogers, Jack Bartlett and Donald K. McKim. *The Authority and Interpretation of the Bible: An Historical Approach.* San Francisco: Harper & Row, 1979.

Rowe, C. Kavin. "Biblical Pressure and Trinitarian Hermeneutics." *Pro Ecclesia* 11 (2002): 295-312.

Runyon, Theodore. *The New Creation: John Wesley's Theology Today.* Nashville, TN: Abingdon, 1998.

Ruth, Lester. *Early Methodist Life and Spirituality: A Reader.* Nashville, TN: Kingswood, 2005.

Sanders, E. P. *Paul and Palestinian Judaism: A Comparison of Patterns of Religion.* Philadelphia: Fortress, 1977.

Sandys-Wunsch, John and Laurence Eldredge. "J. P. Gabler and the Distinction between Biblical and Dogmatic Theology: Translation, Commentary, and Discussion of His Originality." *Scottish Journal of Theology* 33 (1980): 133-58.

Scalise, Charles J. *Hermeneutics as Theological Prolegomena: A Canonical Approach.* Studies in American Biblical Hermeneutics 8. Macon, GA: Mercer University Press, 1994.

Schneiders, Sandra Marie. *The Revelatory Text: Interpreting the New Testament as Sacred Scripture.* San Francisco: Harper San Francisco, 1991.

Schwartzentruber, Paul. "The Modesty of Hermeneutics: The Theological Reserves of Hans Frei." *Modern Theology* 8 (1992): 181-95.

Scobie, Charles H. H. "History of Biblical Theology." In *New Dictionary of Biblical Theology*, ed. T. Desmond Alexander, et al., 11-20. Leicester: Inter-Varsity, 2000.

_____. *The Ways of Our God: An Approach to Biblical Theology.* Grand Rapids, MI: Eerdmans, 2003.

Seitz, Christopher. "Christological Interpretation of Texts and Trinitarian Truth Claims: An Engagement with Francis Watson's *Text and Truth*." *Scottish Journal of Theology* 52 (1999): 209-26.

_____. *Figured Out: Typology and Providence in Christian Scripture.* Louisville, KY: Westminster John Knox, 2001.

_____. *Nicene Christianity: The Future for a New Ecumenism.* Grand Rapids, MI: Brazos, 2001.

_____. "Two Testaments and the Failure of One Tradition History." In *Biblical Theology: Retrospect and Prospect*, ed. Scott J. Hafemann, 195-211. Downers Grove, IL: Intervarsity, 2002.

_____. *Word without End: The Old Testament as Abiding Theological Witness*. Grand Rapids, MI: Eerdmans, 1998.

Seitz, Christopher and Kathryn Greene-McCreight, eds. *Theological Exegesis: Essays in Honor of Brevard S. Childs*. Grand Rapids, MI: Eerdmans, 1999.

Shelton, Larry. "John Wesley's Approach to Scripture in Historical Perspective." *Wesleyan Theological Journal* 16 (1981): 23-50.

Smith, Timothy, L. "John Wesley and the Wholeness of Scripture." *Interpretation* 39 (1985): 246-62.

Spina, Frank. "Wesleyan Faith Seeking Biblical Understanding." *Wesleyan Theological Journal* 30 (1995): 26-49.

Spinks, D. Christopher. *The Bible and the Crisis of Meaning: Debates on the Theological Interpretation of Scripture*. London: T&T Clark, 2007.

Springs, Jason A. "Between Barth and Wittgenstein: On the Availability of Hans Frei's Later Theology." *Modern Theology* 23 (2007): 393-413.

Stacey, John. *John Wesley: Contemporary Perspectives*. London: Epworth, 1988.

Steele, Richard B. *"Heart Religion" in the Methodist Tradition and Related Movements*. Lanham, MD: Scarecrow, 2001.

Steinmetz, David C. *Luther in Context*. Bloomington: Indiana University Press, 1986.

_____."The Superiority of Pre-Critical Exegesis." In *The Theological Interpretation of Scripture: Classic and Contemporary Readings*, ed. Stephen E. Fowl, 26-38. Blackwell Readings in Modern Theology. Oxford: Blackwell, 1997.

Stendahl, Krister. "Biblical Theology, Contemporary." In *Interpreter's Dictionary of the Bible*, ed. G. A. Buttrick, 418-32. Vol. 1. New York: Abingdon, 1962.

Stiver, Dan R. *Theology after Ricoeur: New Directions in Hermeneutical Theology*. Louisville, KY: Westminster John Knox, 2001.

Stuckenbruck, Loren T. "Johann Philipp Gabler and the Delineation of Biblical Theology." *Scottish Journal of Theology* 52 (1999): 139-57.

Sykes, Stephen. *Karl Barth: Studies of His Theological Method*. Oxford: Clarendon, 1979.

Tanner, Kathryn E. "Theology and the Plain Sense." In *Scriptural Authority and Narrative Interpretation*, ed. Garrett Green, 59-78. Eugene, OR: Wipf and Stock, 1987.

Thiemann, Ronald F. *Revelation and Theology: The Gospel as Narrated Promise.* Notre Dame, IN: University of Notre Dame Press, 1985.

Thiselton, Anthony C. *New Horizons in Hermeneutics.* Grand Rapids, MI: Zondervan, 1992.

_____. *The Two Horizons: New Testament Hermeneutics and Philosophical Description with Special Reference to Heidegger, Bultmann, Gadamer, and Wittgenstein.* Grand Rapids, MI: Eerdmans, 1980.

Thompson, Richard P. "Inspired Imagination: John Wesley's Concept of Biblical Inspiration and Literary-Critical Studies." In *Reading the Bible in Wesleyan Ways: Some Constructive Proposals*, ed. Barry L. Callen and Richard P. Thompson, 57-79. Kansas City, MO: Beacon Hill, 2004.

Thorsen, Donald A. D. *The Wesleyan Quadrilateral: Scripture, Tradition, Reason and Experience as a Model of Evangelical Theology.* Grand Rapids, MI: Zondervan, 1990.

_____. "Interpretation in Interactive Balance: The Authority of Scripture for John Wesley." In *Reading the Bible in Wesleyan Ways: Some Constructive Proposals*, ed. Barry L. Callen and Richard P. Thompson, 81-104. Kansas City, MO: Beacon Hill, 2004.

Tilley, Terrence W. *History, Theology, and Faith: Dissolving the Modern Problematic.* Maryknoll, NY: Orbis, 2004.

Tjørhom, Ola. *Visible Church, Visible Unity: Ecumenical Ecclesiology and "the Great Tradition of the Church."* Collegeville, MN: Liturgical, 2004.

Treier, Daniel J. *Introducing Theological Interpretation of Scripture: Recovering a Christian Practice.* Grand Rapids, MI: Baker Academic, 2008.

_____. "Theological Hermeneutics, Contemporary." In *Dictionary for Theological Interpretation of the Bible*, ed. Kevin Vanhoozer, 787-93. Grand Rapids, MI: Baker Academic, 2005.

_____. *Virtue and the Voice of God: Toward Theology as Wisdom.* Grand Rapids, MI: Eerdmans, 2006.

Turner, Max and Joel B. Green. "New Testament Commentary and Systematic Theology: Strangers or Friends?" In *Between Two Horizons: Spanning New Testament Studies and Systematic Theology*, ed. Joel B. Green and Max Turner, 1-22. Grand Rapids, MI: Eerdmans, 2000.

United Methodist Church, The. *The Book of Discipline of The United Methodist Church.* Nashville, TN: United Methodist Publishing House, 2004.

Vanhoozer, Kevin J. *The Cambridge Companion to Postmodern Theology*. Cambridge Companions to Religion. Cambridge: Cambridge University Press, 2003.

_____, ed. *Dictionary for Theological Interpretation of the Bible*. Grand Rapids, MI: Baker Academic, 2005.

_____. *The Drama of Doctrine: A Canonical-Linguistic Approach to Christian Theology*. Louisville, KY: Westminster John Knox, 2005.

_____. *First Theology: God, Scripture and Hermeneutics*. Downers Grove, IL: InterVarsity, 2002.

_____. "Four Theological Faces of Biblical Interpretation." In *Reading Scripture with the Church: Toward a Hermeneutic for Theological Interpretation*, by A. K. M. Adam, et al., 131-42. Grand Rapids, MI: Baker Academic, 2006.

_____. "Introduction: What Is Theological Interpretation of the Bible?" In *Dictionary for Theological Interpretation of the Bible*, ed. Kevin Vanhoozer, 19-25. Grand Rapids, MI: Baker Academic, 2005.

_____. *Is There a Meaning in This Text? The Bible, the Reader, and the Morality of Literary Knowledge*. Grand Rapids, MI: Zondervan, 1998.

Vickers, Jason E. "Wesley's Theological Emphases." In *The Cambridge Companion to John Wesley*. Cambridge Companions to Religion, ed. Randy L. Maddox and Jason E. Vickers, 190-206. Cambridge: Cambridge University Press, 2009.

Wainwright, Geoffrey. *Doxology: The Praise of God in Worship, Doctrine, and Life*. New York: Oxford University Press, 1980.

_____. *Eucharist and Eschatology*. London: Epworth, 1971, 1973 printing.

_____. *Methodists in Dialog*. Nashville, TN: Kingswood, 1995.

_____. "Tradition and the Spirit of Faith in a Methodist Perspective." In *New Perspectives on Historical Theology: Essays in Honor of John Meyendorff*, ed. Braley Nassif, 45-69. Grand Rapids, MI: Eerdmans, 1996.

_____. "The Trinitarian Hermeneutic of John Wesley." In *Reading the Bible in Wesleyan Ways: Some Constructive Proposals*, ed. Barry L. Callen and Richard P. Thompson, 17-37. Kansas City, MO: Beacon Hill, 2004.

_____. "Trinitarian Theology and Wesleyan Holiness." In *Orthodox and Wesleyan Spirituality*, ed. S.T. Kimbrough Jr., 59-80. Crestwood, NY: St. Vladimir's Seminary Press, 2002.

Bibliography

Wall, Robert W. "Facilitating Scripture's Future Role among Wesleyans." In *Reading the Bible in Wesleyan Ways: Some Constructive Proposals*, ed. Barry L. Callen and Richard P. Thompson, 107-20. Kansas City, MO: Beacon Hill, 2004.

_____. "Reading the Bible from within Our Traditions: The 'Rule of Faith' and Theological Hermeneutics." In *Between Two Horizons: Spanning New Testament Studies and Systematic Theology*, ed. Joel B. Green and Max Turner, 88-107. Grand Rapids, MI: Eerdmans, 2000.

_____. "Reading the New Testament in Canonical Context." In *Hearing the New Testament: Strategies for Interpretation*, ed. Joel B. Green, 370-93. Grand Rapids, MI: Eerdmans, 1995.

_____. "Toward a Wesleyan Hermeneutic of Scripture." In *Reading the Bible in Wesleyan Ways: Some Constructive Proposals*, ed. Barry L. Callen and Richard P. Thompson, 39-55. Kansas City, MO: Beacon Hill, 2004.

_____. "Wesley as Biblical Interpreter." In *The Cambridge Companion to John Wesley*, Cambridge Companions to Religion, ed. Randy L. Maddox and Jason E. Vickers, 113-28. Cambridge: Cambridge University Press, 2009.

Wallace, Mark I. *The Second Naiveté: Barth, Ricoeur, and the New Yale Theology*. Studies in American Biblical Hermeneutics 6. Macon, GA: Mercer University Press, 1990.

Watson, Francis. "Are There Still Four Gospels? A Study in Theological Hermeneutics." In *Reading Scripture with the Church: Toward a Hermeneutic for Theological Interpretation*, by A. K. M. Adam, et al., 95-97. Grand Rapids, MI: Baker Academic, 2006.

_____. "The Bible." In *The Cambridge Companion to Karl Barth*, ed. John Webster, 57-71. Cambridge Companions to Religion. Cambridge: Cambridge University Press, 2000.

_____. "The Old Testament as Christian Scripture: A Response to Professor Seitz." *Scottish Journal of Theology* 50 (1999): 227-32.

_____. *Paul and the Hermeneutics of Faith*. London: T & T Clark, 2004.

_____. "Paul the Reader: An Authorial Apologia." *Journal for the Study of the New Testament* 28 (2006): 363-73.

_____. *Text and Truth: Redefining Biblical Theology*. Grand Rapids, MI: Eerdmans, 1997.

_____. *Text, Church, and World: Biblical Interpretation in Theological Perspective*. Grand Rapids, MI: Eerdmans, 1994.

Webster, John B. *The Cambridge Companion to Karl Barth*. Cambridge Companions to Religion. Cambridge: Cambridge University Press, 2000.

_____. "Hermeneutics in Modern Theology: Some Doctrinal Reflections." *Scottish Journal of Theology* 51 (1998): 307-41.

_____. *Holy Scripture: A Dogmatic Sketch*. Current Issues in Theology. Cambridge: Cambridge University Press, 2003.

Webster, John B. and George P. Schner, eds. *Theology after Liberalism: A Reader*. Blackwell Readings in Modern Theology. Oxford: Blackwell, 2000.

Weinsheimer, Joel C. *Eighteenth-Century Hermeneutics: Philosophy of Interpretation in England from Locke to Burke*. New Haven, CT: Yale University Press, 1993.

Wesley, John. *A Plain Account of Christian Perfection*. Kansas City, MO: Beacon Hill, 1966.

_____. *Explanatory Notes upon the New Testament*. New York: Lane & Tippet, 1847.

_____. *Explanatory Notes upon the Old Testament*. Wesley Center Online. (http://wesley.nnu.edu/john_wesley/notes/index.htm): accessed July 2006.

_____. *The Letters of John Wesley*. Edited by John Telford. 8 vols. London: Epworth, 1931.

_____. *The Works of John Wesley*. Edited by Frank Baker and Richard P. Heitzenrater. Bicentennial Edition. Nashville, TN: Abingdon, 1984-.

_____. *The Works of John Wesley*. Edited by Richard P. Heitzenrater. Bicentennial Edition on CD-Rom. Version 1.0c. Nashville, TN: Abingdon, 2005.

Williams, Rowan D. "Barth on the Triune God." In *Karl Barth: Studies of His Theological Method*, ed. Stephen W. Sykes, 147-93. Oxford: Clarendon, 1979.

_____. "Does It Make Sense to Speak of Pre-Nicene Orthodoxy?" In *The Making of Orthodoxy: Essays in Honour of Henry Chadwick*, ed. Rowan Williams, 1-23. Cambridge: Cambridge University Press, 1989.

_____, ed. *The Making of Orthodoxy: Essays in Honour of Henry Chadwick*. Cambridge: Cambridge University Press, 1989.

_____. *On Christian Theology*. Challenges in Contemporary Theology. Oxford: Blackwell, 2000.

_____. "The Suspicion of Suspicion: Wittgenstein and Bonhoeffer." In *Wrestling with Angels: Conversations in Modern Theology*, ed. Mike Higton, 186-202. Grand Rapids, MI: Eerdmans, 2007.

_____. *Wrestling with Angels: Conversations in Modern Theology*. Edited by Mike Higton. Grand Rapids, MI: Eerdmans, 2007.

Wolterstorff, Nicholas. "Living within a Text." In *Faith and Narrative*, ed. Keith E. Yandell, 202-13. Oxford: Oxford University Press, 2001.

Wood, Charles M. *The Formation of Christian Understanding: Theological Hermeneutics*. Valley Forge, PA: Trinity, 1993.

Wright, Christopher J.H. *The Mission of God: Unlocking the Bible's Grand Narrative*. Downers Grove, IL: InterVarsity, 2006.

Wright, John W. "Wesley's Theology as Methodist Practice: Toward the Post-Modern Retrieval of the Wesleyan Tradition." *Wesleyan Theological Journal* 35 (2000): 7-31.

Wright, N. T. *What Saint Paul Really Said: Was Paul of Tarsus the Real Founder of Christianity?* Grand Rapids, MI: Eerdmans, 1997.

Yandell, Keith E., ed. *Faith and Narrative*. Oxford: Oxford University Press, 2001.

Yeago, David S. "The Bible: The Spirit, the Church, and the Scriptures: Biblical Inspiration and Interpretation Revisited." In *Knowing the Triune God: The Work of the Spirit in the Practices of the Church*, ed. James J. Buckley and David S. Yeago, 49-93. Grand Rapids, MI: Eerdmans, 2001.

_____. "The New Testament and Nicene Dogma: A Contribution to the Recovery of Theological Exegesis." In *The Theological Interpretation of Scripture: Classic and Contemporary Readings*, ed. Stephen E. Fowl, 87-100. Oxford: Blackwell, 1997.

Young, Frances M. *Biblical Exegesis and the Formation of Christian Culture*. Cambridge: Cambridge University Press, 1997.

_____. *Brokenness and Blessing: Towards a Biblical Spirituality*. Grand Rapids, MI: Baker Academic, 2007.

_____. "God's Word Proclaimed: The Homiletics of Grace and Demand in John Chrysostom and John Wesley." In *Orthodox and Wesleyan Scriptural Understanding and Practice*, ed. S.T. Kimbrough Jr., 137-148. Crestwood, NY: St. Vladimir's Seminary Press, 2005.

_____. *Virtuoso Theology: The Bible and Interpretation*. Cleveland, OH: Pilgrim, 1993.

Zimmermann, Jens. *Recovering Theological Hermeneutics: An Incarnational-Trinitarian Theory of Interpretation*. Grand Rapids, MI: Baker Academic, 2004.

Index of Authors and Subjects

Abraham, William J. 25-26, 27, 28, 29, 31-33, 51, 72, 116-17, 148, 153
academic divisions 11-12
ad hoc correlation 43
adoption 67, 84, 100-1, 110-11, 116, 154
Aldersgate 102
alterity 126
analogy of faith 17, 18, 53, 59, 60, 61-70, 75, 92, 93, 94-95, 102, 103, 104, 105, 121, 130-32, 139, 143, 149-53, 154, 162, 163, 164
Arnett, William M. 89
Auerbach, Eric 38
Augustine 103, 105, 113
authorial intent 29-30
authority 20, 31-33, 51

Baker, Frank 28
baptism 98, 109, 110-11, 114, 19, 150, 152, 153-53, 163
Barth, Karl 14-17, 43, 99
Behr, John 51, 147
Bible as Christian Scripture 18, 48, 123, 140, 142, 147, 149, 154, 164
biblical canon 13
biblical theology 4-5
Bicentennial Edition 27-30
Bonhoeffer, Dietrich 100, 148
Borgen, Ole E. 56-57
Boston, Thomas 67
Braaten, Carl E. 98
Burnett, Richard E. 14, 15, 16

Calvin, John 16, 38
Campbell, Ted A. 56, 57, 58, 108, 148
canon *see* rule of faith
canonical-linguistic theory 6-7
Charry, Ellen T. 33

children of God 18, 57, 85, 97, 100, 110, 115-16, 118, 119, 129, 133, 136, 139, 141, 142, 153, 154, 164
Christian perfection
   see perfection
closed text (*also* closure) 121-25, 126-27, 146-47
Collins, Kenneth J. 55
community of interpretation 47-52
Comstock, Gary L. 44, 45
covenantal nomism 110
craft 32-3, 163
Croatto, J. Severino 126
Crockett, William R. 112

Dawson, John David 46, 48, 121, 132-34, 141, 163
Dunn, James D. G. 106, 109

Ebeling, Gerhard 94
ecclesially located interpretation 12-18
ecclesiology 112-13
Eco, Umberto 120-26, 128, 140, 146
economy of salvation 18, 20, 48, 53-56, 57, 60, 63, 71, 82, 84, 92, 95, 97, 100-1, 108, 110-11, 114, 117, 122, 140-42, 152, 154, 162-64
Eldredge, Laurence 4
empirical author 121-25
empirical reader 121-25
entire sanctification 18, 164
Erickson, John 114, 117, 153, 154
Explanatory Notes 82-83

Fairclough, Norman 30
Farley, Edward 15
Farrow, Douglas 114

figural reading   8, 13, 18, 38, 44, 45, 46, 48, 91, 121, 129, 132-34, 137, 140-42, 161, 163, 164
final form of Scripture   12, 16, 21, 44, 106, 127
Fish, Stanley   98-99
Fowl, Stephen E.   1, 3, 7, 9, 10-11, 12, 44, 49, 98, 99, 129, 143-44, 146
Frei, Hans W.   11, 13, 15, 17, 34-52, 53, 61, 68, 71, 93, 94, 97, 111, 113, 118, 120, 121, 125, 128, 130, 132, 133-34, 135, 141, 143, 149, 154, 162, 163

Gabler, J. P.   4
Gadamer, Hans-Georg   3, 98, 104, 123, 126, 131
General Rules   57, 68-69
general tenor   62-63, 94, 105, 121, 131, 145, 147, 161
Gorman, Michael J.   106-7, 109-10, 111, 118
grace   53-56, 60
   see also means of grace
grammar of faith   50-52, 61-70
Grant, Robert M.   92
Green, Joel B.   1, 9, 10, 12, 13, 21, 23-25, 30, 31, 33, 106, 120, 144
Greene-McCreight, K. E.   13
Grider, J. Kenneth   21

happiness   54-55
Hart, Trevor   9
Hays, Richard   18, 108, 109, 110, 145, 149, 150-52, 153
Hebrew Bible   13, 134-35
Heidegger, Martin   3
Heitzenrater, Richard P.   27, 72
hermeneutical circle   126
Hermeneutics
   doctrine and   12-13
   philosophical   2-3
   as understanding   2-3
   see also theological hermeneutics

Higton, Mike   36, 39
historical criticism (*also* modernist criticism)   11, 13, 14, 34, 38, 44, 48, 105, 123, 127, 162
historical Wesley, the   27-28, 30
history of reception   52, 124, 142
holiness   18, 24, 33, 53-56, 59-60, 66-70, 77, 98, 105, 121, 131-33, 139-42
Holmer, Paul L.   50-51, 61, 94
Holy Spirit   98-102, 116
Howell, Kenneth J.   36
humanum   117, 152
Hunsinger, George   36, 37, 39
Hutter, Reinhard   39

identity formation   36-38, 132-34, 141-42, 155
interaction of reader, text, and context   35, 44, 45, 47, 125-28
image of God   54-56, 60, 64, 73-78, 80, 94, 97, 110-11, 118, 119, 133, 135-36, 138-41, 153-54
imitation   138-39, 141
Inge, John   157
Irenaeus   13, 147, 149
Iser, Wolfgang   122

Jeanrond, Werner G.   2-3, 14, 127
Jenson, Robert W.   98
Johnson, Luke Timothy   106
Jones, L. Gregory   7, 99
Jones, Scott J.   19-21, 61, 62-63, 81, 93, 104, 105, 107, 145
justification by faith   55, 59, 62-64, 67, 73, 75, 78, 87, 95-7, 101-11, 115, 118, 126-27, 131, 146, 148, 150, 163

Kavanagh, Aidan   114
Kelsey, David   36, 49, 51, 52, 63
Kinzig, Wolfram   149, 150
Klemperer, Klemens von   148
Knight, Henry H., III   56-57, 113, 114

knowledge and love of God 18, 164
Kort, Wesley A. 147
Koskie, Steven J. 19, 155

Langford, Thomas 53, 55, 93
Lash, Nicholas 129
Lee, David 35-36, 44
Levering, Matthew 7-8, 12
Lindbeck, George A. 35, 39
literal ascriptive identity of Jesus 34
literal sense (*also* literal reading) 13, 38-41, 47-52, 92-6, 121, 125, 127, 128, 129, 136, 142, 149, 155, 161, 162-63
   moral aims of 92-93
   as soteriological sense 92, 155
   as verbal sense 93-95
Long, D. Stephen 63, 135, 138, 140
Longdon, Leicester R. 25
Lossky, Vladimir 100
Loughlin, Gerard 36
Lowenthal, David 28-29
Lubac, Henri de 92

MacIntyre, Alasdair 17, 30, 31-33, 44, 53, 71, 105, 120, 143, 144, 148, 162, 163
Maddox, Randy L. 26, 27, 115
Marshall, Bruce 39
Martin, Troy W. 19
McCormack, Bruce 14, 15
McGrath, Alister E. 39
Mead, James K. 4-5
Meadows, Philip R. 27
meaning 3, 6, 7, 9, 11, 15-16, 18, 20, 21-22, 23-25, 29, 36, 38, 40, 42, 45-46, 47, 93, 95, 104, 123-28, 146, 151, 155, 163
   directions of 126-27
   spaces of 127-28
   surplus of 129
means of grace 18, 56-60, 154 164

   as searching the Scriptures 57-60, 70, 139-40
Moberly, R. W. L. 13
model reader 18, 121-25, 130-32, 139-42, 153-54, 161, 163
modernist criticism
Morton, Russell 21
Mullen, Wilbur H. 19
Muller, Richard A. 61

narrative 36-38, 41, 48, 49, 51, 63-5, 78, 103, 133, 142, 145-46, 147, 150-51, 154
new birth 71-72, 73-78, 95, 96, 115, 129
"The New Birth" 73-8, 95
New Perspective 106-11
Nicene Creed 13, 117, 149-55, 163

O'Keefe, John 12-13, 51, 132, 133
Ochs, Peter 11
Oden, Thomas C. 25, 26, 108, 148
"On Perfection" 78-82
open text 123, 126-27, 140, 146
oracles of God 61, 62, 64, 66, 68, 77, 78
ordo salutis
   see economy of salvation
Origen 133-34
original sin 20, 55, 75
Outler, Albert 25-28, 30, 32, 58, 67, 72, 100, 102, 103, 112, 113, 114, 115, 138

participatory exegesis 7-8, 12, 15
perfection (*also* Christian perfection) 18, 55-56, 58-59, 69, 73, 78-82, 131, 138, 164
performance of Scripture 6, 43, 48, 124, 129, 139-42, 146, 150, 163
person (natural, legal, evangelical) 67

Index of Authors and Subjects

Phelan, James 48, 49
Phillips, Thomas E. 21
polysemy 126
prejudice 104, 131, 139, 140
preunderstanding 126, 129, 139
prevenient grace
  see grace
Psalm 22 88-91

Radner, Ephraim 132
Räisänen, Heikki 4
Reno, R. R. 9, 3-4, 12-13, 51, 132, 133, 149-50
righteousness 138-39
Rogers, Eugene F., Jr. 98
Romans 9 83-88
rule of faith 8, 13, 51
  as hypothesis 51, 147-48, 150 163
Rules of the Band Societies 68
Ruth, Lester 148

sacrament/sacramental
  See means of grace
sanctification 55-56
Sanders, E. P. 106
Sandys-Wunsch, John 4
Schwartzentruber, Paul 45
searching the Scriptures
  see means of grace
Seitz, Christopher R. 8, 9, 13, 132
semiotic system 40-43, 44-45, 48, 51, 53, 57, 60, 70, 123, 146, 154, 162
Sender, Message, Addressee 122
sermons 72-73
Shelton, Larry 19
signum/res 113-14
skilled judgments 50, 144
Smith, Timothy L. 19
soteriology 48, 57-60
speech-act theory 6
Spina, Frank A. 21
Springs, Jason A. 36, 41
Steinmetz, David C. 12-13, 103
Stendahl, Krister 4

systematic theology 5, 6, 10, 27, 45, 94

Tanner, Kathryn 36, 47, 49, 52, 91, 120
text 44, 125-29
text intent 29, 123
textual mediation 140-41
theological exegesis
  see theological hermeneutics
theological hermeneutics 1-11, 33
  as craft 33
  Hans Frei's 34-46
  John Wesley's 19-21, 53-70
  Wesleyan 17-18, 21-25, 153-5, 160-4
theological interpretation
  see theological hermeneutics
theology 41-43, 50-52
Thiselton, Anthony C. 1
Thompson, Richard P. 21
Thorsen, Donald A. D. 19, 26-27
Tjørhom, Ola 112
Tracy, David 92
tradition 31-33, 39-41, 44, 49, 50, 52, 104-5, 107, 120, 126-27, 132, 142, 143-44, 147-50, 162
Treier, Daniel J. 3, 4, 10, 11, 12, 14, 16
Turner, Max 1, 9, 10
typology or typological reading
  see figural reading

unity and diversity of Scripture 105-8, 145, 150-52

Vanhoozer, Kevin J. 1, 3, 6-7, 39
veil of Moses 134-36
Vickers, Jason 85
Vinzent, Markus 149, 150

Wainwright, Geoffrey 19, 56, 101, 117
Wall, Robert W. 13, 21-23, 24-25, 93, 95, 96, 146, 149

Watson, Francis 1, 5-6, 12, 13, 14, 15, 16, 44, 106, 107-8, 109, 118
Webster, John 5, 16
Wesley, Samuel 115
Wesleyan Quadrilateral 26-27
"what it meant" and "what it means" 4
whole tenor of Scripture
  see general tenor of Scripture
Williams, Rowan 99-102, 105, 113, 117, 152

Wissenschaft 42
Wittgenstein, Ludwig 113
Wood, Charles M. 2, 34, 36, 47, 48-49, 50, 95, 129, 131
Wright, Christopher J. H. 150
Wright, N. T. 106

Yeago, David S. 149
Young, Frances 72-73, 93, 132

Zimmermann, Jens 2, 3

Index of Scripture

Genesis
1:25   64
1:26-7   73
1:27   80
2:17   74
3:15   65, 66
3:3   64
9:6   64
15:5   110
17:5   110
18:10   85
25:23   86

Exodus
33:19   86
34   134

Numbers
21:4   161
21:4-9   155

Deuteronomy
4:7   84
30:6   81

Leviticus
19:19   79

Psalms
22   71, 72, 88-91, 92
22:1   89
22:6   89
22:7   89
22:8   89
22:16   89
22:17   89
22:22   90
22:23   90
22:25   90
22:27   90
22:27-21   90
22:28   90
22:29   90-91
22:30   91
22:31   91
49:12   74
94:10   76
106:20   84
107   161
107:1-3, 17-22   155
107:17-21   161

Isaiah
7:14   65, 66
8:14   87-88

Malachi
1:2-3   86

Wisdom
2:23   64

Matthew
1:21   68, 80
3:7   68
5:48   64
7   139
12:48, 49   90
19:19   79
22:37   79
27:29, 43   89
27:35   89
27:46   89

Mark
12:30   64
15:34   89

Luke
10:27   64

John
1   161
1:14   66
3   77-8, 145, 155, 156, 158, 160
3:3   76
3:5   115, 116
3:6   73, 76
3:7   73, 75
3:8   73, 75, 76, 77
3:10   158
3:12   157, 161
3:14-21   155, 158, 161
3:16   103, 158 59, 162
3:17-18   159
3:19-20   159
3:21   159
4:24   111
8   161
8:28; 12:32-34   158
9:34   75
12   161
14:6   158
19:24   89

Romans
1:1-6   109
3:24   103
3:25   103
4:1-5   109
4:16, 17   110
4:7, 8   103
5:9, 10   103
6:3   110
6:3, 4   109
6:4   118
8:1   103
8:14   110
8:14-17   99
8:19-23   110
8:29   110

9   71, 72, 83-88
    101
9:5   84
9:6   84-85
9:6   85
9:7   85
9:7-8   110
9:7-13   85
9:8   85
9:9   85
9:12   86
9:14-17   86
9:17   86
9:18   86
9:21   87
9:22   86-87
9:25, 26   109
9:30   87
9:32   87
9:33   87-88
10:5-13   110
12:1   80
12:6   63, 66
13:10   79

1 Corinthians
12:13   117
15:22   75

2 Corinthians
3   134-36
3:1-6   134
3:6   134, 136
3:7   134
3:13   134
3:14   134

3:14-16   134
3:16   134, 135
3:17   134
3:17-18   99
3:18   134, 135
4:4   134
4:6   135

Galatians
2:15-20   110
2:16   110
3:27   110
4:6-7   99
5   81, 139
5:22-23   80

Ephesians
2:1-10   155
2:5   75
2:5   160
2:10   77, 80,
     160, 161
4   81
4:13   76
4:15   76
4:24   74, 75, 76,
     77, 80

Philippians
2:5   77, 79, 93
2:12   68
4:8   79

Colossians
2:13   75
2:15   65, 66

3   81
3:10   77, 80
3:12   130

1 Thessalonians
5   81
5:23   80

2 Thessalonians
2:17   64

2 Timothy
3:5   68, 115
3:17   64

Hebrews
2:11, 12   90
5:12   78
5:13-14   78
6:1   78

James
3:15   77

1 John
3:4   81
3:9   76
4:16   64

1 Peter
1   81
2:5   80
4:11   66

Revelation
12:7   65, 66

www.ingramcontent.com/pod-product-compliance
Lightning Source LLC
Chambersburg PA
CBHW030320080526
44584CB00012B/646